Praise for *Landaluce*

"One of the more difficult things to achieve as an author is to take a life and career cut way short and stretch it into a full-length book. Although the brilliant Landaluce raced only five times before her tragic death, Mary Perdue has been able to tell her story in great detail and keep the reader enthralled throughout. Although it does not have a feel-good ending, it is a feel-good story about a filly who was destined to become one of the greats of all time and the people who guided her up to and through her meteoric rise. Perdue does them all proud."—Steve Haskin

"Fame can be fleeting, even for an Eclipse Award winner like Landaluce. The first Eclipse Award winner sired by Triple Crown winner Seattle Slew and the first conditioned by Hall of Fame trainer D. Wayne Lukas, Landaluce drew comparisons with the indomitable Ruffian before her racing career was cut short by a fatal illness at the end of her two-year-old season. Mary Perdue, a skilled writer and one of Landaluce's most loyal fans, weaves the filly's perfect juvenile season into a rich narrative that brings her breeder, owners, and trainer to life. *Landaluce: The Story of Seattle Slew's First Champion* is a great read and a worthy tribute to the best filly of her generation."—Milton C. Toby, author of *Taking Shergar: Thoroughbred Racing's Most Famous Cold Case*

"Landaluce gave life to William Cullen Bryant's reverence for a 'rose that lives its little hour.' Now author Mary Perdue has delved into the life of this flying but tragic filly with diligent research. Thanks to her artful prose, an unbeaten and compelling racehorse in 1982 is again a figure to cheer, to admire, to savor."—Edward L. Bowen

"As the West Coast version of Ruffian, Landaluce deserves a full-throated telling of her story. Mary Perdue is up to the challenge, providing us with the tale of the transcendent filly's feats and the inner feelings of her human connections. A sensitive and well-researched presentation of the heights and tragedy that accompany great Thoroughbreds."—Lenny Shulman, author of *Head to Head: Conversations with a Generation of Horse Racing Legends*

"In an all too brief but brilliant career, Landaluce wowed crowds every second she spent on a racetrack. Felled suddenly by illness, this filly left a lasting impression on all those who saw her race, and Mary Perdue's chronicle of her short life will do the same. Readers will relish every page as racegoers relished every time they got to see this great filly run."—Jennifer S. Kelly, author of *Sir Barton and the Making of the Triple Crown*

Landaluce

To Rita —
Hope you enjoy!
— Mary Perdue

Landaluce

The Story of Seattle Slew's First Champion

MARY PERDUE

Foreword by Jon White

UNIVERSITY PRESS OF KENTUCKY

Scholarly publisher for the Commonwealth,
serving Bellarmine University, Berea College, Centre
College of Kentucky, Eastern Kentucky University,
The Filson Historical Society, Georgetown College,
Kentucky Historical Society, Kentucky State University,
Morehead State University, Murray State University,
Northern Kentucky University, Spalding University,
Transylvania University, University of Kentucky, University
of Louisville, and Western Kentucky University.
All rights reserved.

Editorial and Sales Offices: The University Press of Kentucky
663 South Limestone Street, Lexington, Kentucky 40508-4008
www.kentuckypress.com

Library of Congress Cataloging-in-Publication Data

Names: Perdue, Mary, author.
Title: Landaluce : the story of Seattle Slew's first champion /
    Mary Perdue.
Description: Lexington : The University Press of Kentucky, 2022. |
    Series: Horses in history | Includes index.
Identifiers: LCCN 2022001501 | ISBN 9780813195537 (hardcover) |
    ISBN 9780813195551 (pdf) | ISBN 9780813195544 (epub)
Subjects: LCSH: Seattle Slew (Race horse), 1974-2002. | Race horses—
    United States—Biography. | Horse racing—United States. |
    Triple Crown (U.S. horse racing)
Classification: LCC SF355.S416 P47 2022 | DDC 798.4092/9—dc23/
    eng/20220121
LC record available at https://lccn.loc.gov/2022001501

For Katie, and all beautiful beings who
leave too soon

Contents

Foreword

On a pleasant summertime afternoon at Hollywood Park in 1982, one day before the usual Fourth of July pyrotechnics, a filly won her racing debut so impressively that it might as well have been accompanied by fireworks.

The young filly Landaluce took Thoroughbred racing by storm that summer. She became something like a four-footed rock star.

What was America like in 1982? Ronald Reagan was in the White House. You could buy a gallon of regular gas for $1.30. The Commodore 64 became the first popular "home use" computer. Michael Jackson released the album *Thriller,* which sold millions of copies. There weren't any cell phones as we now know them, but E.T. was phoning home. The three biggest movies of the year at the box office were *E.T. the Extra-Terrestrial, Tootsie,* and *An Officer and a Gentleman.*

All these years later, for whatever reason, the dizzying heights reached by Landaluce do not seem to be appreciated. Though she was the toast of Thoroughbred racing in 1982, Landaluce is now largely forgotten, which is why this book is significant.

Writing with great passion and dedication, Mary Perdue left no stone unturned in telling Landaluce's story. I can attest that in her desire to do right by Landaluce, the author not only put countless hours into the project but also contacted a whole slew of people, including yours truly.

When Landaluce burst on the scene in 1982, I was a writer for the *Daily Racing Form.* I witnessed all of her races. This means I was trackside for all of her victories, because Landaluce never lost a race.

D. Wayne Lukas trained Landaluce. Lukas reached the pinnacle of the sport in the 1980s. Landaluce's meteoric rise to superstardom in 1982 helped pave the way for Lukas to assemble the strongest large-scale national racing stable ever seen. Lukas made winning important races from coast to coast a commonplace occurrence in those years.

Lukas ran his extensive operation with precision and a fastidious attention to detail. He was sort of like a general in command of a brigade of horses and the people who cared for them. Many of Lukas's "lieutenants" would go on to become very successful horse trainers themselves, such as Todd Pletcher, Kiaran McLaughlin, Dallas Stewart, Mark Hennig, Randy Bradshaw, Mike Maker, George Weaver, and Bobby Barnett.

What Lukas has to say about Landaluce in this book makes it abundantly clear that she was truly a super-special filly. She became a huge star, like her father, Triple Crown–winner Seattle Slew. Observers at the time went so far as to compare Landaluce to Ruffian, considered by many to be the greatest female Thoroughbred of all time.

When Landaluce won the Anoakia Stakes at Santa Anita Park by ten lengths, the runner-up was Rare Thrill, owned by actor Vic Tayback, best known for playing the role of Mel in the television series *Alice*. Even though Rare Thrill was no match for her, Tayback told me it was his biggest thrill as a horse owner to see Rare Thrill finish second to Landaluce.

If you were a racing fan in 1982, this book is terrific in that it will help refresh your memory as to what a big deal Landaluce was that year. For everyone else, thanks to Mary Perdue's in-depth portrayal of Landaluce, you are in for a treat.

Jon White
November 20, 2020

Prologue

On Saturday morning, November 4, 1982, undefeated two-year-old colt Copelan, the best juvenile in the East and presumptive national champion, napped in his stall at the Meadowlands before his final race of the year in the rich Young America Stakes. No one expected him to lose.

Outside the stall door stood veterinarian Dr. Robert Copelan and the colt's owner and breeder, eighty-five-year-old Fred W. Hooper. The two had a long history together. For thirty years, Hooper had been breeding his own racehorses at his Ocala farm, where the vet cared for them. He repaired a chipped knee on the colt's sire, Tri Jet, and a sesamoid on his dam, Susan's Girl, a two-time champion and winner of a record twenty-four stakes races. "Sometime, when you get a little old runt, how about naming him after me?," Copelan once asked Hooper, who laughed and promised he would. "I got this foal who can't hardly stand up," Hooper joked when the son of Susan's Girl was born. "Want me to name him after you?" Since then, the doctor had been present for each of the colt's last six races, hoping his namesake would keep his winning streak alive.

Copelan had already won the most important races and beaten all the best two-year-old colts in the East—easily, and by daylight. But the horse he had to beat to prove himself best in the land wasn't here, and it wasn't another colt, or an older horse—it was another undefeated two-year-old, like himself. A filly. In California. Her name was Landaluce.

She, too, had been named as the result of a promise. When her owners, Texas oilmen and longtime friends Barry Beal and Lloyd R. "Bob"

French Jr., went to Spain one year on a hunting trip, their guide, Paco Landaluce, asked them to name a horse after him someday. Usually, the pair named their horses after Spanish or Texan towns—like their first stakes winner, Terlingua, trained by their friend and former quarter horse conditioner D. Wayne Lukas. But when Lukas found a yearling daughter from freshman sire Seattle Slew that he thought was extra special, the Texans kept their promise.

The two juveniles couldn't have been more different. Copelan was a brawny bay with a white blaze, a homebred born and raised on the Florida farm where his sire and dam still lived. He was trained by Mitch Griffin, a former telephone cable splicer. If Hooper decided to send him west to face Landaluce, Griffin planned to travel with him and never leave his side. Copelan seemed to prefer eating to running. "He didn't have that big desire for races, still doesn't," Griffin confessed. When Hooper visited the colt after a race, he would find him "doing what he likes best—eating hay. He may be the biggest eater I've ever owned." The son of Tri Jet was usually mild-mannered, except when looking for more oats in the feed tub, when he was known to bite, and Hooper still bore fresh purplish bruises on his left hand that wouldn't disappear for another month. Copelan ran only as fast as he needed to win, and his times were nothing special. "In his first few starts, I could even see him turning his head and looking for company," Griffin said. His colt didn't set records or impress crowds with blazing speed. He just won—every time he went to the track.

Landaluce was a dark bay comet, a superstar so fast she'd set three records in only five races. Born at Spendthrift Farm, she was Lukas's number-one pick out of hundreds of royally bred yearlings at Keeneland's select summer sale. Wayne paid $650,000 for her and considered it a bargain. She had never raced outside California and drew near-record crowds every time she ran. She was so popular in California that fans kept her win tickets as souvenirs rather than cashing them, sported "I Love Luce" T-shirts and bumper stickers, deluged the Lukas barn with requests for photos and locks of her mane, and created minus show pools. She became a national media darling after her second start, when she won the Hollywood Lassie Stakes, a six-furlong sprint, by twenty-one lengths in a world-record time for a two-year-old filly around a turn. She won her five races by a combined forty-six lengths—seemingly without effort, and usually under only a hand ride by Hall of Fame jockey Laffit Pincay, who called her "the best two-year-old I've ever been on." In barely seven minutes on the track, she had been compared to Ruffian and Secretariat by veteran horsemen who had seen them both. She was one horse in a rapidly growing nationwide stable run by Lukas—a former high school basketball coach who was already third in earnings among American trainers this year. With many horses in his large, far-flung stable, Wayne had lots of good ones and had already won the 1980 Preakness with Codex. But Wayne knew Landaluce was the best Thoroughbred, colt or filly, he had ever trained. He called her "one in ten million," convinced that another like her might never come his way again. She was first in his mind, heart, and bank account, and there was nothing he would not do for her. He built her an oversized stall and hired a night watchman whose only job was to watch over her while she slept. He made sure she went to the track early in the morning when its surface was freshly harrowed, before any other horse could set foot on it. He ponied her out to the track himself for workouts, and he ponied her back so he could watch every step she took. After she raced, he often cooled her out himself and hand-grazed her the next day. No matter where his others runners traveled, or how important their races, Wayne wouldn't leave Landaluce. "When you're that close to a horse, you're closer than a man is to his wife and children," he told one reporter.

Both Lukas in the West and Hooper in the East believed they had the next Kentucky Derby winner in their barn. Lukas was forty-seven, near the beginning of his Thoroughbred training career, and seeking his first Kentucky Derby after two tries. Octogenarian Hooper had been in Thoroughbred racing for half his life, ever since he went to his first yearling sale in 1943, when he showed up at the offices of the *BloodHorse,* "wrapped his long legs around a high stool, and started asking for books" so he could learn about breeding and pedigrees on the spot. He won the Derby with the first yearling he ever bought, a colt he named Hoop Jr. after his young son, and for whom he paid $10,200. "I never thought I'd make it this quick," he said in the winner's circle under the twin spires. Despite three tries in thirty-seven years since, he had never won the race again.

Both Hooper and Lukas were entrepreneurs gifted at operating outside the box, and undaunted by challenge. "He would not hesitate to take on the establishment if he thought it was wrong," trainer John Russell said of Hooper, but the statement was true of either man. A barber college graduate who competed in prizefights, Hooper tamed wild mustangs in his teens and got his start in construction by taking the most dangerous jobs "working high up with steel." Described as "unabashedly unsophisticated," Hooper briefly farmed potatoes, then started his own construction company and got rich. As a teenager, Lukas eyeballed mustangs shipped in from the Dakotas on their way to be sold as feed for Wisconsin mink farms, shrewdly picked out the best, paid a couple cents more per pound, retrained them as saddle horses, and sold them for a profit. His teenage eye for horseflesh matured into a closely guarded system for picking Thoroughbred yearlings based almost exclusively on conformation over pedigree, usually from unproven sires, which would make him a legend in the auction ring. He was also developing a reputation for flouting tradition by running his best fillies against colts.

In 1949, when Lukas was fourteen, working on earning his trainer's license while trick riding at county fairs, Hooper agreed to a match race pitting his Thoroughbred colt Olympia against champion quarter horse Stella Moore. The adult Lukas knew a thing or two about quarter horses, and even he might have thought Hooper crazy to accept such a challenge. The rugged Olympia, broad-chested and sturdy as a tank, but with blazing speed, won in a photo finish. Hooper spent the rest of his life building one of the strongest racing stables in the country from horses he mostly bred himself, many of them descended from

Olympia. Copelan carried Olympia's bloodlines on both sides of a pedigree Hooper had developed over four equine generations, and Hooper's prized colt and Derby hopeful had inherited the speed of the stallion fast enough to beat a quarter horse.

After tonight's race, Hooper would decide whether or not to take Copelan to California to face the speedy daughter of Seattle Slew in the $750,000 Hollywood Futurity. Turf writers across the United States were already calling it a virtual match race, and Hollywood Park executive Marje Everett was so eager to host the showdown that she offered to boost the purse to $1 million if both Landaluce and Copelan went postward. Once again, Hooper would find himself taking on another quarter horse trainer to prove his colt the best—but this time, with a lot more at stake. The Hollywood Futurity would be the richest race ever run for two-year-olds, and if either Copelan or Landaluce prevailed, he or she could become the first juvenile millionaire in U.S. racing history, and the first two-year-old since Secretariat, to be named Horse of the Year.

Mirrored through the success of its best two-year-old filly ever, the West was on the rise, and on its way to supplanting New York and the old guard eastern aristocracy as the new powerhouse in thoroughbred racing. If Landaluce beat Copelan, the first million-dollar juvenile filly in history would be a California girl, and the first to win a championship while racing exclusively in the West. If she faltered, Fred Hooper could realize his dream of campaigning history's first juvenile homebred millionaire, and his colt would be next year's clear favorite for the Kentucky Derby.

Hooper dreamed of winning the Derby once more before he died. Having already survived three heart attacks, he knew Copelan was his best chance in thirty-seven years, and he thought he was unlikely to live long enough to have another. Wayne Lukas dreamed of winning the Derby for the first time with Landaluce. He even dared to dream that she might be the first filly to win the Triple Crown. Just last year, Lukas had what he thought was his best Derby prospect ever in a colt named Stalwart. Forced to retire Stalwart the next spring when the colt bowed a tendon, Wayne said the experience taught him never to think more than a race or two ahead and to keep his dreams to himself. After a lifetime breeding, training, and campaigning racehorses, Hooper knew what Wayne meant. "I have had a lot of dreams," he said. "Some came true, and some did not."

The dreams of both men were redolent of the hope, luck, and sweat that went into the making of any racehorse, whether plater or superstar. On this morning in early November, they had brought Landaluce and Copelan to the threshold of greatness, and both the western filly and the eastern colt seemed perfectly poised to race their way into history and make those dreams a reality.

But as is often the case in the alternately triumphant and cruelly disappointing world of horse racing, neither man's dream for his horse would come true—and for one of them, as writer Andrew Beyer later noted, memories of the horse of his lifetime would run in and out of his dreams through the years like a dark and painful shadow.

Part One

1

Leslie and Myrtlewood

As with most legends, there was an element of fiction in his life.
—Arnold Kirkpatrick in the *Thoroughbred Times*

One afternoon in the spring of 1949, Leslie Combs turned his Lincoln Continental off Ironworks Pike and drove through the wrought-iron gates up the hill past the dogwood-lined paddocks of Spendthrift Farm. At the top of the hill, in front of his eighteenth-century mansion, he had a good view of his farm and the mares and foals grazing there. His mares, the ones that started this place. He wanted them to be the first thing he saw whenever he came back to the farm, to be reminded of why he returned to Kentucky, why he bought this land, and what he yet hoped to accomplish here.

Leslie shut the car door and strode into the house. In the thirteen years he'd been back in Kentucky, he had made Spendthrift a force to be reckoned with. His yearlings were among the most sought-after at all the major sales, but getting to the top hadn't been easy. Without access to the best stallions in the Bluegrass, finding them closed to new breeders, he bought his own and sold shares in them to investors. Leslie's ingenuity and powers of persuasion had already landed the young stallion Alibhai, bought for half a million dollars from movie mogul Louis B. Mayer, in Spendthrift's breeding shed, where he would eventually sire Kentucky Derby–winner Determine as well as fifty-four stakes winners.

Tall, slim, and alternately charming and irascible, Leslie was skilled at getting what he wanted. He made people feel he was doing them a favor while steering them toward his own desired goal. His charisma engendered decades-long relationships with clients in the top tier of business, entertainment, and society like Mayer, Harry Guggenheim, John Hanes, and Marshall Field III. He entertained on a large and lavish scale, creating a world at Spendthrift so alluring that even the rich and famous wanted to be part of it. But he was careful not to overindulge while entertaining—he would drink a Virgin Mary or plain tonic with lime to maintain an edge over his clients. Frequently tanned from winters at Hialeah and Bal Harbour, his face was taut and lean, and his eyes darted hawklike behind his glasses, narrowed in intense focus when examining a yearling in a barn or auction ring. He spoke in a raspy voice and liberally used the word "boy" and the n-word when dealing with subordinates. He was a legendary and unabashed womanizer who would "flirt with every young thing that came by" and poke women with his cane made from a dried and varnished bull penis. One of his best and earliest clients, cosmetics magnate Elizabeth Arden Graham, "knew he was a terrible rascal" but relied on his sage advice for years when buying yearlings, resulting in Kentucky Derby–winner Jet Pilot in 1947. He kept his only son, Brownell, at arm's length, shipping him off to military school while at the same time making prospective clients feel so much like family that they dubbed him "Cuzin' Leslie." He was an opportunist who had married money. Always impeccably dressed, often in a tweed coat, necktie, hat, and pocket handkerchief, Leslie was a showman, shrewd enough always to practice a broad smile for the camera.

Leslie removed his hat and settled into a wicker chair in his sunroom overlooking a stone patio and a pool, where he could have a glass of grapefruit juice on ice and look out on his broodmares in pasture. On this side porch, Leslie often entertained clients, spreading rolled oats on the surrounding pastures to keep mares and their foals where clients could see them and dream of owning one. The

Leslie Combs at Hialeah, 1947. (Keeneland Library, Morgan Collection)

jewel among them was the foundation mare Myrtlewood, now seventeen, with her filly by Bull Lea at her side.

If a single horse could be the symbol of what Leslie hoped for and eventually achieved, it would be Myrtlewood. Without her,

Spendthrift would not be Spendthrift. Leslie could never have accomplished what he did without her, and he knew it. Foaled at his uncle Brownell's Belair farm in southern Fayette County, Myrtlewood was the first champion bred by the Combs family, and the first horse to be named champion sprinter in 1936. She set two American records for females and held records at five different tracks. In twenty-two starts, she won fifteen times, and she was out of the money only once in her career. She beat Seabiscuit once in Detroit's Motor City Handicap, where she broke the track record under wraps as the highweight and heavy favorite, conceding twelve pounds to the Biscuit. After that victory, sportswriter Lewis H. Walter called her "the greatest racing mare on the United States turf today."

As the magnificent dark bay champion, now a little swaybacked after ten foals, moved with her new filly to the next patch of fresh grass, Leslie saw the flash of one small white sock on her left hind. Her conformation was nearly perfect, with power, good bone, and graceful proportions, as turf writers from her racing days had noted. Generally calm and unruffled, the mare had a quiet temperament and never liked the whip. When a mockingbird chattered in the distance, Myrtlewood raised her head, revealing her forehead with its brief white comma-like strip that didn't quite meet up with the long narrow one that ran down the middle of her face. The markings on Myrtlewood's face reminded Leslie of his own life: how he'd started out in the Bluegrass, been interrupted, then came back for a long stretch he expected to last the rest of his days.

Incredibly, Myrtlewood surpassed her success at the track with her production as a broodmare. Her first two fillies, Crepe Myrtle and Miss Dogwood, would make Myrtlewood one of the most important foundation mares of the American Thoroughbred and ensure the success of Leslie and Spendthrift for years to come. Crepe Myrtle produced Myrtle Charm, the first champion bred in Leslie's own name. Her daughter Fair Charmer produced My Charmer, who, when bred to Bold Reasoning, would foal none other than Seattle Slew. Myrtlewood's second filly, Kentucky Oaks–winner Miss Dogwood, already

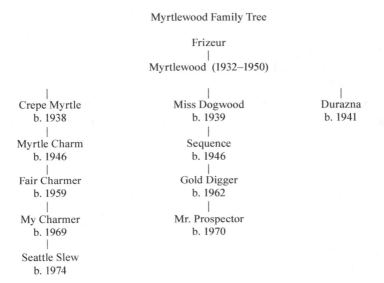

Myrtlewood Family Tree

Frizeur
|
Myrtlewood (1932–1950)

Crepe Myrtle	Miss Dogwood	Durazna
b. 1938	b. 1939	b. 1941
Myrtle Charm	Sequence	
b. 1946	b. 1946	
Fair Charmer	Gold Digger	
b. 1959	b. 1962	
My Charmer	Mr. Prospector	
b. 1969	b. 1970	
Seattle Slew		
b. 1974		

had foaled the good stakes-winning mare Sequence, who would become a beacon in the dazzling Myrtlewood female line when her daughter Gold Digger produced one of the greatest sires in history, Mr. Prospector.

Leslie set down his drink and went into his office. On its walls hung an oil painting of Myrtlewood in pasture with Miss Dogwood. Next spring, when Myrtlewood breathed her last at age eighteen on Saint Patrick's Day, the painting would serve as a reminder of the great mare and all he owed her. Leslie buried her among the roses outside his office window, where he thought he would be near her as long as he lived.

Leslie poured himself another grapefruit juice and returned to the sun-porch. From here, he could look past his own land across Ironworks Pike, to the beautiful farm so full of history bought and christened

Elmendorf by his great-grandfather Daniel Swigert. Leslie named his farm Spendthrift in honor of the yearling Swigert bought for one thousand dollars, who went on to win the 1878 Belmont Stakes and become the great-grandsire of Man o' War. Swigert sold Elmendorf ten years before Leslie was born, and the farm had changed hands several times since. Now it was known as the Old Widener Farm, and Leslie often crossed Ironworks Pike to visit there, determined to buy it back someday.

Leslie took another sip of his drink, his gaze still fixed across the road. Looking towards Paris Pike, Leslie could see the land where his own father worked as a dairy farm manager, tending cows for tycoon James Ben Ali Haggin after he acquired Elmendorf. As a child, Leslie didn't know how low his father Daniel had fallen, tending cattle on a farm he might have once inherited. Leslie, a direct descendant of the founder of Elmendorf, was growing up the son of a stockman. He was too young to understand why his father parted company with Haggin and took the family away from the Bluegrass. Lying in bed at night, he could hear his parents argue about money, but he didn't know his father was depressed by debts he couldn't pay or that he'd been fired and was unable to find another job. When, at age thirty-seven, Daniel was shot in the right temple, no one told his son it was suicide. Even the newspapers said it was an accident.

After the funeral, Leslie's mother, Florence, now nearly penniless, sent her son to live with relatives in her hometown of Lewisburg, West Virginia, where he attended Greenbrier Military School. Between his years in Tennessee at the cattle ranch, and those in the strict academic environment in West Virginia, Leslie felt further and further removed from the Bluegrass. But even in his young heart, he always knew he would come back.

Anyone even mildly acquainted with Leslie knew he could never sit still. Always restless, he radiated energy. Rattling the ice in his glass, he left the sunporch, passing a portrait of his grandfather, Hon. Leslie

Combs, in the hallway. His grandfather did two things that paved the way for Leslie to found Spendthrift Farm. First, he married Mamie Swigert, the wealthy daughter of Daniel Swigert, uniting the two families. Second, shortly after Swigert sold Elmendorf, Hon. Leslie acquired Belair.

Hon. Leslie and his son, Brownell, stood their own stallions and imported broodmares from England at Belair. Sixteen years his senior, Brownell became a solid and enduring presence in young Leslie's life, comanaging Belair as Hon. Leslie aged. Brownell bred his first stakes winner at Belair when Leslie was just eighteen. While Leslie was in his twenties, Brownell acquired the mare Frizeur, a daughter of Frizette. When Brownell decided to breed Frizeur to Blue Larkspur in 1931, her next foal was none other than Myrtlewood.

As a young adult, Leslie felt the lure of the Bluegrass and developed a taste for parties and high society that would remain with him the rest of his life. He loved dancing with pretty girls and being around the wealthy. Hon. Leslie, who felt responsible for helping his grandson amount to something, nudged him toward a more productive path, insisting he enroll in college. After only a year at Centre College in nearby Danville, Leslie dropped out. Hon. Leslie responded by sending his young namesake to Guatemala to work on a coffee plantation, where he learned to speak Spanish and contracted malaria.

At this point in his life, Leslie may not have known exactly what he wanted to be, but he didn't want to be poor or beholden to others. He was determined to be unlike his parents, living hand to mouth. He would be in charge of his own life, and one way or another, he would have money. After recovering at White Sulphur Springs spa in West Virginia, Leslie met the beautiful Huntington heiress Dorothy Enslow. His marriage to Dorothy in 1924 provided Leslie with the money and social connections he craved.

An added bonus was that Dorothy's mother, Juliette, loved horses and racing. The couple frequently accompanied her to the track at Charles Town, and Leslie eventually became chairman of the West Virginia Racing Commission. With an infusion of Enslow cash and influence, Leslie started his own insurance company. Finally, Leslie seemed to be established, putting down roots in his wife's hometown.

But things were about to change.

One Friday evening in October 1936, after a bridge party, Leslie's mother-in-law, sixty-three-year-old Juliette Enslow, said goodnight to live-in housekeeper Elizabeth Bricker and went upstairs to bed with two massive diamond rings she always wore still on her fingers. When Bricker brought the elderly widow her breakfast tray the next morning, she found her dead on the floor with a towel twisted around her neck, her bed sheets and pillow soaked with blood, and the rings gone. Mrs. Enslow's chauffeur, Judge Johnson, arriving to work, noticed an empty wallet on the front lawn. He went inside and woke Charles Baldwin, Juliette's son from her first marriage, a forty-year-old army air captain and amputee, who had lived with his mother since his divorce. Johnson found it odd that Charles sprang immediately out of bed, with the prosthetic leg he usually kept at his bedside, already attached.

Eight hours later and more than a hundred miles away, four-year-old Myrtlewood went to post in the Ashland Stakes at the inaugural meet of newly opened Keeneland racetrack, for what was expected to be her last start. Carrying 126 pounds in the slop and conceding sixteen pounds to her rivals, the great mare romped, winning by twelve lengths.

On the face of it, his mother-in-law's murder and the retirement of Uncle Brownell's greatest race mare couldn't possibly have anything in common for Leslie, but it seems his destiny was entwined with Myrtlewood's: as the mare was ending her fabled career on the track, a family drama was about to unfold that would bring man and horse together in a fateful way and, in the process, create a Thoroughbred breeding empire.

Myrtlewood at Keeneland after winning the Ashland Stakes in 1936. (Keeneland Library, General Collections)

The murder of wealthy Juliette Enslow, originally thought to be motivated by robbery, created a sensation and became national news. A week later, Dorothy's half brother Charles was charged with first-degree murder. Baldwin's motive, according to investigators, sprang from his addiction to narcotics prescribed following the amputation of his leg, and administered by his mother from a supply kept in her bedroom drawer. Prosecutors theorized the widow was killed in a struggle when she refused Baldwin's demands for more opioids and sought the death penalty for the handsome, well-liked former aviator. In March 1937, jurors deliberated less than two hours to find Baldwin not guilty. The crime was never solved.

By September, Leslie had moved his family back to this 127-acre farm on Ironworks Pike. Myrtlewood, a gift from Uncle Brownell to his nephew, left her birthplace at Belair and moved there too, carrying her first foal, Crepe Myrtle, who would become the fourth dam of Seattle Slew. Myrtlewood and Leslie would start out in the business of breeding future champions together. Things were coming full circle: Leslie's grandmother Mamie had recently died and left him enough money to buy the farm. A return to the Bluegrass helped his wife, Dorothy, escape the haunting memories of her mother's death. But perhaps of overarching importance in the timing of Leslie's move was the availability of the old Hugh Fontaine farm on Ironworks Pike, right across the street from Elmendorf. Leslie founded Spendthrift Farm on Ironworks Pike because it gave him a toehold from which to reclaim the land that had once belonged to his family.

Now, looking out where Myrtlewood and her filly still grazed, across the spreading hills toward Elmendorf, as the sun slipped behind the tree line in the pastures around him, Leslie's eyes grew misty behind his glasses. Memories of his great-grandfather Swigert and even his own father, Daniel, were fading like the sunlight. As they grew fainter, still the land revived them. Leslie knew he was home . . . but only part of the way. He was getting closer, but he wouldn't rest until he reclaimed all that he could of the Elmendorf land. "One day I'm going to buy it all back," he thought, "and restore my family to its rightful place."

Even though Myrtlewood would live only another year, she through her daughters would be the one to take him there. It would be another twelve years before he managed it, but through the persistence, panache, and swagger that defined him, Leslie would finally succeed in fusing the blood of Myrtlewood created from the Combs soil of Belair, with the tradition and glory of Swigert's Elmendorf, and unite it under the four thousand acres of his own Spendthrift Farm.

Many years later, on a day in April much like this one in the heart of breeding season, when the breeze was soft, the grass sweet and tender, and the dogwood in bloom, a dark bay filly foaled on that cherished Elmendorf land would be the first and only Spendthrift-bred champion ever to spring from it.

2

Cambridge Stables and the Spendthrift Connection

I'm Spendthrift all the way.
—William O. Hicks

Two stories explain the connection between Leslie Combs and one of his most significant breeding and investment partners, Francis Kernan. One is vastly more entertaining, so it's not surprising that Leslie himself was its author.

In 1921, before dropping out of tiny Centre College, Leslie managed to become a member of its varsity football team at the most auspicious time in the school's history, when the Praying Colonels were captained by quarterback phenom Bo McMillin. Wildly less talented than the team's star, Leslie spent most of his time on the bench. "He is perhaps the only man who attended Centre during the golden period of football who admits he did not play first string," the *Lexington Leader* reported years later. Leslie himself was baffled as to how he made the squad. "I couldn't kick, pass, or run," he said, admitting he only went out for the team "to get extra clout with the girls."

That year, the Praying Colonels traveled to Allston, Massachusetts, to take on the Harvard Crimson, winner of the 1920 Rose Bowl and undefeated in their last three seasons. Tiny Centre College stunned the Crimson 6–0 in what the *New York Times* called "arguably the upset of the century in college football." After the shocking victory, jubilant Centre students painted the "impossible formula" C6H0 on walls around campus and throughout the town of Danville, traces of which can still be seen today.

Among those on the 1921 Harvard roster undoubtedly stung by the loss was backup center Francis Kernan, who had the misfortune of starting his first game against Centre. Kernan might have faced Leslie's good friend and teammate Royce Flippin at center. More than forty years after the legendary game, Leslie told turf writer Jobie Arnold that Flippin worked for Kernan in the brokerage business after he finished school. Leslie claimed that when Kernan expressed interest in buying racehorses, it was Flippin who advised him to "go on down to Kentucky and see my old pal Leslie Combs. He was on that Centre team that beat you all. He'll put you in the horse business."

Kernan, a great-grandson of New York's first Catholic senator, was the oldest of four brothers who graduated from Harvard Law. Although he initially planned a legal career, he later told a financial reporter that he "let himself get sidetracked" into investment banking in 1936, when he joined White, Weld & Co. There, along with pioneer developer Paul Kayser, he crafted a groundbreaking sale of natural gas line securities to insurance company Equitable Life. The *New York Times* credited Kernan's first round of insurance-funded financing as the single biggest factor in the expansion of natural gas into a major public utility. Kernan would spend the next thirteen years financing and developing natural gas transmission lines in the United States, growing them from fewer than 8,000 miles at the end of World War II to more than 150,000 by 1957, making himself a fortune in the process.

Throughout the 1950s, Kernan labored on what was to become his crowning achievement as an investment banker and financier: the construction of the 2,300-mile Trans-Canada pipeline from Alberta to Montreal, the longest in the world at that time. As the pipeline neared completion in 1957, Kernan was described as "breathing a bit easy" afterward. Already wealthy before he started, the workaholic

Harvard grad needed something to sink his teeth into that he could just enjoy—and this is where the second, and more likely, version of how Francis Kernan met Leslie Combs comes into play.

"I've been interested in racing since I was eleven," a beaming Perry Pease told writer William H. Rudy, right after two-year-old colt Timbeau won the 1963 National Stallion Stakes for fledgling Cambridge Stables, formed in partnership with Pease's fellow Harvard alumnus Francis Kernan.

Pease had every reason to be jubilant: from approximately fifteen yearlings he and Kernan purchased in only five years, they had already campaigned three stakes winners—all bred and sold by Leslie Combs's Spendthrift Farm.

When the two investment bankers decided to form their own stable, dubbed Cambridge from their shared years at Harvard, and with racing silks of the school's crimson and black, Pease served as front man for the pair. Kernan, rarely photographed and described as "quiet mannered," was content to stay in the background. A mutual family friend and fellow Harvard man, influential horseman John A. Morris, introduced Pease and Kernan to racing and referred them to his trainer, the salty William O. Hicks.

Morris and Hicks helped the pair scout yearlings at their first Keeneland summer sale in 1957. "John Morris has the keenest eye for conformation . . . I know," Hicks said. "I'd take his opinion over most anyone's. We go three days ahead of time and look at every horse. . . . If he misses something, maybe I get it, and vice versa." Hicks had a clear and unabashed preference for Spendthrift-bred yearlings. "I'm Spendthrift all the way," he declared. "I like the way Lez breeds horses. I like to do business with [him]."

Pease and Kernan went to the sale with a plan to buy three or four top yearlings a year. Morris paid $21,000 at Keeneland for a Spendthrift-bred chestnut son of Kentucky Derby–winner Jet Pilot, and later sold the handsome colt, named simply Pilot, to Pease and Kernan.

The pair sent the colt to Hicks to train. From the beginning, Cambridge's two bankers invested for the long term: "We believe in going slowly with two-year-olds," Pease said. Their patience was rewarded when Pilot won his first two races at Belmont and quickly graduated to stakes company. The colt, whom Hicks affectionately called "a real ham, with the disposition of a saint," delivered a breakthrough performance at Saratoga, when he won the prestigious Sanford Stakes in a crowded field of fifteen, putting himself in contention for two-year-old championship honors. It was a remarkable first season for Cambridge—after purchasing only a handful of yearlings, the stable already had its first stakes winner.

Buoyed by their success with Pilot, Pease and Kernan returned to the 1959 Keeneland yearling sales and walked out with another Spendthrift-bred, a filly from the first crop of Nashua. Hicks, who liked the filly from the beginning, called her "a tough hussy [who] acted like a colt." His assessment proved well founded when the bay, named Shuette, won the 1960 Schuylerville Stakes. Their success in campaigning two stakes winners in as many years of racing, along with their connection to Morris, undoubtedly paved the way for Pease's and Kernan's election to the Jockey Club in 1960.

Shuette's follow-up stakes win in the Liberty Belle Handicap once again brought Pease and Kernan to Keeneland eager to buy her Spendthrift-bred half brother by freshman sire Tim Tam, the bay colt Timbeau. "As Cambridge has succeeded, so have its purchases become more ambitious," noted the *BloodHorse*. That year, Cambridge spent almost $100,000, an astronomical amount at the time, for just two yearlings at Keeneland.

Timbeau's victory in the National Stallion Stakes proved the worth of his purchase price, but it also cemented the reputation of the Hicks-Cambridge-Morris-Spendthrift alliance as a force to be reckoned with, and sealed the developing bond between Kernan and Combs in a way that would have fateful future results for both. Three stakes winners in five years, all purchased as yearlings at Keeneland, all selected with advice from Hicks and Morris, and all bred by Leslie,

Leslie Combs and Mrs. James Kilroe inspecting a horse at Keeneland, 1967. (Keeneland Library, Thoroughbred Times Collection)

from what the *BloodHorse* called "a rather modest number of purchases," could hardly be a coincidence.

By the late 1960s, while he continued to acquire yearlings to race, and bred his own retired fillies at Spendthrift in partnership with Pease, Kernan, now sixty-seven, began to branch out on his own, participating in additional breeding and racing partnerships with Leslie and others. The year 1968 was a banner one for Kernan, when he acquired the mare Tutasi, who later foaled Mansingh, the first stakes winner bred by Kernan and Leslie in partnership.

But by far his most significant act in 1968 and certainly among the most important in his entire breeding and racing career, was Kernan's purchase at Fasig-Tipton's August yearling sale in Saratoga, where he was accompanied by his younger brother Thomas. The Kernan brothers signed the ticket for a chestnut filly they would name Strip Poker. At $70,000, and the seventh-highest-priced filly at the sale, the daughter of Bold Bidder was a significant investment for Francis, and the only horse he bought there. Francis recruited his brother as a partner because "Strip Poker exceeded the ordinary price range I had maintained with Pease," Kernan later explained.

The Kernans formed a new entity called Spring Bank Stables under which Strip Poker raced. She showed promise when finishing second in her first start as a juvenile at Belmont, but then followed that effort with a dismal ninth in a maiden race at Saratoga, stopping when her rider lost his whip. Thomas, quickly disappointed, asked his brother to find a buyer for his interest in the mare, and Leslie Combs stepped in. Following her retirement to Spendthrift as a broodmare, all of Strip Poker's progeny were bred by Kernan and Leslie in partnership.

After ten years together, the Cambridge partners' interests were beginning to diverge. Kernan's commitment to breeding apparently ran far deeper than Pease's, and he had forged a much stronger friendship and business connection with Leslie than Pease seemed interested in having. Together, Kernan and Combs would breed a total of twelve stakes winners over the course of Kernan's lifetime. The investment banker who started out simply buying Spendthrift yearlings to race became one of Leslie's most successful and enduring breed-to-sell partners.

It was around this time that Strip Poker's first foal, the bay colt Clout by Indian Chief II, made it to the races. Although Pease had no ownership of his dam, the colt, trained by William Hicks, raced for Cambridge from 1974 to 1978, and notched his first stakes win in the Golden Joey Handicap on the turf at Belmont, where he set a new course record. The gritty colt went on to amass earnings of more than $300,000. The sale of Clout to the D. Wayne Lukas barn in 1978 was a watershed moment for Cambridge—the seasoned campaigner would be the last stakes winner to race for both Pease and Kernan as partners, and the last Cambridge stakes winner with ties to Spendthrift.

Cambridge Stables' Clout, first foal of Strip Poker, winning the GIII Edgemere Handicap at Belmont in track record time, 1977. (Bob Coglianese)

Kernan clearly had the heart of a breeder. Not content simply to race good horses, he had the time, money, and patience required to breed stakes winners. He knew that the timeframe from mating a mare to seeing her colt or filly make it to the races could be three to five years or longer, and among those to start, less than 5 percent would win a stakes. The man gentle and humble enough to "walk away from a bright light," as Spendthrift farm manager John Williams once described him, also possessed the determination and intellect to complete the enormous task of financing the world's first transcontinental pipeline, and he approached the process of breeding the best Thoroughbreds in the nation with the same mind-set.

Francis Kernan wanted to breed a champion.

3

Seattle Slew Day

Things have been said, and deeds have been done by the people around him, but he remains just what he is, a splendid thoroughbred unaltered by human frailties.
—Barney Nagler

As the charter jet neared touchdown at Bluegrass Airport in Lexington, Kentucky, on the bitterly cold afternoon of November 29, 1978, the dark bay champion Seattle Slew tossed his mane in anticipation. Calm throughout the flight, Slew had been listening to radio music that his owners, Karen and Mickey Taylor and Jim and Sally Hill, who accompanied him from Aqueduct, always played to help him relax. Slew had just ended his racing career there with a victory as highweight in the Stuyvesant Handicap, barely missing Riva Ridge's track record while carrying an eye-popping 134 pounds, the second-highest impost ever carried by a winner of the race. It was a fitting last hurrah for the Triple Crown winner and his connections, but the last sixteen months had been tumultuous. First came a crushing and shocking defeat to champion sprinter J. O. Tobin by sixteen lengths in Slew's ill-fated West Coast start in the Swaps Stakes last summer, followed by an injured hock, an acrimonious change of trainers, a debilitating and nearly fatal illness, and unrelenting criticism in the press for the management of the horse's final year on the track.

The wheels touched down, and Karen Taylor breathed a sigh of relief. Almost every day of the past year had brought some new injury, argument, or problem. It had been a year of triumph and discord, of pleasure and pain, to the point where it was almost impossible to distinguish between the two. She wanted to do everything she possibly could for this horse of her dreams, who had transformed her life in ways she never could have imagined. Slew had always done his best for her, and he deserved nothing less in return. But she wanted the pressure and scrutiny to be over and to be free of the second-guessing that seemed to follow every action or decision she made. When you owned a horse like Seattle Slew, you never really had a moment's peace. Karen, a former flight attendant, and her accountant husband, along with veterinarian Hill and his wife, knew they had been lucky beyond measure and that their journey with Slew had taken them places they never thought they'd go. Their $17,500 yearling purchase with a crooked leg and conformation so unappealing he'd been rejected from the prestigious Keeneland summer sale and consigned to Fasig-Tipton instead, where trainer Leroy Jolley had snapped, "put him back" after the son of Bold Reasoning was led out for inspection just three and a half years ago, had racked up wins in fourteen of his seventeen starts, earned more than $1.2 million in purses, was voted champion three times in a row and once Horse of the Year, and now had made them rich. It had been a swift and eventful journey, but it was time for it to be over and a new one to begin.

As the plane taxied to a stop, Karen thought back to Slew in his stall at Hialeah at the end of his three-year-old campaign, so sick he almost died. That was only eleven months ago, yet it seemed like an eternity. The owners had been at a crossroads then: should they retire the champion or give him a chance to keep racing to increase his value at stud? Few horses recovered from the rare disease Slew had contracted, yet like a champion he'd fought it off. Now, as the jet's ramp was lowered to the tarmac, Slew walked out of one world and into another. He had just been syndicated for a record $12 million, and the Taylors and Hills still owned half of him.

The controlling owner of the other half, Brownell Combs II of Spendthrift Farm, who had spearheaded Slew's syndication, watched and waited with his wife, Linda; father, Leslie; and farm manager, John Williams. Leslie had made history in Kentucky when he landed Nashua in 1955, the first stallion to be syndicated for more than $1 million. Now approaching eighty, he'd recently handed off farm operations to Brownell, who had spent the better part of his adult life trying to live up to his father's lofty expectations. Today, Seattle Slew just might be Brownell's Nashua. Indeed, the stallion who once was fed by a gold shovel and only allowed to drink mineral water would be upstaged by Brownell's newest acquisition.

The splendid bay was about to join an exclusive group of thirty-two of the world's most famous stallions housed in Spendthrift's U-shaped barn, including Nashua, Raise a Native, Majestic Prince, Caro, and Wajima, all of whom had been syndicated by Brownell or Leslie at record-setting prices, and whose offspring averaged a stakes win every two days worldwide. Every major farm in the Kentucky Bluegrass, including Brownell's biggest rival, Gainesway, had tried to get Slew, but Brownell had won. He was used to winning. The minute he'd heard Slew was sick back in January, he called the owners, seizing the opportunity to make a deal and capitalize on their uncertainty about the horse's future. As the most valuable new stallion in the country made his way toward a waiting van, Brownell had every reason to be proud of what he had achieved. He had already syndicated champion sprinter J. O. Tobin, the horse who beat Slew in the Swaps, whom he considered conformationally superior, and reached a deal to syndicate Affirmed to stand at Spendthrift next year, becoming the first breeder in history to stand two back-to-back Triple Crown winners in consecutive years. Finally, Brownell had managed to do something even his father had never done.

Silently, he mentally reviewed all the preparations he'd already made for Slew's arrival. Wajima, whom he'd syndicated for a then-record $7 million three years ago, was moved from his place of honor in the front paddock to make way for Slew, where the farm's newest stallion would be monitored twenty-four hours a day by closed-

Spendthrift Farm manager John Williams, age thirty-seven, at Lexington's Bluegrass Airport awaiting the arrival of Seattle Slew, November 29, 1978. (John Williams personal photo collection)

circuit TV. Lightning rods in trees near the stallion barn and breeding shed, a special gate on Slew's stall that ran all the way to the ceiling, and heaters to warm the shed floor had already been installed for Slew's safety and comfort.

Brownell thought it was fitting that Slew would stand at Spendthrift, almost as if he were returning to his roots. Through his dam, My Charmer, Slew descended from Spendthrift's foundation mare Myrtlewood, responsible through her daughters for Spendthrift's current status at the very top of Thoroughbred breeding. Brownell felt a sense of satisfaction as Slew stepped off the ramp and into the waiting van. The great champion from his farm's best female line was coming home, and to honor the occasion, Brownell had plastered "Welcome Home, Champ" banners on the side of the van, the

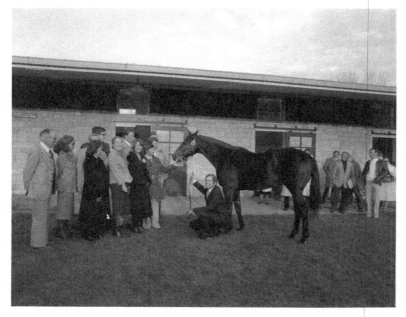

Seattle Slew and his connections upon arrival at Spendthrift Farm, November 29, 1978. *Left to right:* Chet Taylor, Linda Combs, Mr. and Mrs. Franklin Groves, Joe Layman, Sally Hill, Doug Peterson, Karen Taylor, exercise rider Mike Kennedy, Mickey Taylor, Brownell Combs, and Dr. Jim Hill (*kneeling*). (John Williams personal photo collection)

farm gates, and the entrance to Slew's new stall. As soon as the stallion was released in his new quarters, Slew immediately dropped and rolled in the hay.

Due to weather and flight scheduling problems, Slew had arrived a day earlier than planned. The next day was officially proclaimed "Seattle Slew Day" by Brownell's college friend and Kentucky governor Julian Carroll, who presided over a welcoming ceremony at the stallion's stall. A crowd of 150, who sported black and yellow buttons to match Slew's racing silks, joined trainer Doug Peterson and exercise rider Mike Kennedy to watch as Dr. Hill led Slew from his stall and hand-grazed him. Grand old Nashua, aged twenty-six but still an active sire, was paraded for the crowd, who then retired to a private dinner at the Spendthrift mansion to celebrate. Welcoming his throng of guests in the foyer where, as a boy, he'd watched Fred Astaire tap-dance down the steps to dinner, Brownell proposed a toast to Slew and savored his success.

4

Slew in the Shed

Of everything I can think of over the career God has given me,
Spendthrift stands out. . . . That was magic. Man, what a time.
—John Williams

"Mick, we have a little problem," Spendthrift farm manager John Williams said into the phone from his barn office not long after Seattle Slew arrived at his new home. Just a month after the stallion's eagerly anticipated arrival, Williams would later say he could already feel the roots of his coal-black hair starting to turn gray. This wasn't a phone call he thought he'd have to make. High on Williams's priority list after the stallion's arrival was to arrange a test breeding for Slew. Before Slew could breed the forty-five world-class mares already waiting for him in the wings, he had to successfully breed three non-Thoroughbred test mares and qualify for fertility insurance. Some stallions straight off the racetrack could be shy to breed, and it sometimes took patience and horsemanship to calm a new one and teach him his job. But after an hour in the Spendthrift breeding shed with the most experienced horsemen in the business, including Nashua's groom Clem Brooks, whom Williams called "the best guy that ever had hands on a stallion shank," Williams and the stud crew emerged frustrated and unsuccessful. There was a lot at stake, and right now there were at least 12 million reasons Slew needed to be a good breeder.

Williams and his team led Slew back to his corner stall, where he was already getting used to standing along the wall, looking out the window toward the road leading to the stallion barn. When he was turned out, Slew could see Nashua, Williams's most admired stallion, in the adjoining paddock. Williams remembered vividly the first time he walked into Nashua's stall and felt the splendid stallion beneath his hand. "When I first got there, I felt like a kid in a candy shop," he admitted. "I can't believe I'm the manager of this farm," he thought to himself. Williams knew he was in the presence of the best stallions in the world, entrusted with bloodlines that went back generations. Slew might be Spendthrift's new standard-bearer, the stallion to take the farm into a new era. Williams wanted to do everything he could to help him succeed.

Next to Slew in Spendthrift's U-shaped stallion barn was nemesis J. O. Tobin, one of only three horses ever to beat Slew to the wire. Many in the breeding industry, including Brownell Combs, thought J. O. Tobin, a dual champion in both the United States and Europe, would make the better stallion. "Without taking anything away from Seattle Slew, I think J. O. Tobin may be the better horse," Brownell said. When the elegant dark bay arrived at Spendthrift, he took his place in what had been the stall of his deceased sire, Never Bend. That stall just happened to be next to Slew's. The two rivals would spend the better part of their breeding career side by side. In their first year at stud, J. O. Tobin was "every bit as popular as Slew," according to Williams.

Still, demand for a date with the Triple Crown winner in the breeding shed was extremely high. "Day after day, from all over the world, the calls keep coming, 'What are the chances of breeding to Seattle Slew?,'" wrote the *New York Times*. "Sorry, my friend, there's no chance right now," Brownell Combs would reply. In his first five days at Spendthrift, there were already forty applicants for just three openings in Slew's breeding schedule. "The only way to get to Slew . . . is to have a top broodmare and put her into a breeding partnership with one of the syndicate members," the *Times* reported.

Syndicating Seattle Slew and stallions like him was a big part of Brownell's plan to restore Spendthrift to its days of glory. Ever since the death of Dorothy Combs in 1968, many had observed that Leslie Combs was not the same. "He lost a zest for life that my mother fueled in him," said Brownell, and consequently, the farm became rundown. Slew was the culmination of syndications negotiated by Brownell throughout the 1970s—including Wajima, Caro, and Exclusive Native, the sire of Affirmed. In early 1979, as Williams struggled with Slew, Brownell was poised to announce the syndication of Affirmed himself, which would make Spendthrift the only breeding farm in history to stand two back-to-back Triple Crown winners simultaneously. These five stallions alone were worth more than $50 million, and their success was vital to infusing the farm with new blood, as Leslie's old-guard stallions Nashua and Raise a Native were aging.

Brownell had been working aggressively during the past five years to land the most important new stallions for Spendthrift, ever since seventy-three-year-old Leslie had asked him to take over the farm's operations. By his own admission, he and his father had "never been close," and Brownell professed something approaching amazement when Leslie phoned to ask for his help in running the farm. Now in his mid-forties, Brownell still called his father "Mr. Combs," as he had all his life. Leslie berated Brownell in public throughout his youth and adulthood, to the embarrassment of those caught in the crossfire. "Goddammit, Brownell, you are just never going to amount to nothing, you big dumb son of a bitch," he was once overheard to say. The two reached an impasse in the 1960s, when Brownell finally left the farm to escape his father's ridicule and abuse, and prove he could make it on his own. The two Combs men could not have been more different—Brownell was huge and burly, standing six foot four and weighing more than three hundred pounds, whereas Leslie was six inches shorter, immaculately groomed, and described as "well preserved." Perhaps from a lifetime of failing to please, Brownell often stuttered and would smile disconcertingly when angry. He agreed to come back to Spendthrift only with a written three-year contract signed by Leslie. "He decided to let me do what I wanted to do,"

Leslie Combs (*left*) and Brownell Combs (*right*) with Brownell's sons Daniel and Leslie at Hialeah, 1969. (Jim Raftery)

Brownell said. "The big doubt I had . . . was whether he would let me do it."

Brownell returned to the farm in the early 1970s, right after he met and married Linda Kerr, an Oklahoma horsewoman fourteen years his junior, a beauty with an independent streak who shared Brownell's passion to rejuvenate the aging farm. Leslie, who always liked a pretty face, initially approved of Linda, and she may have been part of the reason he approached his son about returning. The elder Combs thought enough of her that he entrusted all of Spendthrift's barren mares to her care shortly after the marriage. Linda achieved a fertility rate of 70 percent while managing the herd at Belair Farm, where she and Brownell lived.

Brownell did not have an easy road at the beginning, as he found out when he tried to syndicate his first stallion, Sham, without his father's help. "The first time I personally had to go to people and syndicate a horse . . . they felt insulted. . . . They would say, 'Well, kid, have your dad call me.' The Sham deal was the toughest one I've ever done."

But together, Linda and Brownell made an effective team. Indeed, Linda had played a vital role in landing Slew. She "got along famously" with Karen Taylor and Sally Hill the first time they met at Hialeah to discuss Slew coming to Spendthrift. John Williams, who accompanied the Combses on the Florida trip, knew that it was Linda's vivacious personality, combined with the owners' confidence in Brownell's financial and business acumen, that tipped the scales toward Spendthrift for Slew's new home as a stallion. It didn't hurt that at Spendthrift, two out of three stallions succeeded at stud, compared to one out of six nationwide.

As a team, Linda and Brownell worked to streamline and modernize the farm, selling off acreage and culling broodmares that weren't producing. They also adopted a new philosophy with regard to yearling sales: "Instead of maneuvering for world sales records, as Leslie Combs had done, Brownell and Linda concentrated on trying to get solid, if not spectacular, prices for their entire consignment," noted turf columnist Billy Reed.

One of the biggest changes the couple made—hiring John Williams as farm manager—was definitely Linda Combs's idea. A horseman all his life, starting out as "a horse-crazy kid mucking out on a local farm," who managed his first horse farm at age twenty-five, Williams relished the opportunity to come to the Bluegrass to work for one of the greatest breeding farms in the world. But Brownell didn't think he needed a farm manager. Linda found a way around her husband's objections: she hired Williams as yearling manager and promoted him to farm manager six months later. Williams had a unique condition of employment—he wanted to bring his twenty-three-year-old mare Fleet Flight with him to the farm. His plan was to breed the daughter of Triple Crown–winner Count Fleet to Nashua. As a rule, Spendthrift didn't allow employees to keep horses on the farm, but Williams insisted and Linda agreed.

Williams respected Linda as a valued ally in the execution of the many ideas they shared to rebuild the farm and create a new age of prosperity for Leslie's declining empire. "She was the starch that made the bread rise," he said. One day, Leslie objected to Williams's request to repair a badly damaged stall, saying, "You and Linda, you just want to spend my money." Out of Leslie's earshot, Linda told Williams, "He's going to be gone to Florida two weeks. As soon as you see those tail lights going out that driveway, you go ahead and fix that barn." With Linda's approval, Williams dismissed many Spendthrift farm staff who had become complacent and replaced them with younger recent graduates from the Irish National Stud. Linda and Williams were also the first employers among major farms in the Bluegrass to hire women as grooms. Linda supported Williams's improvements to farm infrastructure, including a second breeding shed, additional fencing, and run-in sheds. "I can't express how important she was," Williams summarized.

All of this made John Williams acutely aware of how vital it was for Seattle Slew to succeed at Spendthrift, and he didn't want to let anyone down. Though he wished Slew's breeding problem didn't exist, the process of solving it intrigued him. There was nothing about horses he didn't like. He enjoyed figuring them out and doing whatever it took to make them thrive. Slew was an interesting puzzle.

As it turned out, transforming Seattle Slew into a reliable stallion required a concoction of various remedies devised by Williams and his staff through trial and error. Slew's preferences were whimsical and peculiar—sometimes, the stud crew had to introduce the stallion to a mare outside the shed before breeding. Other times, they had to breed him outside the shed, often with two mares in quick succession. On days when he preferred chestnuts or bays, the crew would bring in a mare of the right color, then switch "at the critical moment," which made Slew "mad as fire. Sometimes he would not be interested . . . in the breeding shed, but willingly would breed . . . on a grassy spot next to the shed. We would breed him in the snow or rain," Williams recalled. Another favorite breeding spot was underneath a magnolia tree. Slew also had little patience for skittish or maiden mares. "If it's too much trouble, he's just not interested," said assistant stallion manager Ernie Campbell.

Williams and his old mare Fleet Flight had been at Spendthrift three years by the time Slew arrived. After being bred twice to Nashua, the mare failed to conceive, and Williams realized it was time to retire her. Since she had a quiet temperament, he decided to try her in pasture with newly weaned fillies. The strategy worked—she had a calming effect on the youngsters, who followed her everywhere. It seemed Fleet Flight had found her calling at Spendthrift. But now, wracking his brains for ways to make Slew a reliable breeder, Williams suddenly thought of his old mare in a new way. Since she was so quiet and easy, maybe she'd be a good candidate to get Slew to breed. If something were to go wrong, Williams would be assuming the risk on his own mare instead of one of the farm's. "Old Fleet Flight was a shot in the dark," Williams admitted, "but we'd already tried everything else."

It turned out that Slew had more than platonic affection for the mare Campbell called "raggedy taggedy." "We'd get him all fired up on her and then switch him to the other mare at the last minute," Campbell recalled. When Slew pinned his ears in anger at being tricked, the stud crew would immediately feed him to calm him down. "I don't care how mad he was. If you just rattled some cellophane, all was forgiven." Williams's ruse had worked, and Fleet Flight assumed the role of reproductive diplomat. Over time, the stallion eventually became more reliable and tractable in the shed. But in those first early years when so much was at stake, colts and fillies from Slew's first crops owed their existence at least in part to the kindhearted, gentle, old swaybacked mare and the ingenuity and patience of John Williams and his staff.

Despite his success in resorting to unconventional methods, Williams still felt there might be more he could do to understand Slew's reluctance to breed. Perhaps, for some underlying reason, the stallion wasn't satisfied or content. "He was the smartest horse I've ever been around in my life," Williams said, "and I wondered if he just didn't have enough to do." So one day the former exercise rider asked a Spendthrift groom to help him tack up the stallion in the breeding shed, then rode him into his paddock. "I turned left down that field . . . and he dropped his neck, chin against his chest (dropping the bit), and I felt my irons go out. He had a hold of me. And I thought, 'Dear Lord, please get us back safe.'" It took awhile, but Slew eventually let Williams regain control and returned to the stable. "I realized that it had been too long since I'd ridden a real race horse. Slew about dragged my guts out." As harrowing as that first ride was, the experiment worked.

Williams finally had hit on the missing piece in the puzzle Slew presented. "He missed his job . . . [and] all he wanted was [to get it] back." Seattle Slew needed to be under saddle, to work and have a purpose. This trait was in his blood, and it would turn out to be one he would pass on to his offspring.

Even though John Williams had discovered the key to Slew's libido through a regular exercise program, it wasn't long until another issue arose—Slew liked to eat. Ever since he was a foal, the bay son of Bold Reasoning "seemed to eat more than the others" and would be "first at the gate when it was time to be fed," according to farm manager Paul Mallory at White Horse Acres, where Slew was born. As a weanling sharing grain from a cattle trough with pasturemates, Slew was "always the first to eat, and sometimes wouldn't let the others come around," Mallory recalled.

At Spendthrift, Slew had the run of a two-acre paddock, and he loved to eat grass. He ate so much that his grooms had to occasionally muzzle him to keep him from getting too fat, which made him lazy in the breeding shed. The stallion crew made sure Slew's appetite was satisfied with the equine equivalent of hot cereal in the morning—six quarts of cooked barley, bran, flax seed and corn brewed into a mash. Still, even with regular exercise, the Triple Crown winner had a tendency to put on weight—so Spendthrift used a special treadmill to keep him in shape.

In the late 1970s, when Slew began his first season at stud, demand for Spendthrift stallions was so intense that vans carrying mares from farms all over the Bluegrass lined the farm's main entrance road and were backed up "all the way to Ironworks Pike," according to Williams. In 1977, the year before Slew arrived, Spendthrift stallions serviced approximately 1,800 mares, and the breeding shed remained open nearly round the clock to accommodate them. The *New York Times* reported, "In one hectic ninety-minute span . . . thirty mares were bred to thirty different stallions, a three-minute average which stands as a Spendthrift record." It took an eight-man stud crew an average of six minutes to manage the breeding of each mare. "I just open the door and yell, 'who's next?,'" quipped stallion manager Hooper Roff.

Despite such frenetic activity, opportunities to breed to Slew when he first came to stud were remarkably limited, due to the unorthodox way the Taylors and Hills chose to organize his syndication. Dubbed the "Slew Crew" in the press, the owners took what turf writer Andrew Beyer called "a monumental gamble" by retaining half-ownership of their stallion. Customarily, owners sending a horse to stud syndicated him into forty shares and usually kept three or four for themselves. "This is standard procedure," wrote Beyer, "because it is too expensive and risky for any one owner to keep a major stallion and all his offspring." The Slew Crew, however, were so attached to their horse that initially they didn't want to sell even half of him. "The only reason we [did]," explained Mickey Taylor, "was that he was too expensive to keep. We couldn't pay the $2.1 million insurance."

Instead, Slew's owners kept twenty shares, and the remaining twenty were split between partners George Layman Jr., Franklin

Groves, and Brownell, with Layman owning ten shares, and Brownell and Groves retaining five apiece. Each share represented one breeding opportunity a year. As syndicate manager, Brownell also received four additional breeding rights annually.

Since the Slew Crew owned only a single mare at the time Slew went to stud, they embarked on various partnerships with owners of elite mares they wanted the stallion to breed. They offered these owners a free service to Slew in return for shared ownership of the resulting foal. In this way, they controlled twenty breeding opportunities to Slew each year, and determined for themselves which twenty mares would go to him. This meant that unless Brownell, Layman, or Groves sold a share or "season" to Slew, outside breeders were effectively locked out. It also meant that Brownell and Spendthrift had nine breeding opportunities to Slew each year—five from Brownell's ownership position, and four from his management position. One of the nine mares sent to Slew through Brownell was Francis Kernan and Leslie Combs's Strip Poker.

The chestnut daughter of Bold Bidder, described by John Williams as "short and compact, built like a quarter horse" was a logical candidate for the Spendthrift connections to send to Slew in his first season at stud. "She wasn't big, but she was attractive and had good conformation," Williams said. Despite her undistinguished race record, Strip Poker had already produced two winners, including graded stakes winner Clout. The tough, determined colt had achieved his best results on the turf at Belmont, setting or equaling course records there three times. After five years with Kernan's Cambridge Stables, the hardy bay, now seven, was still racing on the West Coast for trainer D. Wayne Lukas, having started an eye-popping fifty times.

Besides being a proven producer, Strip Poker also had a desirable pedigree. Her mother, the British mare Pange, when bred to Italian champion Ribot, produced Prix de l'Arc de Triomphe–winner Prince Royal II, who went on to be named European champion three-year-old colt in 1964. Producing an Arc winner made Pange instantly valuable, and she caught the eye of John Gaines, Spendthrift's upstart rival at nearby Gainesway Farm, who was looking to infuse his stock with quality European bloodlines as an outcross. Gaines bought Pange immediately after her son's Arc win and made her a permanent member of his broodmare band. He had to be patient, as Pange's foals from her first two American matings both died, and it wasn't until three years after arriving at Gainesway that she foaled Strip Poker, her first American-bred offspring by the champion handicap stallion Bold Bidder, a son of Bold Ruler. As an American-born half sister to an Arc winner, Strip Poker's bloodlines were valuable enough for Gaines to include her in his first-ever yearling consignment at Saratoga's 1968 summer yearling sale in the brand-new Humphrey S. Finney pavilion, where she was sold to Francis Kernan.

One day in early May 1979, the diminutive chestnut left her barn on the historic Elmendorf land known as the Old Widener Farm and boarded a van for a brief trip across Ironworks Pike to Spendthrift's breeding shed for her first date with a Triple Crown winner. Upon her arrival, the mare was scrubbed with antiseptic and her rear legs hobbled to prevent her kicking out and harming the stallion. Seattle Slew was led from his stall barely fifty yards away, down a path to the white building with green trim, a sloping roof and large sliding doors on either end, described as "hardly bigger than a one-room summer cabin."

Not since the filly Idun in 1958 had there been a Spendthrift-bred champion. Brownell Combs had grown up at Spendthrift and now piloted the Combs family legacy from his home at Belair Farm, the birthplace of Myrtlewood, who started it all. He had syndicated five world-class stallions and hoped that at least one of them carried the blood to take Spendthrift where it needed to go. If he were extremely lucky, one of his new acquisitions might sire the first Spendthrift-bred champion in over twenty years.

No one could have known on that spring day in 1979 when Seattle Slew bred Strip Poker, that the son of Bold Reasoning would be the horse that not only regenerated Spendthrift but also transported it into a realm hardly imaginable by Brownell or anyone else.

5

April 11, 1980

They begin to show intelligence and determination from the minute
they see the light of day.
—Leslie Combs

When the day crew arrived to work at Spendthrift in the morning
hours of spring foaling season, one among them usually had won a
chicken dinner. Before their shift ended, and after they'd inspected
all the mares who had yet to foal to see whose udders, or "bags," were
fullest, they'd place bets on who would be next to give birth. Strip
Poker had been on everybody's list for a day or two now. But when
the crew arrived the morning of April 10, 1980, there still was no
colt or filly by her side.

Foaling season always meant more work for everyone—by now,
the crew weren't just leading rotund mares in and out of barns and
mucking stalls. So many mares had already foaled that there were
nearly twice as many horses to care for as there had been back in
December.

Yet, as hard as they worked, the day crew rarely was rewarded by
seeing foals actually being born. Mares, following an instinct to give
birth when predators are least likely to be nearby, usually foal at
inconvenient times for people: late at night or early in the morning,
while humans stamp from side to side to keep warm, and breathe on
their knuckles, waiting. Animal and human breath mingles in the
night together against the ankle-deep, warm, honeyed yeast of hay

and urine, and the stakes are high: death against life, the disappointments of the past against what one gentle laboring mare might produce. So the day crew left, hoping for hot chicken and gravy and wondering what new life might be there to greet them tomorrow.

Spendthrift broodmare manager Rick Nichols and resident veterinarian Don Witherspoon, known as "Doc Spoon," had supervised hundreds of foalings throughout their careers. What both men wanted was an uneventful, routine birth that ended with the mare delivering safely and expelling her afterbirth, and a healthy foal able to stand and nurse within an hour.

Tonight, Strip Poker was finally ready—and the foal about to arrive would be among nearly two hundred born at Spendthrift this year alone. Nichols, aged twenty-nine, quiet and reserved, had been rapidly promoted to assistant farm manager, in charge of all the broodmares who foaled there.

The mare who pawed her bedding and circled in her foaling stall tonight held a special place in Nichols's heart. He couldn't say why exactly, but there was something about the graceful chestnut that had pulled at him the first time he saw her. She was so sweet, with such a wonderful temperament. Although he was officially responsible for all of the more than four hundred broodmares stabled at Spendthrift during foaling season, his staff knew to call him, no matter what the hour, when certain ones began their labor. Strip Poker was definitely on that list—partly because she was a graded stakes producer with exceptional bloodlines, partly because she was in foal to a Triple Crown winner, and partly because Nichols just had a soft spot for her.

Retired to Spendthrift, Strip Poker joined one of the largest and most elite broodmare bands in the country, assembled by Leslie Combs over forty years through intuition, guesswork, and a certain amount of luck. Most had won stakes races or produced stakes winners. By 1980, Spendthrift had become the largest commercial Thoroughbred breeding operation in the nation. Three separate farms were required to house and foal all the mares who lived there. They were kept in two separate groups, one for farm-owned mares, and one for client-owned mares boarded at Spendthrift, each with its own robust staff of veterinarians, managers, and grooms, many of whom lived on-site year-round so they could be summoned at a moment's notice. Farm manager John Williams, described by general manager Arnold Kirkpatrick as "totally dedicated to the farm to the exclusion of everything else" and who reportedly thought about his horses even when he slept, lived in the stone gatehouse barely thirty yards from Barn 16, where Strip Poker was foaling now, and across the street from the brick residence Leslie had recently built for Kirkpatrick. Williams attended all foalings of mares bred to Seattle Slew during the stallion's first year at stud. Directly behind the foaling barn lived newly hired twenty-seven-year-old assistant Dr. Thomas Riddle, fresh out of veterinary school, who in two years would start one of the most prestigious equine clinics in the world in the Queensway Drive garage of his partner, Dr. Bill Rood, in Lexington. Brownell Combs lived about twenty miles away on the old Belair Farm, rechristened Myrtlewood, and Doc Spoon and Nichols lived on a third farm where client-owned mares foaled.

Thirteen-year-old Strip Poker lived in paddocks reserved for farm-owned mares surrounding this barn on Ironworks Pike, across the road from the main Spendthrift parcel, on land once part of Elmendorf known as the Old Widener Farm when Leslie bought it in 1962. When grazing on this historic land, Strip Poker could lift her head and perhaps see a pasture close to where she herself had been foaled and grew up across nearby Paris Pike at Gainesway. With the exception of her brief trip as a yearling to the Saratoga sale and her single summer of New York racing, Strip Poker spent nearly her entire life in this same square mile of Kentucky bluegrass.

Leslie Combs wasn't the only one who appreciated this land—John Williams loved it too. "It was as good a piece of land from an agricultural standpoint as anything the Combs family owned," he said, but there was another reason hidden underground which explained his fondness for it. Pieces of Williams's heart lay in the earth there, too—beneath a fresh patch of grass, he'd buried the great mare

Affectionately with his own hands on the hill up the road from his house known as Linden Lane, lined by gnarled linden trees planted by Daniel Swigert more than a century ago, beneath ancient towering pines at a spot surrounded by hedges called Lion's Circle, where former Elmendorf, Widener, and Spendthrift champions slept side by side. Among them were the great stallion Turn-To, who lay buried near his dam, Source Sucree; Kentucky Derby–winner Swaps; and Alibhai, one of Leslie's original stallions. Myrtlewood's daughters and grand-daughters were also there, including Miss Dogwood, Miss Fleetwood, and Sequence, dam of Gold Digger, who foaled Mr. Prospector and lived among the same pastures with Strip Poker for eleven years.

Now, in this plain, undistinguished concrete block rectangular barn just down the hill from history, Strip Poker's time was drawing near. She had already labored here seven times before. Beneath a metal roof in the sixth stall on the left, her filly tonight would be only the second she'd produced so far, a tenuous thread in the preserva-tion of her own female line. The success of Clout, her first foal, ensured Strip Poker a place at Spendthrift for many years. When Brownell and Linda Combs culled half of the farm's broodmare pop-ulation in a partial dispersal, Strip Poker survived the cut. It was a good thing for racing history that she did. As Nichols, Williams, and Doc Spoon looked on, Strip Poker's Seattle Slew filly slipped into the straw. She was born a seal-brown dark bay, the color of her father, with no white markings except for a small whorl in the middle of her forehead. As Strip Poker calmly licked away the afterbirth, the filly soon began to struggle to stand, impelled forward from her first few moments of life. For reasons he hadn't figured out, Rick Nichols had observed that fillies usually were quicker to get up and move around after birth than colts, and this one was no exception. As she wobbled unsteadily and took her first hesitant steps in the straw, he noticed that her right front foot turned out a little bit, just like Slew's.

Years ago, when Leslie Combs was in his prime, he used to visit the foaling barn and watch newborns in their first hour of life. "The ones who survive the birth most quickly, and are up and around looking for worlds to conquer, they're my type," he said. He claimed

Seattle Slew at Spendthrift, May 1980, shortly after Landaluce was foaled. (Tony Leonard collection)

Majestic Prince, the first Kentucky Derby winner bred by the farm, had stood and nursed within a half hour, and that's how he knew the colt would have the heart and will of a winner.

Perhaps he might have been impressed if he'd been present to see his newest foal take her first steps. Satisfied that all was well with Strip Poker and her filly, Nichols and Doc Spoon moved on. There were many mares still to foal, most with credentials to produce a future stakes winner. While many farms would be happy to breed a few of these a year, in the busy spring breeding season of 1980 at Spendthrift, the mares Ferly, Sassabunda, and Kadesh would all foal stakes winners at the Old Widener Farm alone. So would Sigh Sigh, Mellow Marsh, Savage Bunny, Yale Coed, Tudor Jet, Air Maid, Fast Call, Silent Beauty, Clairvoyance, and Call Me Goddess. Yet among this bounty of riches, this treasure of pedigree, not one of the elite runners from these mares would come close to matching what Strip Poker's filly would achieve. Even among this golden group, Strip Poker's filly would outshine them all.

6

Growing Up

You are never going to see a better filly than that in your life.
—William O. Hicks

Behind the barn on Ironworks Pike where Strip Poker's filly was born lay a great, open field that stretched as far as the eye could see. Mares and foals roamed freely here on fine-weather days, nourished on the rich ground of the Old Widener Farm, once part of Elmendorf. Beneath it flowed a hidden, underground river that emptied into nearby Elkhorn Creek, and some believed that the water deep below the surface accounted for the richness of this pasture, and helped young horses thrive.

Strip Poker and her filly were turned out daily into this expansive pasture, part of a group of twelve that had been kept together based on the mares' expected foaling dates. Unless they were barren, the broodmares in this group would foal around the same time each year, and their foals would grow up together. Seattle Slew's new daughter would be among his first offspring to begin life on this historic ground.

When her filly was four weeks old, Strip Poker once again traveled in a van across the street to be bred to Seattle Slew—the first time in nine years the mare was bred back-to-back to the same stallion. Her filly remained behind, while a broodmare staff member watched and stayed in a stall with her if necessary. As soon as Strip Poker returned, she immediately called out to her foal, who whinnied back so her mother could find her. After nursing, the pair was turned out again in pasture.

Each summer, Francis Kernan made a trip from New York to Spendthrift to see his mares and new foals. Accompanied by trainer William O. Hicks, who also served as Kernan's bloodstock advisor, the investment banker saw Strip Poker's filly for the first time when she was "two or three months old" and still nursing at her mother's side at the Old Widener Farm. Hicks was immediately impressed. "This is going to be a tremendous horse," he told Kernan, "and I advise you and Leslie right now to make plans to hold on to her."

Shortly after Kernan returned to New York, weaning began for the mares and foals in Strip Poker's group. From mid-July through September, when the foals were four to six months old, weaning took place gradually, with a few foals separated from their mothers each day. Kernan and Hicks returned to the Bluegrass in the fall, and this time Hicks was even more forceful in expressing his opinion of the Seattle Slew filly. "You are never going to see a better filly than that in your life," he told Kernan. "She is absolutely perfect— she's well put together, and she has wonderful hind legs and withers. If you ever want to hang on to anything, this is the one to hang on to." This put Kernan in a quandary. By this time, he and Leslie in partnership were breeding mostly to sell. Although they did occasionally keep a filly, Kernan's finances at the time were such that he needed to get a good price for this first foal by Seattle Slew. And so Leslie and Kernan decided she would be nominated to the Keeneland July yearling sale the following summer.

Once weaned, Strip Poker's filly left the Old Widener Farm and was taken to the main Spendthrift parcel across the street on Ironworks Pike to Barn 22, where the farm's twenty-four most select yearlings bound for next year's sales were stabled and prepared. This was the time when next year's matings were planned. Strip Poker, nearly fourteen, was five months pregnant with her second Seattle Slew colt or filly, and she would be bred in the spring to another Triple Crown champion, Affirmed. If she delivered a healthy foal,

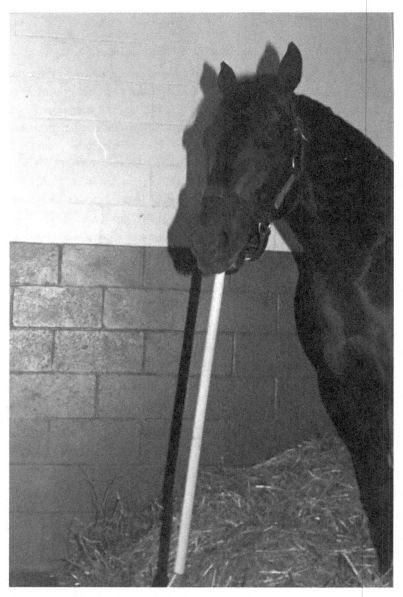

Seattle Slew "helping" Spendthrift groom Andrew "Sandy" Shaw clean his stall, August 14, 1981. (Andrew "Sandy" Shaw)

Strip Poker would produce three offspring in as many years from Triple Crown winners—a "triple triple."

Around the time Strip Poker's filly was getting used to her new home in the yearling barn, twenty-year-old Irishman Andrew "Sandy" Shaw arrived at Spendthrift, hired as a relief groom in the stallion barn. Seattle Slew's Triple Crown win had inspired a teenaged Shaw to train at the Irish National Stud, and the recent graduate hoped he might somehow have an opportunity to care for the great champion. Shaw was delighted when he worked his way up to regular groom for Slew and three other stallions, including J. O. Tobin. The young man developed a strong and immediate bond with the Triple Crown winner, engaging in long conversations with the stallion as he was grooming him. Like John Williams, Shaw was struck by Slew's intelligence. "He could almost talk to you," Shaw recalled. "He seemed to understand what you were saying to him. If you were telling him a sad story, he looked sad. If it was a funny story, you could almost see him laughing." When cleaning out his stall, Shaw would enjoin Slew to "get the brush." "He would . . . try to nudge it in my direction, or even grab it with his teeth and push it across the floor."

In the early months of 1981, preparation of Spendthrift's sales yearlings began, and the most elite among them, including Strip Poker's filly, were assigned to a groom responsible for six. Colts were placed in individual paddocks, and fillies ran together in groups of twelve. As early as March, agents from Europe arrived to inspect yearlings slated for Keeneland's July sale, including those representing heavyweight buyer Robert Sangster and his trainer Vincent O'Brien. In April, across the street at the Old Widener Farm, and almost exactly a year after foaling her first Seattle Slew filly, Strip Poker delivered another. This one was a chestnut, and looked a lot like her mother—compact, small, and shapely.

By May, Spendthrift's twenty-four sales yearlings were being hand-walked intensively and prepared for sale in earnest. To keep their coats from getting sunburned, the group was only turned out at night. Now, one groom was responsible for just four yearlings.

Strip Poker's filly was taught to lead by the handler at her shoulder, and to stand squarely and quietly after walking. By June, she was being lunged in a ring four times a week in addition to hand-walking. The yearling grooms set up a tent outside their barn to replicate those used at Keeneland so the youngsters wouldn't "get spooked by those big green things" when they arrived on the grounds. Their fetlocks, whiskers, and manes were trimmed, leaving a two-inch bridlepath, and they were all trained to wear leg wraps before loading on the van to the sales. Along with her pasturemates, Strip Poker's filly was measured for a custom halter so that the cheekpieces and noseband fell in exactly the right places to show off her head.

In the months leading up to the select sale, Spendthrift stallion grooms were sometimes asked to help hand-walk yearlings. Young Sandy Shaw was eager to oblige, and particularly keen to spend time with any of Slew's yearlings. He often hand-walked Strip Poker's filly, and he was struck by her resemblance to her sire. "My one strong memory of her was she was so like him," he recalled. "The same color and build with few white markings." Shaw hoped that Strip Poker's filly, as one of Slew's first yearlings to go to auction, would make it to the track and help the Triple Crown winner become a top sire.

Sadly, as the time drew near for her filly to leave Spendthrift for good, and just a month after delivering her full sister, Strip Poker developed a severe case of colic. She was taken to a clinic for surgery but did not survive the procedure. "She died the dam of Clout," John Williams observed—the mare's best runner to date, and her only graded stakes winner. Strip Poker's last two foals, both Seattle Slew fillies, remained to carry with them to the racetrack whatever legacy she might still bequeath.

As the important summer sale approached, another wave of sadness flowed through the workings of Spendthrift Farm. The marriage of Linda and Brownell Combs appeared to be over. Despite her role in revitalizing the farm, Linda was driven away at least in part by Leslie's cruelty to the couple and his frequent abuse of her in front of employees, which often reduced her to tears. Many observers felt that Leslie resented Brownell and Linda's success in improving the farm. Things came to a head when Leslie used an extremely offensive epithet in a heated exchange, and Linda stormed out of the office, never to return. Many at Spendthrift, including John Williams, were sorry to see her go.

By July 1981, Strip Poker's filly—fit, clipped, and gleaming—was ready to leave the farm and begin her journey on the road to becoming a racehorse. But first, she had to be discovered by the trainer who would take her there.

Part Two

7

Wayne and Terlingua

If you want something that you never had before, you must be willing
to do something you have never done before.
—D. Wayne Lukas

In July 1977, Wayne Lukas walked into his first Keeneland yearling
sale and walked out with a single horse, a chestnut Secretariat filly
out of a mare named Crimson Saint. Although he had bought quarter horse yearlings at auction for years and had a lifetime of experience judging horseflesh, this was his first trip to the Kentucky select
sales, and few on the grounds took notice of the tanned, immaculately dressed forty-two-year-old quarter horse trainer with creased
blue jeans, aviator sunglasses, and a white Stetson looking to buy a
Thoroughbred or two. Had they known, it would have meant next to
nothing to Bluegrass breeders and consignors that Lukas was national
quarter horse trainer of the year five times, doubled the record for
most wins in a single year, and was battling to become the all-time
leading trainer in purses won. Back then, Keeneland's moneyed blue-
bloods wouldn't have viewed quarter horse racing as a stepping-stone
to any kind of success worth having, since in their minds it was just
a rung or two up the ladder from the greyhounds.

Technically, Lukas had already won a Thoroughbred stakes race
three years ago, although the second division of the Foothill at Pomona,
California, with three-year old-colt Harbor Hauler would hardly have
turned heads at Keeneland. Lukas had made a few modestly successful

forays into racing Thoroughbreds in the past and had a small stable at Hollywood Park earlier in the year, but his quarter horse stable at Los Alamitos and Ruidoso Downs had proven too lucrative to leave behind. Two of his quarter horse owners with an itch to expand into Thoroughbreds had given him some to train: former Chicago policeman turned entrepreneur Eugene Cashman, who had already won the 1976 Preakness with Elocutionist and trainer Paul T. Adwell, brought Hillhouse, winless as a juvenile, to the Lukas barn, and in the summer of 1974, Lukas took the colt from maiden to stakes winner, notching eight wins in ten starts. Former Oklahoman corporate attorney turned Southern Californian Cadillac dealer Robert H. Spreen, a pioneer in the creation of loaner fleets, also gave Wayne a few Thoroughbreds to train, including Harbor Hauler. Wayne's attempt to run a quarter horse stable at Ruidoso and Los Alamitos simultaneously with a Thoroughbred operation at Hollywood and Del Mar overwhelmed him. "I ran myself just about ragged, up and down the highway," he said. Although few in the Thoroughbred world could appreciate it at the time, they would soon come to understand that for Wayne Lukas to admit such a task was beyond him was like the pope declaring there was too much peace in the world.

It seemed the trainer couldn't quite bring himself to make a whole-hearted transition to Thoroughbreds and a clean break from quarter horse racing, though his son Jeff, who worked for him in the summers while still a student at the University of Wisconsin, had been urging him to do just that. Wayne knew he needed a "box office horse," a star who would make a splash for his fledgling Thoroughbred stable and attract more new owners, as quarter horse runners Native Empress and Dash for Cash had done for him in the past.

There were lots of reasons for Wayne to switch to Thoroughbreds, including the opportunity for bigger purses, and an international bloodstock market that made Thoroughbred breeding potentially even more profitable than racing. Depending on which story you believe, either Lukas persuaded his quarter horse owners to go along on his new adventure, or they persuaded him. But the former high school basketball coach would later tell *Sports Illustrated*'s William "Bill" Nack that he was looking for a challenge, as well as greater prestige and the chance to race nationwide. "I'd won the NCAAs," he said, "but I wanted to try it in the NBA." "All successful people 'have a fire burning in them,'" he told writer Carol Flake: "They've either got it from the eighth pole to the wire or not." Flake reported Lukas showed "a certain reluctance to leave the sport where he had become king of the mountain," and that he did continue racing quarter horses simultaneously for awhile, this time assisted by trainer Tom McKenzie, a former starting gate attendant whom he credited for helping him make the move for good. Lukas told Flake he'd been preparing for this move all along or, as she put it, "to cross the barrier of class and pedigree which separated the two racing worlds."

In any event, Lukas started his Thoroughbred stable with a handful of older horses already in training, with a long-term plan to expand through purchasing for his owners a steady stream of yearlings that he would select and train. The Keeneland summer yearling sale was the most elite and expensive place he could have gone to start out, but it was typical of Wayne to aim for the top. Up until the time he actually boarded a plane, Lukas hadn't been entirely sure he would go, later claiming he made the decision "on a whim" and suggesting the trip had been more Mel Hatley's idea than his.

Hatley, another enthusiastic Oklahoman who had made his fortune in "oil, construction, land development and banking," and who would later become one of Lukas's closest friends, was part of the trainer's rapidly expanding posse of quarter horse owners about to turn Thoroughbred, along with Bob French and Barry A. Beal, two of the richest oilmen in Texas at that time. Most of them had been in quarter horses a very long time (French owned starter Panama Ace in the 1959 inaugural All-American Futurity) before meeting the charismatic Lukas, and most told a similar story of trying him out with a couple of horses before being won over by his dedication, work ethic, and unconventional, self-taught approach to training that produced extraordinary results.

On this first buying trip to the Bluegrass, however, it seems Wayne was accompanied only by his longtime friend Clyde Rice, who had helped the trainer pick horses ever since they were kids in Wisconsin eyeballing wild mustangs shipped in from the Dakotas to become feed for the Great Lakes region's mink farms. Wayne picked out the best, paid a cent or two more per pound, and then he and Rice would tame them and resell them as saddle horses. Keeneland was Wayne's first attempt in the Thoroughbred world to create the pattern that would become his trademark: using his superior eye and a ten-point rating system he'd devised based strictly on conformation rather than pedigree, he selected yearlings he felt had the most potential to be great runners, usually sired by stallions new to the market, at prices significantly less than those commanded by the most stylish and coveted pedigrees.

Wayne later admitted that he came to his first Keeneland sale with an eye toward buying the Secretariat filly, because his father-in-law, Rod Kaufman, trained her dam, Crimson Saint, a speedball who won seven of eleven starts and set a track record for five furlongs at Hollywood Park. Wayne felt certain that the combination of blazing quarter horse–type speed with the classic conformation of a champion like Secretariat could be a winning one. Secretariat's first foals were just starting to race as two-year-olds that summer. Wayne claimed that although he'd always been a fan of Secretariat as a sire, "I always felt you had to breed him to a certain kind of mare. Mares that were very precocious and very quick." The Secretariat filly's conformation and bloodlines fit what Wayne was looking for, and he had confidence in her potential from personal experience watching her dam train and race.

"I could see her before I laid eyes on her," Wayne later said. Whether out of embarrassment at being a neophyte at the elite sale or out of craftiness to conceal his interest, Lukas never asked Tom Gentry, the filly's breeder and consignor, to lead her out for his own inspection, waiting instead and observing when other potential buyers asked to see her. "And when they led her out, nobody had to tell

Wayne Lukas at Keeneland with John T. L. Jones Jr. (*far left*) and Robert Gentry (*center*), 1977. (Keeneland Library, Thoroughbred Times Collection)

me [who she was]. She looked like her mother all the way," Wayne recalled. While Gentry poured lime and rum cocktails for a throng of potential buyers, Wayne stood off to one side, watching the filly walk. He liked her more and more each time she came out of her stall, and each time she reminded him more and more of Crimson Saint. He began to worry that her price would be too high for his group of owners to afford. Gentry, who evidently expected the filly to be among the stars of the sale, had pulled out all the stops to promote her. "He had balloons, popcorn, signs, and every time she walked out of her stall, it was accompanied by fanfare," Lukas recalled. Gentry even had pennies minted that bore a likeness of Secretariat's head.

The filly was slated to be sold on the final night of the sale, and as Wayne observed the prices of those who preceded her, his anxiety grew. He called Bob French, vacationing in La Jolla, to warn him that he thought the filly might sell for as much as a half-million dollars. The owner replied, "This sounds crazy, but just bring her back with you."

Wayne's memory of that evening includes the filly entering the ring escorted by four Kentucky state troopers in uniform, swinging nightsticks. The trainer took a seat in the front row of the auction pavilion, but an usher tapped him on the shoulder and asked him to leave the VIP reserved section. As the usher tried to lead him out, Wayne ducked in an attempt to evade him, but he was eventually escorted out. He had to bid on the one horse he had come to buy from the very back of the auction ring.

Like most things he set out to do, Wayne accomplished his goal and secured the filly for French for $275,000, impressive even at the industry's most select yearling auction, where the sale average was $87,000. French was delighted: "I always wanted to own a Secretariat," he said, and invited partner Barry Beal to purchase an interest upon securing the filly. Wayne told *Sports Illustrated*'s Bill Leggett he had been "stunned" to get the filly at that price and admitted, "Tom Gentry never knew I was interested [in her] until after the sale was over." It would be the last time Lukas ever attended a Thoroughbred sale incognito, and never again would his interest in a horse in the auction ring go unnoticed. The trainer had just taken his first step on the road to making Thoroughbred racing history, and the chestnut filly soon to be named Terlingua in honor of a Texas ghost town famous for chili contests would kickstart his success.

As he prepared to ship his first Keeneland yearling purchase to California, Lukas was aware of the enormous task ahead of him, and he knew he needed help. In a few months, he would call his son Jeff, a senior at the University of Wisconsin and only a semester away from graduation, telling him, "You've been there long enough."

It was time for both father and son to get serious about racing Thoroughbreds.

8

Thoroughbreds All the Way

There has never been anyone quite like him, no one even remotely
close, in the long and colorful history of the sport.
—William Nack

Wayne Lukas had no time to waste. Each morning by 4:20 a.m.,
with his Australian shepherd, Duke, in tow, he met Jeff in an all-
night donut shop, ordered a hot glazed donut, and started to map
out their day. By 5:00 a.m., he expected hotwalkers and grooms,
supervised by assistant trainer Laura Cotter, to punch a time clock
at the barn and be ready to work. Wayne budgeted twenty hours a
day for work, seven days a week, allowing thirty minutes for lunch
and forty-five for dinner. "He orders a Coke, menu and check in the
same breath," said John Nerud, one of the first to send a group of
horses to Wayne to train when he was starting out. He didn't take
vacations or days off—"My work is my entertainment," he said.
Arriving at Hollywood Park in early 1978 with six horses, by August
he had twenty at the track and twenty more in training at San Luis
Rey Downs. Three years later, he had more than a hundred horses in
stables sprawled across the United States. In just two years, Wayne
managed to land among the top five trainers in the United States by
total earnings. In four years, he would be among the top three,
behind only Hall of Famers Charlie Whittingham and Laz Barrera.
"I still have to pinch myself from time to time to make sure this is
happening," Lukas said of his rapid rise.

From the start, Wayne made it his mission to upend virtually every convention associated with training Thoroughbreds. Always immaculately groomed, he was called "Mr. Clean" behind his back, and his obsession with appearances extended to every corner of the shedrow—from freshly painted green and white barn doors, to stalls piled with extra deep, clean straw, a tack room resplendent with well-oiled, gleaming girths and bridles, to the bright, potted flowers outside and a herringbone pattern raked into the barn aisle. "Even the dirt . . . looks clean," quipped a Los Angeles columnist.

Wayne bridled his horses in white leather to make them stand out and bathed his favorites in Breck shampoo. "Old horsemen made fun of him behind his back . . . and teased him about his shrubbery," said Spendthrift's John Williams. "But he embarrassed those trainers to clean up their act. The hotwalkers' underwear hanging from a string disappeared."

Wayne's training techniques were equally unconventional. Completely self-taught, he devised his own methods through trial and error, and a keen understanding of horses. "He is an absolute natural horseman," said Williams. "He has a great eye for a horse," added Spectacular Bid's trainer Bud Delp. "The man can train a horse, and he puts them where they can win." Instead of standing at the clocker's platform as most trainers did, Wayne rode to the track every morning in fringed chaps atop a quarter horse pony in western tack with silver trim to get a closer view. He often didn't carry a stopwatch and instead observed intently the way each horse traveled, using hand signals to tell its exercise rider whether to slow down or speed up. His goal wasn't a "bullet" work, but rather a natural development of speed as a horse gained fitness and confidence.

Wayne's attention to detail was never more evident than when applied to the care of his horses. Owner Mel Hatley once saw an ice truck pull up in front of Wayne's barn, and all the horses began to nicker. It was a hot day, and Wayne sometimes had ice delivered to add to their water. "Some of these races are won by a photo finish," he explained. "If they enjoy fresh ice water . . . it might make 'em stick their noses out a little farther. I do every little thing I can to make these horses happy." Wayne also eschewed the conventional wisdom of withdrawing hay and water on race day. "Horses thrive on routine," he said. "I want them to think they're going to have a normal day and not fret when they see the hayrack drawn." Similarly, Wayne got up early so his horses would be first on the training track in the morning—"the going is best at that time and the traffic is lightest," he said.

In the summer of 1978, two very different horses—five-year-old stakes winner Effervescing and two-year-old Terlingua—thrust him into the forefront of California Thoroughbred racing and gave it a crash course in Wayne's way of doing things. In June, Wayne debuted Terlingua not in a maiden or allowance race but in a stakes, which she won in track record time. In July, Effervescing and Terlingua won four stakes races in one month. After capturing the American Handicap on the turf July Fourth with Effervescing in stakes record time, Wayne ran the horse five days later in the Citation Handicap on dirt, where he won again, setting another record. Terlingua set a track record in the Hollywood Lassie Stakes, then one week later, took on colts in the Hollywood Juvenile, which she won in a time two-fifths faster than Triple Crown–winner Affirmed had run the race a year earlier. A third horse who came west in July would also prove important to the trainer. After scoring on the turf at Belmont, Strip Poker's six-year-old son Clout found his way to the Lukas barn and won his first start at Del Mar. Wayne liked Clout—he was an honest, hardworking horse who always tried to give his best.

Terlingua's spectacular and early success gave Wayne instant recognition as a Thoroughbred trainer and fueled the enthusiasm of owners French and Beal for their transition out of the quarter horse ranks. "She put us on the map," Wayne said. Because of Wayne's discerning pick of Terlingua in his first try at Keeneland, Beal and French had a star-quality Thoroughbred who could win at the highest level. They were hooked.

In September, when Terlingua won the Del Mar Debutante and set a stakes record, Wayne and her owners began to think seriously

Terlingua beating the boys in the Hollywood Juvenile Championship in only her second start, July 22, 1978. (Courtesy of Hollywood Park)

about an Eclipse Award. Although she was undefeated in four California starts and had already beaten colts, Wayne knew the only way for Terlingua to win a championship was to go east and challenge the best juvenile fillies in the Grade One Frizette. Confident that Terlingua would prevail, Wayne wanted to prove that a California-based filly could win a championship. Perhaps he also wanted to show that he was more than just a quarter horse "cowboy." "I guess I'm going to have to win the Arc . . . before they're going to call me a thoroughbred trainer," he told one eastern reporter.

Terlingua's trainer knew what he was up against when it came to eastern prejudice against western runners. "When a horse named Swaps came out of California to win the 1955 Kentucky Derby, it was the first time that the racing establishment took West Coast racing at all seriously," observed the *New York Times*. In 1959, two-year-old Warfare became the first California-based juvenile to win a divisional championship since the awarding of seasonal titles began in 1936. After scoring in two stakes at Hollywood Park, the gray son of Determine shipped East, winning the Cowdin, Champagne, and Garden State Stakes—a record convincing enough to secure the championship. In 1978, when Wayne was making plans for Terlingua, no California-based juvenile had won a title since.

Eastern suspicion of western runners was so engrained among Eclipse Award voters that it was presumed that any California juvenile promising enough to challenge for a divisional title needed to travel east to get it. "The faithful at Belmont cling to the notion that when it comes time for a regional showdown on the race track, the Californians will be exposed as phonies," wrote the *Times*. Western runners had two strikes against them in eastern racing circles: the legal use of Butazolidin in California, (any race-day medication was illegal in New York at the time), and the harder, denser California racing surfaces that easterners believed produced artificially fast times.

Difficulties for western juveniles in securing a championship were not confined just to eastern bias, however. It wasn't until 1969, when the Oak Tree meet at Santa Anita was first held, that the West inaugurated its own season-ending championship determiners for two-year-olds: the Norfolk for colts, and the Oak Leaf for fillies, both at a mile and one-sixteenth. Although they drew fields of the best western juveniles throughout the 1970s and were designed to determine the "best in the West," these races were not awarded Grade One status until 1980, seven years after the graded stakes program for U.S. racing was instituted in 1973. Of course, the Champagne and the Frizette, for decades considered the preeminent juvenile races in the East, received Grade One status from the outset.

Even after the West created its own year-end juvenile contests for both sexes, sweeping the best races California had to offer still wasn't enough to secure a national championship, and rarely was this dilemma better exemplified than in the case of two-year-old filly June Darling in 1970. After her score in the Hollywood Lassie, the filly was bought by Clement Hirsch, who ran her in virtually every available California fall stakes. Following a second-place finish in the Del Mar Debutante in early September, the filly returned a week later to defeat colts in the Del Mar Futurity. In October, she scored in both the Anoakia and Oak Leaf against fillies, then beat the best colts in the West in the Norfolk after a week's "rest." With three stakes wins in barely thirty days, and only two weeks after the Norfolk, Hirsch then shipped the filly east to confront favored Forward Gal, winner of the Spinaway and Frizette, in November's Gardenia Stakes in New Jersey. Injured in the barn prior to the race, June Darling went postward anyway and finished last, while Forward Gal ended up third. The day after Forward Gal won the Frizette, and before she even contested the Gardenia, the *New York Daily News* reported that Forward Gal had "thus wrapped up the . . . championship of her division." Despite June Darling's six stakes wins to Forward Gal's four, and despite having beaten stakes colts twice when Forward Gal never attempted it, a win in the Frizette trumped the California filly's record, and Forward Gal was named champion.

By 1978, Terlingua's first year at the track, there still wasn't a single Grade One race available for juvenile colts or fillies in the West. At this early stage in his Thoroughbred career, Wayne believed Terlingua superior to the best eastern fillies and seemed eager to prove it. He was ready to meet the eastern racing establishment head-on, confident he would come out on top—even though Terlingua would have to ship cross-country to unfamiliar tracks with dramatically different weather and surface conditions.

Wayne and Terlingua arrived at Belmont several weeks before the Frizette, so the filly would have time for three works there prior to the race. Immediately, the trainer was struck by the difference in the track's surface: "It's much deeper and more tiring here," he confessed to the *Form,* adding, "I'm not sure she likes it." As it turned out, she didn't. Terlingua suffered her first career defeat and came home a well-beaten third behind 60–1 shot Golferette and eventual co-champion It's in the Air. Darrel McHargue, leading rider in the country at the time, shook his head back in the jockey's room and muttered, "The filly is much better than she showed."

Disappointed but undaunted, Wayne immediately shipped Terlingua to Keeneland for the Alcibiades, looking for redemption. He may have thought things couldn't possibly go worse there, but they did. Encountering rain, hail, and a sloppy track for the first time in her life, Terlingua ran a badly beaten second in the mud at Keeneland. The press was quick to seize upon what they considered a predictable failure, calling Terlingua "slightly overrated." Maryjean Wall in Kentucky went further: "Whatever wins in California does not always get the job done east of the Rockies," she opined. Years later, California turf writer Jay Hovdey suggested that the barely concealed smugness of the eastern racing establishment at Wayne's early failure with Terlingua hardened into his resolve to quit campaigning his best horses there simply to win eastern approval, even if it meant foregoing an Eclipse Award.

Although she showed flashes of it as an older runner, Terlingua was unable to duplicate her two-year-old brilliance, and did not win beyond a mile or around two turns. Retired at four, Terlingua achieved immortality as a broodmare when she foaled top sire Storm Cat in 1983.

In 1979, John Nerud of Florida's Tartan Farms sent Wayne eighteen horses, one of which was a temperamental two-year-old colt named Codex. Nerud's choice of Wayne for his expansion west "gave him respectability" and helped him become leading trainer at Santa Anita for the first time, ahead of veterans Charlie Whittingham, Ron McAnally, Bobby Frankel, and Laz Barrera.

By 1980, although Wayne had achieved several milestones, a start in a Classic race was not among them. Many trainers waited years to have a legitimate Classic contender, but Wayne characteristically felt he had no time to waste. When Codex captured the Santa Anita Derby at three, the trainer was eager to send him to Churchill Downs. Nerud, however, was not keen on the idea and hadn't even nominated the colt to the Derby. Wayne swallowed his disappointment, watched the filly Genuine Risk win the race on television, and looked ahead to the Preakness.

Shortly after the Derby, Nerud came west to see Codex for himself and decide whether or not to pay $10,000 to supplement the colt to the second jewel in the Triple Crown. Nerud reportedly arrived disinclined to run but, after watching the son of Arts and Letters gallop, "had a change of heart and . . . a certain degree of compassion for a young trainer who had never had a classic horse." After previous travel plans fell through, Codex flew east for his first race outside California in a cargo plane filled with two thousand crates of strawberries. The colt arrived at Pimlico unraced in thirty-four days and with only three official works, none over the Maryland track. In the days leading up to the race, the press questioned Wayne's training methods, insinuating that Nerud was the one calling the shots, with the former high school basketball coach serving merely as his protégé.

Codex won the Preakness in the second-fastest time in the race's history, only one-fifth of a second slower than Cannonero II's record, and equal to Spectacular Bid's winning time. Wayne was delighted, scoring a Classic win in his very first attempt. But all of this was overshadowed in the aftermath of the race. Jacinto Vasquez, rider of second-place finisher Genuine Risk, lodged a foul claim against Codex and jockey Angel Cordero. Wayne told reporter Maryjean Wall that his view of the race was blocked, and he didn't see the incident at the time. Vasquez claimed that Cordero deliberately bumped the filly around the final turn, forced her wide, and actually hit her with his whip. A stewards' review disallowed Vasquez's claim, and the result stood. Wayne thought that was the end of it and relished what was by far the most important win of his career.

The next morning, Wayne went to the barn, exhilarated by his first win in a Triple Crown race, and his first chance to bask in the national spotlight. Wayne expected the win to elevate his stature as a Thoroughbred trainer and perhaps attract new owners. When he arrived at his office, there were more than fifty telegrams waiting there, but they weren't congratulatory—most derided him as a quarter horse trainer who didn't belong in racing's major leagues, and blamed him for victimizing the popular filly. Wayne was deflated and angry. "I'd like to wake up with America applauding Codex . . . instead of having women in Miami sending telegrams telling me I'm a bum," he told reporter Wall. After Genuine Risk's owners, Bert and Diana Firestone, filed an appeal, a hearing was held three weeks later, during which video of the race was replayed seventy-eight times. The Maryland Racing Commission upheld the Pimlico stewards' decision, and Codex was once again declared the Preakness winner— and once again, the treatment of Wayne and his horse by the eastern racing establishment left a sour taste.

That summer, Wayne returned to Keeneland's yearling sale. Unknown just two years ago, the trainer was becoming an important buyer at the elite event, and he purchased sixteen yearlings for nearly $2 million. From unproven freshman sire Blushing Groom, Wayne found a gray filly for client Stonereath Stable who would be named Blush with Pride. A colt he did not buy, purchased for $500,000 by client Marvin Warner, would also turn out to be important in the trainer's future. Wayne had been impressed with the son of Hoist the Flag from the outset, telling Warner the colt was "a steal" at that price. Warner named him Stalwart and sent him to Wayne to train shortly after the sale. While at Keeneland, Lukas bumped into an old acquaintance, Bobby Barnett, whom he knew from his quarter horse days in Oklahoma. Wayne needed help with his ever-expanding stable and offered Barnett a job as assistant trainer working with both Laura Cotter and his son Jeff. Barnett moved to California and stayed with Wayne's organization for the next five years.

As eventful as 1980 had been, 1981 would become a landmark year for Wayne. He now owned a home in Arcadia, near Santa Anita, and employed a staff of seventy-five. Jeff Lukas lived in an apartment near his father. Still yearning for his first Derby starter, Wayne had his eye on three-year-old colt Partez, a son of Quack owned in partnership by seventy-two-year-old Henry Green, his wife, Annabelle, and their accountant Elizabeth Davis. The bay colt had started eight times at two, winning the listed Sunny Slope Stakes at Santa Anita and finishing third in the Norfolk, with year-end earnings approaching $80,000.

A yellow legal pad in Wayne's office turned out to be as valuable a training tool for Partez as a stopwatch or an extra cup of oats. In 1981, Churchill Downs officials invoked a race condition that limited the Derby to twenty starters, determined by total career earnings. Wayne figured it would take approximately $100,000 for Partez to qualify. Wayne and Jeff kept an earnings list of fifty-three colts on the Derby trail and updated it anytime a race for three-year-olds was run. Wayne had to start Partez five times before the Derby to accumulate the $25,000 in earnings necessary for the colt to make the field, even running him once on grass for good measure. Wayne's scratch pad got Partez into the Derby, but barely, as the colt was seventeenth on the entry list right before the race. As other connections fumed at last-minute leapfrogs on the earnings list, with two owners even going to court for an injunction permitting their colts to run, Wayne planned carefully to achieve the desired result.

Besides being Wayne's first Derby starter, Partez made history as the first Black-owned Derby entrant since comedian Eddie Anderson's Burnt Cork in 1943. Unraced outside California and given little chance, Partez went postward the first Saturday in May as part of the pari-mutuel field. Behind a blistering opening pace that cooked most of the front-runners, the colt who had barely made it into the race finished a respectable third. The performance of Wayne's unheralded colt was a welcome relief after the controversy surrounding

Codex's Preakness the year before. Wayne was vindicated, and the pressure to prove that he belonged in racing's top echelon was somewhat lifted.

Back home in the West, Wayne was making progress with two-year-old colt Stalwart for Marvin Warner. The headstrong bay son of Hoist the Flag, often brilliant in his morning works, was difficult to handle. "We've either got a saint or a sinner," Wayne told Warner. "We'll see how he develops." A secret ballot among Lukas grooms would likely have resulted in a unanimous "sinner" vote, as the colt had already injured several. "He can be a handful," Wayne admitted. "We've got a couple of ponies that live in dread of him."

By late June, Wayne was ready to try Stalwart in a maiden race at Hollywood Park. The colt finished seventh in his five-and-one-half-furlong debut after being hit in the eye with a dirt clod. Wayne told Warner to "throw this race out. If he ever runs that bad again, I'll be shocked." Wayne decided to wait awhile before racing the colt again, allowing him plenty of time to forget the unpleasant experience and to be bursting with eagerness to run. "He's got a mind of his own," the trainer explained, "and he might have gone out and started running to half his ability, thinking he could get away with it."

Wayne undoubtedly had another reason for taking his time with Stalwart. As a westerner, he knew that the path to achieving sufficient earnings to make the starting gate at Churchill was about to change—California's Hollywood Park had recently announced a new year-ending meet that brought additional racing dates and the opportunity to campaign two-year-olds later in the year. More importantly, the track had created a new race for juveniles, the $500,000 guaranteed Hollywood Futurity, to be run in late November. If Wayne could develop Warner's promising colt as planned, Stalwart could earn enough at two to guarantee a spot in the Derby next year, regardless of what he might accomplish at three. "This year is going to enlighten people," the trainer predicted. "They're going to look at more two-year-old races in the fall."

While Wayne plotted his strategy with Stalwart, it was once again time for the Keeneland summer yearling sales. The forty-six-year-old trainer, himself now a rising star and about to return to the place where he had chosen the filly who launched his Thoroughbred career, could not have known that there was another waiting for him there who would literally change his life.

9

One Bay Filly

I love bringing a good horse out in front of somebody.
—John Williams

On the weekend before Keeneland's summer yearling sale opened on Monday, July 20, 1981, breeder Tom Gentry hosted a party at his farm, where he offered rides on a camel, an elephant, a hot air balloon, and a Ferris wheel, then served a sit-down dinner to more than eight hundred invited guests. Across the street from the sales grounds, Boeing jets owned by the sheikhs of Dubai and shipping magnate Stavros Niarchos were parked at Bluegrass Airport, alongside the Goodyear blimp, forced to lay over due to bad weather but rumored to have been commissioned by British Bloodstock Agency's Robert Sangster, here to do battle for the offspring of top sire Northern Dancer. Champagne and bourbon flowed at the Spendthrift Farm mansion on Ironworks Pike, where Leslie Combs held a cocktail buffet for houseguests Beverly Hills heiress Dolly Green, her Hall of Fame trainer Laz Barrera, and breeder Francis Kernan, who mingled with Kentucky hardboots, bloodstock agents, and Hollywood celebrities—all here to buy or sell this year's crop of yearlings from the best bloodlines in the world.

Meanwhile, 389 royally bred yearlings arrived at Keeneland's sales grounds from farms around the Bluegrass and were led into stalls in green and white barns behind the auction pavilion, where they would be sold over the next three days. At the end of the sale, after nearly $90 million had changed hands, they would disperse to prepare for racing careers at tracks around the globe.

Wayne Lukas didn't drink, and he wasn't a partygoer. The unknown cowboy who bought a single horse four years ago was now in the top echelon of Keeneland's American buyers. He was not here to compete with the Arabs and Europeans for record-setting multi-million-dollar yearlings from the Northern Dancer line. Instead, he was in search of equine athletes—and he didn't care about pedigrees. Conformation—the way a horse is put together—was more import-ant to him than anything else. "I can't cinch up a catalog page," he once told Spendthrift's John Williams. He approached the sale as if it were a sports draft, with his goal to identify top picks. His eye for the attributes of an ideal runner enabled him to find "bargains" at the sale—horses without the most fashionable pedigrees, usually from first-year, unproven sires that met his criteria for the optimal equine body type. Wayne made it a point to look at each individual yearling at the sale without opening the catalogue page to view its pedigree—the opposite of what most sale buyers did. It took him a few days to make his way through several hundred colts and fillies, using a ten-point rating system to prioritize potential buys as follows: "If I give one a six, we pay attention and look for a bargain. If I come up with an eight . . . well, we must own all the eights. And for a nine, I'd give up my wife and firstborn." Only after he had rated horses in this way would he look at the catalogue page to see whose parents a colt or filly "might have to call on in the last sixteenth of a mile."

So while others sipped champagne and bookmarked catalogue pages, Wayne and co-owners Bob French and Barry Beal made their way through Keeneland's barns, inspecting nearly every horse on the grounds. French had enough money and trust to buy whatever Wayne recommended; he had been with the trainer for over a decade, going back to their quarter horse days together. Wayne credited the Texan, among others, for his success in acquiring top yearlings: "We have the same goals . . . to have a classy stable." French usually became major-ity owner of whichever horses Wayne purchased, with partner Barry

Wayne Lukas and Bob French conferring at the Keeneland July 1981 yearling sale. (Keeneland Library, Thoroughbred Times Collection)

Beal acquiring a 10 percent interest afterward. Wayne made the draft picks, French put up the cash, and Beal enjoyed the ride.

Spendthrift's John Williams watched as Lukas approached Barns 9 and 10, immediately behind the auction ring, commonly known as "Leslie's barns," where the farm's yearling consignment was stabled every year. Williams was happy to see Wayne coming his way. "He made a strong presence early on," Williams recalled, "so all consignors knew him, and looked for him to visit. We were very happy whenever Wayne would buy a yearling from us, because he had extraordinary success with many of his purchases."

"Show me what you've got," Wayne said to Williams, already moving off to the side of the gravel path in front of the barns. Williams knew Wayne preferred to see a horse in profile on a diagonal, and was one of the first to employ the technique. "I'm an angles guy," Wayne later said, explaining that he could get a better sense of a horse's proportions that way. Wayne viewed several horses in Spendthrift's consignment before a bay filly with just the barest hint of white on her forehead and a whisk broom tail was led out from Barn 10.

Among the twenty-four yearlings Spendthrift had to offer this year, this filly was one of only six Seattle Slew yearlings in the entire sale, but of course Wayne did not know that at the time. The farm had not featured her in advance sales promotion, focusing instead on yearlings by more established stallions Raise a Native and Exclusive Native, as well as those by J. O. Tobin, widely expected to be this year's top freshman sire.

Wayne watched as the filly walked alongside a handler down the gravel path. Her seal-brown coat was glossy in the sun, darker near her neck and shoulders, and lighter along her spine. The trainer was immediately struck by her enormous heart girth, almost out of proportion to the rest of her. He admired her long barrel and strong hindquarters that would provide her power to push off into an extended and fluid stride. She was "built downhill," with withers slightly lower than her hipbone, the right body type for extra speed, but at the same time Wayne noticed that she stood over more ground than Terlingua, who was built like a pure sprinter. This filly was longer and taller than Terlingua, suggesting she might be better at longer distances. Williams thought the filly's athletic, slightly rugged build might draw Wayne's attention, and he was right.

"She really caught me," the trainer admitted later. "I believe that if you know horses and you walk around a horse three times, you know if it can run," he said. "As soon as I walked around her, I got this chill." "[It's] a gut reaction that's hard to explain," he said.

With Bob French standing alongside, Wayne watched the filly briefly walk twice up and down the gravel path. It didn't take him long to realize that she was the first "nine" he had ever seen in his life. He couldn't find a flaw in her. Wayne was careful to conceal his interest: he didn't want to draw attention to her. "I loved everything about her," he later recalled. "Put her up," he told Williams in a level voice. To French he said, "Take a good look at her because we're not going to look at her again. We are going to buy this one."

By the end of the day, based strictly on conformation, Hip No. 158 was Wayne's top draft pick in the entire sale. "She was like a picture you'd draw of a perfect yearling," he said. After he made his short list of prospects, Wayne checked the filly's catalogue page. What he saw there only increased his excitement. The filly whose physical appearance rated a "nine" was from the first crop of Seattle Slew. Wayne thought Slew was a good bet to become a top stallion, and he liked buying yearlings from new sires. What's more, the filly was inbred to Bold Ruler. "Looking at that pedigree, I knew there would be plenty of mix in that tank," the trainer later said. To top it all off, she was a half sister to Clout, the tough, durable colt who by now had been in Wayne's barn for three years, and who won a division of the Henry P. Russell Handicap for the trainer at Santa Anita.

Wayne could only hope that the next time he saw Hip No. 158 in the sales ring Monday night, he would sign the winning ticket.

As opening night approached, the Slew Crew had high hopes for their stallion's first yearlings ever to go through the auction ring. Slew had just been elected to the Racing Hall of Fame a few days ago, and the partners were anticipating a price in the millions from his colt out of Queen Sucree, the dam of 1974 Kentucky Derby–winner Cannonade. Because they had made the risky and unorthodox decision to retain half-ownership of the Triple Crown winner, there were only six Slew yearlings available for purchase at this sale, as many were already owned in partnership or foal sharing agreements by the Taylors and Hills. The Slew Crew had a lot at stake: they were painfully aware that the last Triple Crown winner, received enthusiastically by breeders in his first few years at stud, had produced few runners of note. They believed in their stallion, but if he followed in the hoofprints of Secretariat, they were doomed.

Two years had already elapsed since Slew bred his first mares—eleven months gestation, then another year or so for foals to mature into yearlings. Offspring sold here today would not come to the races until next year, as two-year-olds. So the minimum timeframe for a breeder to recoup his or her investment at the track was at least three years. "[It] was a long, long time to wait," said Mickey Taylor. "It seemed like forever to me."

Demand was strong for Slew when he first came to stud in 1979, and the syndicate had no trouble filling his book with high-quality mares. But by his second year, Jim Hill realized Slew was "just another stallion," and the partners had to scramble to woo owners of mares they most wanted Slew to breed. Even though he was a Triple Crown winner, some Kentucky breeders remained skeptical about the stallion's conformation and pedigree. Slew's sire, Bold Reasoning, was relatively unknown at the time, and his dam, My Charmer, though descended from Myrtlewood, was herself only the winner of a single minor stakes.

It didn't help that Triple Crown–winner Affirmed now stood across the aisle from Slew in Spendthrift's stallion barn. Brownell had syndicated the chestnut son of Exclusive Native immediately after Slew for $14.4 million, and Affirmed now enjoyed the attention of breeders seeking another hot first-year stallion. There was also significant competition from Slew's stablemate J. O. Tobin, an elegant, flashy stallion whose first yearlings inherited his looks. Slew's offspring, on the other hand, although mostly good-boned, well-mannered, and athletic types, were generally "not extremely attractive" by Hill's own admission. If a stallion like J. O. Tobin could be compared to Cary Grant, then Slew was more like Muhammad Ali, according to Hill. "He's not a pretty horse. He just gets the job done. . . . The third year, we had to struggle," Hill confessed—with no crop yet to race, mare owners had to trust they wouldn't be left with a less than desirable yearling if Slew's first runners turned out to be mediocre. It was vital that Slew's first crop here at Keeneland sell at prices high enough to attract owners of quality mares likely to produce winners in the years to come.

The summer of 1981 had not been an easy one for Brownell Combs. In the midst of divorce proceedings with Linda, Brownell had also been under investigation for irregularities in state insurance contracts, and he resigned from his post as chairman of Kentucky's racing commission. In addition to his personal difficulties, Brownell had much at stake as president of Spendthrift. It was important that the farm's newest stallions, J. O. Tobin and Seattle Slew, perform well at this sale. Yearlings from these two new sires comprised nearly one-third of the farm's Keeneland sales consignment, and consequently its fortunes rode on their shoulders. Spendthrift could no longer rely on older, established stallions like Raise a Native and his son Exclusive Native to compete with Northern Dancer bloodlines. It was up to Slew and his rival to keep the farm where it had always been—near or at the top of Keeneland's leader board.

The eagerly awaited Monday-evening session, known as "Combs night," and always the highlight of the sale, was about to begin. In Barn 10, Spendthrift set up a complimentary bar in the tack room, where bartenders in bow ties poured liberally throughout the evening. Leslie Combs made the rounds of potential buyers, as he always did, "seldom still, moving quickly from person to person to congratulate them on this horse, cajole them about that horse, and jolly then into looking at [another] yearling," according to Spendthrift general manager Arnold Kirkpatrick.

There were no empty seats in the sales pavilion, and onlookers jammed into the viewing areas outside the auction ring, anxious to see if the foreign battle for yearlings from Northern Dancer would result in a new world-record price. No yearling had ever been sold at auction for $2 million, and many in the crowd thought that either of two Northern Dancer colts consigned by E. P. Taylor's Windfields Farm might be the first.

Midway through the evening session, one of them, Hip No. 156, a bay full brother to champion Storm Bird, entered the ring. Robert

Sangster, who bought Storm Bird at auction two years ago for $1 million, wanted the colt desperately. But so did Stavros Niarchos and Sheikh Mohammed bin Rashid al Maktoum. It took twenty-four bids for the colt to reach $1.7 million, equaling the world record. Applause broke out when the colt reached $2 million, and again, minutes later, when the bidding reached $3 million. "There was an air of disbelief," reported Dan Farley of the *Thoroughbred Record*. When Niarchos declined to go further, bidding continued between Sangster and the sheikh. At $3.5 million, the sheikh folded, and Sangster had his record-breaking colt.

Next in the ring was Hip No. 157, a half sister to Spectacular Bid, who sold quickly for $700,000. The crowded pavilion was still buzzing from the sale of Storm Bird's brother as the filly left the ring. Wayne, sitting on the aisle with Bob French alongside, signaled to a tuxedo-clad bid spotter that he intended to bid on Hip No. 158. A few rows behind the trainer sat former Louisiana state senator J. E. "Boyzee" Jumonville Sr. and his wife, Barbara. The portly and flamboyant Cajun, who once pulled off one of his boots during a debate and hurled it at the clock on the Louisiana senate floor, and showed up for an afternoon press interview in blue pajamas, owned five thousand acres of natural gas wells that produced an income of more than $10 million a year. Jumonville's ostentatious wealth included three Rolls Royces, a private jet, and a fondness for massive diamond rings. The sixty-three-year-old reportedly wore four on each hand at Keeneland, while wife Barbara once briefly lost a sixteen-carat stone when it rolled underneath a Las Vegas baccarat table.

Meanwhile, Spendthrift's Rick Nichols led Strip Poker's filly from Barn 10, stopping just short of the auction ring, where he handed her off to a Keeneland groom. Wayne had not seen the filly since her brief weekend walk at the barn, but he was determined to get her. As she circled in the ring, bidding soon narrowed to Wayne and Jumonville, who dropped a drink that rolled on the pavilion's slanted floors and spilled underneath the trainer's feet. Auctioneer Tom Caldwell dropped the hammer at $550,000 with Wayne the winning bidder. When his bid spotter brought Wayne the sales ticket to sign, Jumonville disputed the result, claiming his was the high bid. "We have some confusion here," said Caldwell, who reopened the bidding solely between Wayne and Jumonville. Bob French leaned over and whispered to Wayne, "Do not lose her." Wayne smiled, recognizing what he called French's "Texas pride coming out." He continued to spar with Jumonville until the former state senator declined to proceed after Wayne bid $650,000. This time, when the hammer dropped, Wayne was the owner of Strip Poker's filly. The trainer was nonplussed—"We were prepared to go a lot higher," he said.

Rick Nichols waited outside the ring, took the lead rope from Keeneland's groom, and led Strip Poker's filly back to the barn. So far, she was the highest-priced of the thirteen Spendthrift yearlings who had already gone through the ring. Immediately after the filly left the ring, another son of Northern Dancer followed her and was sold to Sheikh Mohammed for $3.3 million. In fifteen minutes, Windfields Farm had just realized more from two Northern Dancer colts than the value of Spendthrift's entire twenty-four-yearling consignment. Strip Poker's filly was part of "the most expensive four-horse string ever sold at public auction," and among the yearlings sold in those dramatic fifteen minutes, she cost the least.

Wayne would end up spending nearly $4 million at this sale, acquiring nine yearlings for only $50,000 more than what Robert Sangster paid for Storm Bird's full brother alone. Although he was now the sale's top American buyer, the trainer's purchases paled in comparison with those of foreign interests, who spent nearly $30 million, or one-third of the sale's total gross receipts. Hip No. 158, soon to be named Landaluce by new co-owners Beal and French, was the second-highest-priced yearling Wayne bought that year, his first and only Seattle Slew purchase at the sale, and the only Seattle Slew filly sold there to outside interests.

If Francis Kernan had to disregard trainer William O. Hicks's advice and let the filly go, he must have been elated with her sales price—the highest among Spendthrift's entire Keeneland consignment.

Even though she had not been a successful runner, Strip Poker had proven an excellent investment for Kernan, producing stakes winner Clout and now a filly among the top twenty yearlings in the elite sale.

Led by freshman sires J. O. Tobin and Seattle Slew, Spendthrift had slipped into third place among consignors, but if not for these two young stallions, the slide would have been much worse. The new young studs were helping Spendthrift stay near the top of a hyperinflated market created by demand for Northern Dancer bloodlines, but in 1981, the farm's consignment averaged less than half of Windfields'. Northern Dancer by this time commanded prices that inspired incredulity—his six yearlings sold for nearly $9 million, an all-time record at Keeneland. J. O. Tobin lived up to Brownell's expectations, finishing behind only Northern Dancer himself and recently deceased Hoist the Flag as the third-highest-grossing stallion in the sale, and its top freshman sire, with yearlings selling for an average of nearly $60,000 more apiece than Slew's. J. O. Tobin and Slew were the only two freshman sires to crack the top five, and Spendthrift's old standbys, Raise a Native and Exclusive Native, were now no longer even among the top ten.

Although a finish in Keeneland's top five sire list was a happy result, the Slew Crew still had a long road ahead to establish their horse as a top-tier stallion. Seattle Slew's Queen Sucree colt had sold for only $700,000—far less than anticipated—and foreign interest in his yearlings had been lackluster, with only Sheikh Mohammed purchasing a single colt.

Now, it was important for Slew's yearlings sold here at Keeneland to perform well on the track. The Slew Crew had kept many of the stallion's yearlings to race themselves in the next twelve months, but it would certainly help the Triple Crown winner if any of his six yearlings sold here today turned out to be good runners. But that was out of their control. All they could do was wait—and hope.

10

Stalwart Hopes

I have a lot of respect for anybody that can train fillies. Basically fillies run for you. Colts run for themselves.
—Paul Mostert

It was nearly nine hundred miles and a world away from the bluegrass pastures of Spendthrift and Keeneland to the Wayne Lukas ranch in the flatlands outside Norman, Oklahoma. There, Landaluce and eight other yearlings purchased by the trainer were allowed to relax and mature for three months before it was time to begin training in earnest.

Waiting for Wayne back in California was Marvin Warner's two-year-old colt Stalwart, unraced since late June. Wayne felt the son of Hoist the Flag had enormous potential. In addition to giving the colt some time off to recover from his first and largely unpleasant racing experience, Wayne was charting a new path for the headstrong bay—pointing him toward the newly minted Grade One Norfolk Stakes at Santa Anita in late October, with his ultimate goal the rich $500,000 Futurity at Hollywood Park in November.

The landscape of California racing was changing, and nowhere more so than at Hollywood Park under the leadership of director Marje Everett, whom Bill Dwyre of the *Los Angeles Times* described as "a major female force in sports at a time when it wasn't considered a possibility," and the *BloodHorse* once called "the Iron Lady of Inglewood." Everett's passion for racing, her advocacy for improving the sport in California, and her determination to make Hollywood Park a national showplace, were well-known throughout the industry. Her goal to establish year-round racing in the state came to fruition when the California Horse Racing Board awarded Hollywood new dates in November and December of 1981 to top off the racing year.

As soon as the new meet was approved, Marje and her staff went to work designing stakes races to flesh out the existing Southern California schedule. "We wanted a natural progression to solid end of year two-year-old championships," explained then Hollywood racing secretary Tom Robbins. But Marje also hoped "to make a big splash," according to Robbins, and wanted her new year-end races to have "significant dollars to get horses to come to California in the winter." Marje had more than twenty years' experience in shaping juvenile races into profitable crowd-pleasers of national importance—beginning in 1962, when she ran Arlington Park and crafted its Arlington-Washington Futurity into the richest race in the world at that time. So the ground-breaking $250,000-guaranteed Hollywood Starlet for juvenile fillies, and the $500,000-guaranteed Hollywood Futurity for juvenile colts, were born. Instantly, the Futurity became the second-largest purse in the country, behind only the Arlington Million, and the Starlet became the richest race for females anywhere in the United States. Coming as they did at the end of the year, Everett hoped these races would shape divisional championships and eventually lure top eastern runners westward. According to Robbins, who helped Everett design, schedule, and promote the new contests, these races were funded entirely out of on-site pari-mutuel handle, because simulcasting and off-track betting were not yet legal in California, as they had been in New York since the 1970s. In 1981, the only way to see a live race or bet on a race in California was at the track. Big crowds and large pari-mutuel handle yielded more money to fund purses, and Everett aggressively reinvested profits back into her facility.

But Everett didn't stop there, according to Robbins. Exerting the considerable force for which she was already legendary, Everett "went on the road to New York and other places," promoting the new races and encouraging eastern connections to build them into their racing schedule. "She was a pretty good arm-twister," Robbins recalled.

Wayne Lukas, who already had his own reasons for taking his time with Stalwart, now had been given more. For the first time, Wayne and other western trainers had two races for juvenile colts that could yield earnings high enough to make the starting gate at Churchill and maybe even give them a shot at an Eclipse Award—all while staying in California. The Norfolk Stakes at Santa Anita had just been elevated to Grade One status, and the Hollywood Futurity was by far the richest race in the country for juveniles. If Stalwart captured the Futurity, he could earn as much in a single race as the best and most heavily campaigned eastern juveniles would amass in the entire year. There was no race in the East remotely approaching the Futurity's purse—even the revered Champagne, traditionally the championship determiner for juvenile colts, offered only $150,000— about one-fifth the expected total purse for the Futurity, which would swell above its guaranteed value with additional nomination and supplemental fees. *Sports Illustrated*'s William Leggett agreed that "It is clear that California is where the most money can be made." The race's timing dovetailed with Wayne's preferred strategy for bringing a colt to the Derby: "It's been my plan all along to race . . . my top three-year-olds only twice apiece before we consider the Kentucky Derby," he said. "Every year you see horses coming up to the Preakness who are worn out." A win in the Futurity would make a colt's three-year-old earnings nearly irrelevant, allowing his trainer to campaign him sparingly in the spring preps leading up to the Derby. If he had a colt good enough to hit the board in the Futurity, Wayne could throw away his yellow scratch pad. If he had one good enough to win the Grade One Norfolk, and also capture the Futurity, there was at least an outside chance for an Eclipse Award. Wayne thought Stalwart had the potential to win both races.

Of course, when the trainer returned from Keeneland, the temperamental son of Hoist the Flag was still a maiden, so Wayne's plans might have seemed utopian to some. In his next start at Santa Anita, Stalwart broke his maiden, but barely, with jockey Laffit Pincay practically having to lift the colt over the finish line. "Laffit told me afterward [he] should have won by daylight," Wayne said, "but . . . he was playing around all the time. He never did have his mind on business." Even so, the colt's victory marked the beginning of a three-race winning streak in which Wayne took Stalwart from maiden company to Grade One stakes winner in a little more than three weeks. Stalwart's winning time in the Norfolk was just two-fifths off the stakes record, the second-fastest in the contest's twelve-year history. Jockey Chris McCarron was impressed with Stalwart's effort—"He's a little green still," said the rider, "but . . . when I set him down at the quarter pole, he really dug in." "He shows flashes of brilliance," Wayne added. "I'd have to say he's ahead of Codex at this stage of his career."

Meanwhile, around the time Wayne renewed Stalwart's campaign, Landaluce and the other Keeneland sales yearlings, now about to become two-year-olds, left Oklahoma for the San Luis Rey Training Center in California, where they would remain until the spring, when it was time to come to the track. Under the tutelage of assistant trainer Tom McKenzie, Wayne's yearlings began schooling in earnest to learn how to race. Like many California trainers, Wayne found the low-key atmosphere out in the country at San Luis Rey to be quieter and less stressful for horses. Here, Landaluce galloped every day for a mile or two. She learned to be saddled in a paddock, work on a track in the company of other horses, and to break from a starting gate. Once a week, Wayne drove ninety-five miles from Los Angeles to Bonsall to view his yearlings' progress. He spoke by phone with McKenzie and other staff members regularly for updates. From the beginning, Landaluce was easy and tractable and acted like she wanted to run. Wayne had high hopes for the daughter of Slew, and was particularly interested in her progress. But at this early stage, Landaluce was not yet at the top of his staff's list as a racing prospect. "She's very nice, boss," they would tell him, "but the one we really like is the Full Out filly." Much would change in the next six months.

As fall blended into winter, it was time for Marje Everett's first year-ending Hollywood Park meet to begin on November 11. For the first time ever, Thoroughbreds would race at the Inglewood oval until nearly Christmas Eve. The highlight of the meet was the Hollywood Futurity on November 29. Wayne had given Stalwart a breather since his Norfolk victory so he would be ready to face a tough field of twelve juveniles, including one-eyed Cassaleria, winner of the El Camino Real Stakes; future millionaire and Del Mar Futurity winner Gato del Sol, third behind Stalwart in the Norfolk; as well as highly regarded eastern shipper Laser Light, winner of the Grade One Remsen at Aqueduct. Also in the field was another Lukas-trained starter, Tartan Farms' talented sprinter Sepulveda, as well as the filly Header Card.

By race day, the Futurity purse had swelled to $715,000, and Stalwart and Laser Light were co-favorites. The track was rated slow, and several runners were equipped with mud caulks. At the break, Laser Light hesitated and was never a factor. Sepulveda zipped to the lead and took command until the head of the stretch, when Stalwart and Cassaleria moved to challenge. Stalwart had the lead at the eighth pole, but by the sixteenth pole, Cassaleria drew even and briefly put his head in front until he made what the *BloodHorse* called "a big mistake" when he lugged in and bumped the son of Hoist the Flag. The angered Stalwart dug in and passed Cassaleria, battling back for a half-length victory at the wire, with the filly Header Card well back in third. "I love this colt," Wayne said afterward. "He's a heck of a fighter."

Accolades were heaped upon Marvin Warner's colt, now co-owned with breeder John T. Oxley, immediately after his Futurity score. "Stalwart and Cassaleria, by drawing away from the rest of the field with authority, pointed themselves out as outstanding classic

Stalwart's win in the inaugural Hollywood Futurity, November 29, 1981, convinced Wayne that the colt was his best Derby prospect to date. (Courtesy of Hollywood Park)

prospects," reported the *BloodHorse*. "Many Californians feel [Stalwart] is one of the best West Coast youngsters since Swaps," wrote William Leggett, calling the Lukas trainee "one of the favorites" for the Kentucky Derby. Despite such high praise, none of the colt's connections held out hope for an Eclipse Award. "I think he deserves it," Wayne said, "but it's hard to get their attention back there," noting that he didn't expect easterners to vote for a western horse. Co-owner Warner was equally philosophical: "Horses that are exclusively in California are suspect until they prove themselves elsewhere," he pointed out, adding "most of the votes are centered in the East."

Stalwart didn't win an Eclipse Award, but his Futurity victory brought his lifetime winnings to $528,000—surpassed only by the great Buckpasser's juvenile earnings record, which had stood since

1965. For Wayne, that was more than good enough. "The bottom line is dollars, and they're even more important than Eclipse Awards," he later said. "The hell with the votes from a bunch of sportswriters." The former quarter horse trainer had the best Derby prospect of his career right where he wanted him. Guaranteed a spot in the gate at Churchill by virtue of his Futurity win, Wayne planned to give the colt a rest, begin working him in the spring, and start him in one or two key prep races. Then it would be on to Kentucky.

As 1982 dawned, the D. Wayne Lukas stable was riding high. The cowboy had finished fourth in the nation with $2.6 million in total earnings. By the end of January, the *Louisville Courier-Journal* rated Stalwart as its second-favorite in the Run for the Roses. Last year, Wayne had been happy just to make the starting gate with Partez. This year, the cowboy would have a co-favorite, a colt who could actually win. "A horse like this only comes along every fifteen years or so," he told turf writer Billy Reed. The most coveted prize in racing seemed within his grasp.

On March 1, when turf writer Joe Hirsch visited Wayne at Santa Anita, the trainer confided he was "convinced he could win the Derby." Five days later, Stalwart bowed a tendon in a morning work. Heartbroken, the trainer brought in veterinarians throughout the country, hoping for a way to keep the colt on the Derby trail, but to no avail. On March 19, the best Derby prospect of Wayne's career was retired.

The trainer was devastated. "I was in a daze," he later told Hirsch. "All my life I waited for a horse like this and he finally came along then he was gone. Every time I went to a restaurant for a cup of coffee people would ask me 'How is Stalwart?' and my stomach would do flips. . . . The public never saw his real brilliance." Wayne called the son of Hoist the Flag "the best horse I've ever been associated with" and his injury, "the biggest disappointment I've had in the horse business." For three days, the trainer found it difficult even to walk down the shedrow. Wayne knew Stalwart had been his best chance ever for the blanket of roses, and he respected the fact that it might be a very long time before he had another quite as good.

Wayne dusted himself off and won the Santa Anita Derby in early April with his second-best three-year-old colt, Tartan Farm's gray Muttering, who became his new hope for the Classic. Around the same time Wayne shipped the gray son of Drone to Churchill, Landaluce, now two, clocked her last official work at San Luis Rey before heading to Hollywood Park in anticipation of her first start. She departed the training track in style, working four furlongs in :47 3/5, a bullet—the fastest run by any horse that day at the distance.

When she arrived at Hollywood, assistant trainer Bobby Barnett was struck by Landaluce's appearance the first time he saw her step off the van from San Luis Rey. "What a big, good looking two-year-old filly," he thought. If all went well, Landaluce would race for the first time in about two months.

In the meantime, Muttering's disappointing fifth-place finish in the Derby rubbed salt into the wound from Wayne's loss of Stalwart, when two colts defeated by the son of Hoist the Flag—Gato del Sol and Laser Light—finished first and second at Churchill Downs. When his 1980 Keeneland yearling purchase Blush with Pride by unproven sire Blushing Groom captured the Kentucky Oaks the day before the Derby, Wayne achieved a new milestone. Still, Wayne's early experience with these two races only intensified his determination to win the Derby and may have rekindled his belief that entering the right filly in the Classic would be a smart move. Gato del Sol won nearly triple what Blush with Pride earned in the Oaks, and the publicity for the Derby winner and his trainer, Charlie Whittingham, was "immensely greater," as writer Ross Staaden noted. "Comparatively speaking, the Oaks was nowhere, completely overshadowed by the Derby," he observed. "This could only have increased Wayne's existing propensity for running top fillies against colts." Wayne was already contemplating another unorthodox strategy bound to unsettle the Thoroughbred racing establishment. Inspired by Genuine Risk's Derby win, Wayne "may well have seen that the belief that fillies cannot win was at least partly responsible for their poor showing."

He would not be afraid to run a filly in the Derby—when the right one came along.

Back in California, Wayne took stock of his up-and-coming two-year-olds waiting for him at Hollywood Park. It didn't take long for him to realize that the bay daughter of Seattle Slew who so impressed him as a yearling might indeed be something very special.

Every morning in the half darkness, and never later than 6:05 a.m., Wayne waited in midstretch around the sixteenth pole aboard a retired quarter horse pony to watch his horses work or gallop. Jesse Cerillo, "a bull of a little man with shoulders like a linebacker," rode Slew's bay daughter whenever she galloped at the track. Sometimes, the filly's dark bay coat in the darkness made her nearly invisible, with only Wayne's trademark white bridle seeming to glide swiftly through the air, ghostly, as if unattached to a living thing. At first, the filly's smooth and effortless way of going fooled the trainer into thinking she wasn't really traveling that fast. Once, when Wayne was watching her gallop, she changed leads so smoothly the trainer, who missed nothing, didn't see her do it. "I must have blinked," he said, "because I never saw . . . it." The trainer knew this was a sign a horse was moving very fast—because one who was traveling slowly would have a rougher and more obvious lead change. Wayne soon realized that Landaluce's deceptively easy way of swallowing up ground was a sign of huge potential.

Assistant trainers Bobby Barnett and Laura Cotter noticed other things about the filly that hinted at her promise. "She always did everything right," said Barnett. "She was a treat to be around." Cotter, who had worked for Wayne since his quarter horse days, was struck by Landaluce's intelligence and felt the filly could almost "talk" to her. When Laura led her outside the shedrow and held her bridle while waiting for Cerillo, Landaluce would stop and survey the track in both directions. Laura thought the filly was saying, "Are you looking at me yet? You know you want to watch me. I'm getting ready to run now." Laura had been around horses a long time, and she sensed this one was special—it was as if the filly knew she deserved and even thrived on human attention and respect. If Laura had ever met Seattle Slew's interim groom Sandy Shaw at Spendthrift, the two might have traded notes on what father and daughter had in common.

Although Landaluce had already made a name for herself at San Luis Rey with her speedy works there, when she first set foot on the Hollywood Park strip to work three furlongs from the gate on May 8, her :38 1/5 clocking was attributed to a horse named Landalulu. About two weeks later, twenty-year-old aspiring jockey David Pineda, whom Wayne called "the best exercise rider in California" was astride Seattle Slew's bay daughter. Landaluce worked easily, and Pineda was satisfied with the filly's outing until he pulled up in front of the trainer. Wayne was furious. "Don't you ever, ever work a baby of mine that fast," he yelled at Pineda. "But she was going easy," the rider protested, thinking the filly had worked a half-mile in about forty-nine seconds. Pineda was amazed when Wayne told him the filly's time was :46 3/5. "Your watch must be wrong," he shot back. Once again, the clocker misidentified the fast filly, listing her in charts this time as Landalule. But it wouldn't be long before everyone at Hollywood Park knew her name.

Throughout the month of May, Landaluce progressed to working every seven to ten days, with gallops in between. Each week that passed brought more excitement and optimism from her trainer. Even though Wayne's goal was to "put a good foundation on her" without asking for speed, and even though Pineda now understood that Landaluce's easy stride was deceptively fast, he still often had difficulty holding the filly below :47 or :48 in her works. "We learned she had the speed whenever we wanted it," the trainer later said.

As Landaluce matured, Lukas began to use two horses in her works—one who broke in front of her at the outset, and another waiting at the three-eighths pole. "She always ate up both of them, first one and then the other," the trainer recalled. Wayne soon realized that "we had nothing that could stay with her; nothing of any age." Word quickly spread around the Hollywood backstretch that

Wayne had another crackerjack juvenile filly, one maybe even faster than Terlingua. "I hear D. Wayne Lukas has a Seattle Slew filly who can really run," said trainer Dave Hofmans, who had seven two-year-old Slews in his barn. In early June, the *Form*'s Mike Marten found Wayne tight-lipped when the reporter asked for an assessment of Landaluce's prospects before her first start. Marten wrote that Wayne "sidestepped the issue by indicating he would let the filly do the talking on the racetrack."

Although he wouldn't admit it at the time, Wayne was described much later as "smitten" with Landaluce. The trainer was so enchanted by her that he wondered if his mind was playing tricks on him—maybe his grief at the loss of Stalwart was fueling a higher opinion of Landaluce than he really ought to have. Maybe it was simply wishful thinking to believe this unraced filly might be the equal of his best colt ever. Wayne began to doubt his own instincts. "I had just gone through that thing with Stalwart," he told turf writer Billy Reed. "When I saw her I was thinking that I had better be careful. When I watched her the first time, I couldn't believe it. But I didn't think I could be fooled that easily. When I watched her again, I didn't think she was doing anything—until I looked at my stopwatch."

As summer began, Wayne thought Landaluce was ready to race, and he entered her in a maiden contest at Hollywood. In late June, Wayne traveled east for Blush with Pride's attempt to capture the Coaching Club American Oaks at Belmont, the third jewel in the filly Triple Crown. When he returned to California on Saturday, June 26, the trainer found himself on a redeye flight with jockey Angel Cordero, who'd piloted Codex to the trainer's first Preakness win, and who also rode Seattle Slew for the last four races of the stallion's career. As it happened, Cordero was on his way to Hollywood Park to ride in the Milady Handicap for trainer Howie Tesher. Wayne planned to go straight to the barn as soon as the plane landed to work his Hollywood string. Landaluce was on the work tab, and if all went well, she would start the following weekend. As the plane descended, Wayne had an idea.

"I've got a filly I'd like your opinion of," he said to Cordero, suggesting he come to the barn and work her if the jockey "wanted a treat." Cordero agreed, but once he was astride Slew's bay daughter, Wayne cautioned "she's very talented, so don't let her go too fast." Landaluce was scheduled to work in company with three-year-old maiden colt King Thou Art. Even though Cordero had the filly "under a stranglehold," the older horse could not keep up, and was six lengths back after a quarter mile. Instead of continuing to fight her, Cordero relaxed his hold for the rest of the work. As Landaluce galloped out, Wayne rode up on his pony "to see if she was breathing hard." She wasn't—even though she had just worked a half mile in :46 4/5 while being restrained for half the distance. "She feels real good underneath me," Cordero said. He asked the trainer when Landaluce was scheduled to start, offering to take off his New York mounts to come west to ride her. "I'll ride her anywhere, anytime," he said.

Wayne was now certain his optimism about Landaluce was well-grounded. The opinion of Cordero, "the first significant professional rider to work her," clinched it. His Seattle Slew two-year-old really was as good as he thought she was—maybe even better. Barely three months ago, the bitter disappointment of Stalwart's loss had been all Wayne could think about. "I said to myself it would be a long time before I ever got one as good," he later admitted. "A couple months later . . . I knew I had one twice as good."

Wayne Lukas had been training horses long enough to know there were few professions with higher peaks or lower valleys. Despite his penchant for planning and attention to detail, there was much outside his control. The unpredictability of Thoroughbreds—their brute strength combined with their fragility—conspired to compose a life punctuated almost daily with both delight and discouragement that could deepen, if he let it, into despair. In spite of everything that had happened with Terlingua, Codex and Stalwart, the trainer was carefully, and somewhat reluctantly, letting himself believe he now had a filly who could be better than any of them—and she was ready to run.

Part Three

11

Good from the Beginning

Young horses . . . are usually very green . . ., and then develop . . . but
she was good from the beginning.
—Laffit Pincay

Thirty-two-year-old Laffit Pincay, top rider for the Wayne Lukas
barn, made his way from the jockeys' room to the paddock at Hollywood Park on the bright, sunny afternoon of Saturday July 3,
after having hurriedly changed into Beal and French's hunter-green
silks with white polka dots. Already among the top jockeys in U.S.
racing history and inducted into the National Racing Hall of Fame
seven years ago, Laffit had more important things on his mind than
the upcoming race for maiden two-year-old fillies he was about to
ride.

It was the middle of a big holiday weekend at Hollywood, with
a crowd of nearly thirty-four thousand on hand to enjoy some of the
West Coast's most important stakes races, including today's feature,
the Hollywood Express, in which Laffit would ride favorite Time to
Explode against a field of ten of the circuit's best older sprinters. Then
there was the Hollywood Oaks on Sunday for three-year-old fillies,
and the American Handicap on Monday. Laffit had top mounts in
all of them. Wins in these races were vital for Laffit to wrest the
meet's riding title from younger jockey sensation and defending
national champion Chris McCarron, who was ahead of him in total
wins. Laffit's ultimate goal was to surpass his idol Bill Shoemaker's

record of 8,883 lifetime wins, and he needed to be aboard winners every day to make that happen.

Laffit was having a spectacular summer, with the month of June an embarrassment of riches on both coasts: Just a few weeks before, after guiding Conquistador Cielo to a win over older horses in track record time in the Metropolitan Handicap at Belmont, he had finally broken his "Triple Crown drought" with a stunning fourteen-length victory aboard the bay son of Mr. Prospector in the Belmont Stakes for trainer Woody Stephens, following up with a victory on the sensational gelding Perrault in the Hollywood Gold Cup. But that wasn't all: to top it off, he had ridden sprinter Time to Explode to a new world record in an allowance race right here at Hollywood for trainer Gary Jones. Among these wins, the Belmont was most satisfying, for after a decade of promising mounts in the classics, including a heartbreaking second-place finish on Sham behind Secretariat, Laffit had failed to win a Triple Crown race. Conquistador Cielo's Belmont win proved once and for all that the rider could capture the Classic races, erasing the lone blemish on his star-spangled career.

Still, Laffit was a perfectionist. Consumed with an overwhelming desire to be the best in the sport, he couldn't afford to let up now. To stay ahead of McCarron and to catch Shoemaker, he needed to be on the best horses in each race, every day, and he needed to stay in peak physical condition. Laffit struggled throughout his career to keep his weight at or near 112 pounds, while remaining fit enough to power winners home through the stretch. His self-discipline with respect to diet and exercise, even among a jockey colony obsessed with these rituals, was legendary. In a sport where the average rider's career lasted only five years, Laffit's had already spanned eighteen. For more than half his life, he had secretly subsisted on a diet of fewer than four hundred calories a day, while working out at the gym daily and visiting the sweatbox, once managing to lose six pounds in four hours. A typical diet for Laffit was coffee with a plain piece of toast every other day, nothing for lunch, and one ounce of boiled rice and two ounces of chicken or steak for dinner. He was once observed scraping salt off a single cracker before eating it. When winning owners invited him to dinner to celebrate, Laffit either politely declined or went along and ate only three ounces of chicken while the rest of the table savored thick steaks and champagne. Wayne Lukas, whose filly he was about to ride, had been shocked on the way home from the races on a private plane with Laffit when dinner was served: as Wayne dug in to his meal, Laffit pulled a single peanut from his pocket, split it in two, and ate half.

Laffit had convinced himself such strict regimens were necessary to overcome an illogical but deeply held belief that many of his colleagues were superior riders. "I never believed I was the best," he said. "I always felt that a lot of these guys were better. I had to work harder and do more if I was going to compete with them." In the 1970s, Laffit started jogging on the track in the late morning after horses had finished their workouts as another way to burn calories and remain fit. "I couldn't work horses in the mornings because it took too much out of me," Laffit admitted, opting to conserve his energy for the grueling race day ahead. He didn't want anyone to know there were times when the stress of diet and weight loss left him feeling too weak to ride. He needed all his strength to push his mounts over the finish line in the last sixteenth of a race, a skill at which he excelled. Other jockeys laughed and shook their heads when they saw Laffit in these human morning workouts, but as he began to break earnings and win records, some started to join him.

Today, as Laffit approached the saddling enclosure before the fourth race, the mood at the track was festive. In the early 1980s, Hollywood Park was among the premier racing facilities in the United States, attracting fields of top runners and attendance of 123,000 for this weekend alone, nearly 30,000 more patrons than Belmont Park, its nearest competitor. Saturday racegoers often arrived as early as 10:00 a.m. to grab a spot on the rail or to enjoy activities in the infield, including adult softball games and a playground for children. Buffets were set up in the infield, an orchestra played, and female patrons could get their hair and nails done at a beauty salon in the clubhouse, where fans might catch a glimpse of many celebrities regularly in attendance, including Cary Grant, Elizabeth Taylor, Joe Namath, Walter Matthau, and Mel Brooks, who liked to bet long shots. On days like today, the track's parking lot was so tightly packed that Marje Everett sometimes came out of her office to direct cars into stalls.

Laffit loved riding at Hollywood Park and had won more races here than anywhere else. He was in a good mood. He twirled his racing crop and smiled as he walked past the Hollywood Gold Cup memorial, inscribed with the names of winners of the track's signature race, run since it opened in 1938 and won by Seabiscuit that year. Laffit had already won five times, most recently with Affirmed in 1979 and with Perrault just weeks ago.

The only thing was, he was overweight by one pound on the filly he was about to ride in this race for Wayne Lukas, and he was two pounds over on Time to Explode in the feature for Gary Jones. Laffit knew that both trainers had immense confidence in him, or they would have replaced him with another rider if they deemed the overages significant enough to affect their entry's performance. Still, in spite of everything he'd done to make weight, Laffit couldn't help wishing he was just two pounds lighter. To bring himself luck, Laffit wore his underwear inside out—a habit he'd employed since his first race in Panama as a teenager in 1964.

As he walked into stall number six, where Wayne and assistant trainer Laura Cotter were preparing her for the first race of her life, Laffit saw the dark bay daughter of Seattle Slew for the first time. As is often the case with top jockeys, he had never worked or ridden her before—he was simply too busy. Wayne had wisely refrained from sharing the news that Laffit's rival Angel Cordero had worked the filly a week ago and was so impressed that he offered to surrender his New York mounts to ride her in this race. Laffit's agent, Tony Matos, who secured the mount, had told him that Wayne "was very high on this filly," and Laffit had learned to trust Wayne's opinion when it came to assessing his starters' prospects. Still, Laffit, like most jockeys, rarely shared the degree of optimism felt by trainers, especially when it came to unraced two-year-olds. Green or inexperienced horses learning to break alertly from the gate, race in tight quarters, accelerate or wait until asked, and handle crowd noise and the excitement of live racing for the first time were unpredictable at best and disastrous at worst. Laffit knew that with two-year-olds, anything could happen. It was best not to expect too much.

On the other hand, Laffit respected Wayne's horsemanship, and knew he was developing a reputation for being particularly adept with fillies. Laffit had been riding for Wayne ever since he switched from quarter horses to Thoroughbreds. When he won his first race for the trainer aboard three-old colt Current Concept, Wayne had joked, "I know he can run a quarter mile. After that, you are on your own." Since then, Laffit had guided Wayne's top horses Terlingua, Effervescing, and Island Whirl, among others, to stakes victories during those early years. Although it slipped his mind today at Hollywood, Laffit had also ridden Landaluce's half brother Clout to a turf win for Wayne at Del Mar four years ago, when the colt first came to the Lukas barn from the East Coast.

Laffit noticed that the filly stood quietly in her saddling stall, seemingly unruffled by the crowd, and made no fuss when Wayne cinched her girth or slipped her halter off over his trademark white bridle. He thought she had a nice air about her. All these were good signs.

As Laffit swung his leg up over the filly and prepared to head to the post, Wayne predicted, "You're really going to enjoy this. . . . Just sit perfectly and she'll run like a six-year-old." But Laffit could not have anticipated what was in store for him. Neither he, Wayne, nor any among the crowd in attendance knew that what was about to unfold in this seemingly ordinary maiden race would eclipse anything else at Hollywood Park that day.

A little before 3:00 p.m., Landaluce and Laffit left the bright sun-shine and warm summer air of the paddock for the cool, damp con-crete tunnel leading to the track as they made their way to the post. The filly, accompanied by her stable pony Buddy, had drawn post position six in a field of seven for this six-furlong race. She was the 7–5 morning line favorite and unanimous choice among official track handicappers, who proclaimed she had "the earmarks of a stakes filly," with the exception of a lone holdout who preferred Flameout, who had drawn the rail, and who was, ironically, owned by Brownell Combs. Both Flameout and Landaluce had recent posted works at five furlongs, and Flameout's was slightly faster. Today's race would be their first attempt at the longer distance.

Bettors were also impressed by the early efforts of Seattle Slew's first crop, who were just beginning to race. His first three starters had all finished in the money. Trainer Dave Hofmans's filly Slew Manet ran second, beaten by a nose in a photo here at Hollywood in late May, while filly Embellished ran third in her first start at Belmont and juvenile colt Slewpy broke his maiden there in late June. It looked like Seattle Slew was already producing good runners, and the fact that Landaluce had a Lukas-trained graded stakes–winning half brother in Clout, who had run well here in California, increased the betting public's confidence in her. This was in spite of the fact that Landaluce would be the only filly in the field carrying 117 pounds, with all others carrying 116.

Second choice in the betting was Midnight Rapture, ridden by Chris McCarron, and the only runner in the field with racing expe-rience, having finished a good second in her first outing to Princess Lurullah, who went on to place in the Cinderella Stakes.

Also parading to the post was another Lukas-trained maiden, a chestnut Quack filly ridden by Pat Valenzuela named Some Kinda Flirt. Wayne had purchased her at the same Keeneland yearling sale as Landaluce for $185,000 on behalf of Ruth Bunn, widow of coffee magnate Jacob Bunn, a major owner for Wayne throughout both his quarter horse days and transition to Thoroughbreds. Wayne thought

Some Kinda Flirt had stakes potential, too, though he certainly didn't have as high hopes for her as for Landaluce: in four furlong works for both throughout May and June, Flirt was generally two to three seconds slower.

Rounding out the field were longshots Miss Big Wig, Natalie n'Me, and Meet a Queen. Although he could not have known it at the time, Meet a Queen's rider, Marco Castaneda, was about to become the only jockey in history to run against both Landaluce and the great champion Ruffian in each of their maiden races.

This was the only race in Landaluce's life for which little would be written in advance. There was no buildup, loaded expectations, or throng of photographers. For a few more minutes, she would be just another promising, beautiful, two-year-old filly prancing up the stretch with her pony, her ears flicking to take everything in on her first time going to the post.

When the horses reached the starting gate, Landaluce waited patiently for the five inside her to load, showing none of the skittishness or nervousness of untried young starters. She stood calmly in the gate, and Laffit made sure her head was pointed straight ahead so she would break well.

When the gate opened, Landaluce broke alertly, like a seasoned runner, rushing almost immediately into contention with Miss Big Wig, who was ahead of her on the inside, and Meet a Queen on her outside. In just several strides, Landaluce surged to the lead between horses, ahead a half length by the first eighth, with Laffit urging her, but only mildly. Landaluce was running smoothly without really being asked, and she was drawing away from the field, extending her lead to a length and a half by the end of the first quarter in a sizzling :22 flat. It was no wonder the others could make little headway, yet, in a style that would become her trademark, Landaluce was running so apparently effortlessly that her speed was deceptive. She appeared to be relaxed, running within herself, and certainly nowhere near her top ability. Her stride was so long and smooth that it didn't seem to anyone she was moving as fast as she was. Laffit was happy with the way the race was unfolding. All the things that could ruin the chances of an unraced filly starting from an outside post position in a sprint hadn't happened: she hadn't broken badly, she hadn't got boxed in behind horses, and she wouldn't be pulled wide around the turn. Laffit had yet to ask her to run, but here she was, easily and happily on the lead, opening up ground on the rest of the field. By the time she ran the first half mile, she was ahead by three lengths, in a spectacular time of :44 3/5, and still without being asked for speed. Because she was already so far ahead of Miss Big Wig and Midnight Rapture, who had moved up to second, Landaluce was able to hug the rail around the turn and save ground, still striding easily. At the eighth pole, the field bunched behind her, Laffit tapped her lightly on the shoulder, and Landaluce continued to pull away in the stretch, winning under a hand ride by seven lengths.

Laffit pulled the filly up gradually, impressed at the ease of her stride that had propelled her to victory. He knew she wasn't tired, could have run longer, and had a demeanor that suggested she was easy to ride and wanted to win. These were the qualities of a stakes winner, and perhaps even a champion.

The rest of the field straggled back to the tunnel to head to the barns. Marco Castaneda had finished next to last on Meet a Queen, duplicating his performance on Precious Elaine when she finished next to last in Ruffian's maiden race. Perhaps he was thinking he had come up against a filly of similar caliber.

Nobody but Laura Cotter and her groom paid much attention to Some Kinda Flirt as she trotted back from the track to be unsaddled. She would be the only filly from this maiden race ever to run against Landaluce a second time. The chestnut hadn't run badly, finishing fourth, but she, like the rest of the field, had simply been outclassed, beaten over thirteen lengths by her stablemate, whom *Daily Racing Form* columnist Jon White described as "a two-year-old filly without wings who also can fly." In off-microphone audio during the gallop out, track announcer Harry Henson can be heard saying, "That filly ran the last eighth of a mile in eleven and something [seconds]. She

Landaluce breaking her maiden at first asking by seven lengths in the sensational time of 1:08 1/5 at Hollywood Park, July 3, 1982. (Benoit Photo)

just got in with the wrong kind of filly in here to break her maiden." He could have been talking about any filly in the field.

When Laffit and Landaluce reached the winner's circle, only Wayne, Laura Cotter, and groom Ebaristo Olivos were there to meet them, as owners Beal and French had decided not to attend. Never again would Landaluce's winner's circle attendance be this sparse.

Weighing in after the victory, Laffit looked up at the tote board and saw Landaluce's payout was $3.60 for the win—the first and last time she would pay more than three dollars for a win bet. No one would ever see those kinds of odds on her again. Astoundingly, the official time on the tote was 1:08 1/5. Laffit could not believe it was correct, because the filly's motion had been so smooth and effortless, and because two-year-old fillies simply did not run that fast, especially in a first start. He thought the clock must have malfunctioned. "Is that really the time?," he asked an amused and beaming Lukas, whose trust in the filly had just been vindicated. Landaluce's time for six furlongs was the fastest ever recorded on any U.S. track for a two-year-old filly around a turn. "Nobody, not even the oldest observers around here, can recall a juvenile filly doing that anywhere," Jon White wrote the next day.

Two hours later, after groom Ebaristo Olivos had bathed, cooled out, and fed Landaluce, and she was relaxing in her stall, it was time for the big feature race, the six-furlong Hollywood Express Handicap for older male sprinters. Laffit was aboard the favorite, three-year-old colt Time to Explode, the current world record-holder for seven furlongs, who had won four of his last six starts. Hopes were high among the crowd that they might see another record-breaking performance as the speedy sophomore confronted older horses for the first time. Second-favorite in the race was three-year-old California- bred gelding Remember John, trained by Darrell Vienna. Both colts were legitimate contenders for year-end national sprint championship honors if they continued their current form. The pair had met twice before, trading wins in listed California stakes that spring. Laffit liked his chances in this race, despite the fact that Time to Explode was two pounds overweight at 117, and Remember John carried only 115. A victory here would bring Laffit one win closer to passing Chris McCarron, aboard Remember John, for the meet's leading jockey title.

The starters left the gate at the same spot on the track Laffit's race on Landaluce had begun just hours ago. Unfortunately, Time to Explode veered in at the start, eliminating himself from contention and impeding another starter, Laughing Boy. Remember John went on to win the race in 1:08 4/5.

As Laffit dismounted, handing off his saddle and proceeding to the jockeys' room, he felt everything had changed. Although he was disappointed in Time to Explode's performance, his thoughts were now filled with Landaluce. He, along with racing analysts and knowledgeable racegoers in the crowd, might have been thinking the same thing: Landaluce, an unraced two-year-old filly carrying two pounds more over the same track at the same distance on the same day as the best older West Coast males in contention for the national sprint championship, had run three-fifths of a second faster without being pressed or urged. With her impressive victory, she was an instant favorite for the Hollywood Lassie Stakes next week. She entered the starting gate an unknown juvenile, and now she was a rising star.

12

"She Just Went"

You search and you look, and then all of a sudden, it comes, that star, and you know you have been blessed with something special. . . . You know you will go down in the history books.
—Wayne Lukas

The filly's mane was too short, and Laura Cotter was embarrassed. She wanted the splendid daughter of Seattle Slew to look the part of the great runner she already was. A horse as grand as Landaluce should be groomed to perfection. She shouldn't have a mane that was too short. Laura felt she had let her down.

Maybe it was because she was nervous for Luce, as she was called around the barn. Today was only her second start, but it seemed already so much was being expected of her. True, her first race had been spectacular, a world record for a two-year-old filly. No one had expected that. Now, just seven days later, the stakes were already much higher. Was it tempting fate to ask Luce to win again so soon? Could the filly's first race have been a fluke? All Laura's experience with Luce told her otherwise, but still, you could never be sure with two-year-olds. Here she was, splashed across the front page of the *Daily Racing Form,* and the odds-on favorite for her first stakes appearance after sixty-eight seconds on the track. Barely four days after her maiden, turf writers were already predicting she'd win today's Lassie, and would have installed her as the favorite for Wednesday's Haggin

Stakes against colts had Wayne chosen to enter her. What if it was all too much? What if her beautiful filly, barely twenty-seven months old, couldn't live up to the hype?

As Wayne's assistant, Laura was responsible for the day-to-day care of all the horses in his Hollywood Park string. Only Luce's groom, Ebaristo, had more direct personal contact with the budding superstar. She knew Wayne had taken a chance when he hired her six years ago, because it wasn't common for women to be racehorse trainers. She admired Lukas immensely and didn't want to disappoint him. "You're my girl everything," he told her.

She met Wayne for the first time in 1969, when she was a teenager showing quarter horses. A mutual friend introduced them, saying, "You two need to meet because you're both gonna go places," and predicting, "Someday this guy is gonna win the Kentucky Derby." Laura might have found this an odd statement, since Wayne wasn't even training Thoroughbreds then. But seven years later, after getting to know him better, she joined his team. Laura was used to being a trailblazer: she was the first woman to give a pleasure horse demonstration at the biggest show in the country for quarter horses, the American Quarter Horse Congress. But she didn't think about that most of the time. She just did her job. Her whole life was horses, and she hadn't had a real day off in seven years.

Laura had been with Wayne since the early days, when established Thoroughbred trainers called him "the cowboy" behind his back. Now the cowboy had Thoroughbreds in training at five different tracks, and Laura was excited to be part of a winning team. She'd been around horses long enough to know when one was truly special. Luce was.

She couldn't explain how she knew this, yet she was free of doubt. Landaluce had a certain look that was impossible to describe, a quality all great horses had in common. She had a big air. Without being mean, she was a spitfire—she showed spirit, and when she went to the track to work or race, Laura could tell Luce loved it. Laura and Luce had that in common: they both loved their jobs.

Today, as she and Ebaristo led Luce from her stall at Wayne's Barn 65 North to the track receiving barn, Laura felt more nervous than the filly appeared to be. Today's race would crown the juvenile filly champion for the Hollywood meet, which was nearing its final week. Laura had stood at this same spot four years ago when Wayne won the race with Terlingua, who still held the stakes record. Luce's opponents today included highweight and undefeated Cinderella Stakes–winner Barzell, as well as second-place-finisher Princess Lurullah, both with more experience and earnings than Landaluce. Princess Lurullah, a chestnut front-runner trained by veteran Mel Stute, had posted a bullet work here just three days ago, covering five furlongs in a sizzling :58 2/5. Her maiden score at five and one-half furlongs, a track record for a two-year-old filly, had lifted her into the ranks of potential starters against colts in the upcoming Hollywood Juvenile Championship Stakes. In her second outing, Princess Lurullah, who bobbled at the start, was beaten in the Cinderella by Barzell, a Shecky Greene homebred owned by Tommy Asbury, who boarded mares at his Hedgewood farm in Kentucky for *Partridge Family* star David Cassidy. Trained by Jerry Fanning, Barzell liked to dash to the lead and stay there, leading at every point of call and setting blazing sub-:22 fractions in the opening quarter in both starts at distances of five and five and one-half furlongs. Today would be her first effort at six, and as a stakes winner, she carried two pounds more than Landaluce.

Still, Luce's maiden performance had made her a 1–2 morning line favorite, bet down to 3–10 by post time, coupled with stablemate and first-time starter Carambola, a $470,000 yearling purchase and daughter of Alleged trained by Lukas and owned by Beal and French. Immediately after the Cinderella, trainers Stute and Fanning were bullish on their fillies' Lassie chances, but Landaluce's maiden win a mere three days later gave them pause. The day after Luce's opener, some handicappers predicted Barzell and Landaluce would hook up in a head-to-head battle, and other trainers in the field might have hoped the duo would burn each other up and create opportunity for a closer. Rounding out the field was Bold Out Line, a listed stakes winner at Golden Gate Fields trained by Loren Rettele and ridden by Ray Sibille, moving up to graded stakes company for the first time and considered by morning line handicappers to have virtually no chance at odds of 22–1.

As Laura, Luce, Ebaristo, and Carambola made their way toward the receiving barn on this pleasant Saturday afternoon, a crowd of more than forty thousand chose the races over the summer blockbuster *Star Trek: The Wrath of Khan*, which was still cleaning up at the box office a month after its release. Drawn partly by the chance to see a potential new juvenile star but also by a tote-bag giveaway that proved immensely popular, total weekend attendance swelled to ninety-two thousand, a record for a nonholiday weekend. Track management distributed the tote bags on Saturday and Sunday, with "masculine" colors of burgundy and maroon on Lassie day, and "feminine" colors of lavender and yellow on Sunday, when the Vanity Handicap for older females was slated to be run. Record crowds would become a hallmark of Landaluce's career, but already, after just one race, Landaluce was doing her part to pack them in.

The bustling crowd didn't seem to affect Luce or Carambola as Wayne's son and assistant trainer Jeff joined them on their journey postward. Jeff, Laura, and Ebaristo saddled both horses, who behaved "like perfect ladies," according to turf writer Jay Hovdey, who walked alongside. At Hollywood Park in the 1980s, horses were saddled mostly in a tunnel leading from the receiving barn to the paddock, because it was quieter and less distracting. Its drawback, however, was the tunnel's overhead electrical ducts and protruding steel girders, which Hovdey called "a chamber of horrors" even though these hazards were padded, and the tunnel walls lined with wooden slats. Hovdey remarked on the comportment of both fillies as they navigated these obstacles.

Emerging from the tunnel, the Lassie field was joined in the bright, open sunlit paddock by owners, jockeys, and trainers. On hand for the first time, Barry Beal watched admiringly as his filly circled the paddock. Galvanized by Luce's maiden race, he and co-owner Bob French vowed they would never miss another.

Also in the paddock was Laffit Pincay, who had recently narrowly avoided disaster in the Hollywood Oaks, when he hit the rail aboard the filly Tango Dancer trying to charge through a hole that closed at the last minute but, remarkably, still managed to angle her out and win. Had he been seriously injured, he would have missed Landaluce's race today, and maybe the rest of the meet, forfeiting his opportunity to remain the leading jockey in the country. As impressed as he was after Luce's first race, Laffit knew two-years-olds just learning to race were often inconsistent: He'd seen plenty with a breakout performance like Luce's unable ever to duplicate it.

As he strode into the paddock, Wayne Lukas was smiling and jovial, inspired at least in part by his sensational filly, who was fortifying the winning attitude he strove to maintain throughout his barn. Among the last twenty starters he'd sent to post, eleven had returned winners, including maiden colt Full Choke, who upset favored Via Magnum in the Haggin Stakes at odds of 21–1. This string of victories reminded Wayne of how another daughter of a Triple Crown winner had ignited his success exactly four years ago, when the barn won five stakes races in eighteen days, capped by Terlingua's score over colts in the Hollywood Juvenile Championship Stakes. At this point in the year, Wayne was now third leading trainer in the United States, behind only Hall of Famers Charlie Whittingham and Laz Barrera. In four short years of training Thoroughbreds full-time, with eighty-two horses in training for seventeen owners, the cowboy had made his way from the ranks of the unknown to a potential Hall of Fame spot himself.

Landaluce stood quietly in her holding stall as Wayne approached for his final prerace inspection. When the trainer opened a window to give Luce more fresh air, turf writer Hovdey noted, "The sunlight made [her] dapples dance, and Lukas smiled." Hovdey recalled a July day in the paddock at Hollywood five years before, when he watched Seattle Slew parade in a lather prior to his shocking defeat in the Swaps Stakes to J. O. Tobin in his lone West Coast start. By contrast, Slew's daughter today was calm, and perfectly at home in the West. Would she avenge her sire's loss by becoming his first graded stakes winner today?

Wayne offered Laffit a leg up and gave the rider simple instructions. "Bust her out of the gate," he said, "and put ten pounds of pressure on the bit. She will do the rest."

It was a little after 5:00 p.m., with temperatures in the low seventies and a light breeze as the Lassie field approached the gate, and starter Cotton Barnett, dressed in a coat and hat, climbed the blue metal platform as a jet from nearby LAX droned overhead. Landaluce, starting from post position three, had to circle a few times behind the gate, waiting for a somewhat reluctant Barzell to load directly inside her. When her turn came, the filly walked calmly into the gate with no fuss and waited patiently for the two outside her to load.

At 5:17 p.m., Cotton Barnett opened the gate. The chestnut Barzell, ridden by Frank Olivares and carrying the purple silks of F. P. Lamazor, sprang to an immediate early lead on the rail, with Landaluce close behind on her outside, settled under a hold by Pincay and joined by Carambola. Briefly the twin Beal and French green-and-white silks raced side by side behind Barzell, who showed great early speed as she maintained a half-length lead through a sizzling first quarter. When the opening fraction of :21 2/5 flashed on the tote board, the crowd gasped. Clearly, Olivares knew the only way to beat Landaluce at this distance was to get to the front and stay there, if he could, and to use his inside post position to keep the daughter of Seattle Slew on his outside and perhaps force her wide around the turn. As he urged Barzell in the straightaway before the turn, asking for speed, Olivares extended his right arm, elbow up, whip in hand, in an effort to keep Landaluce as far out on the track as possible. But Landaluce had stayed near Barzell through the blazing opening quarter without being urged by Pincay, and at this point, the field was bunched, with the exception of Princess Lurullah, who trailed early.

With three fillies lapped on the leader, it might have appeared to be anybody's race. But by the time the leaders completed the half in an insane :43 4/5, Wayne's bay filly enjoyed a length and a half lead on Barzell. Landaluce had passed Barzell with ease, apparently on her own, without urging, even at this torrid pace. She had completed the first half-mile a full second faster than she ran it in her scintillating maiden win, yet she was continuing to draw away. Barely a furlong later, as Landaluce swept around the turn, she had opened up nine lengths on a struggling Barzell, running five furlongs in :56 flat. Her strides were lengthening, Laffit's hands remained low and still, and many in the crowd were already watching the clock, anticipating another record.

But it was at the top of the stretch, in the final furlong of a six-furlong sprint, that Landaluce ran her way into history. Already nine lengths ahead at the five-furlong mark, she would somehow, incredibly, put an additional length between herself and the rest of the field in each remaining second of the race. In the next twelve seconds, she nearly doubled the price for Seattle Slew's offspring, vaulted him into the top of the North American sires list, and tripled his value as a stallion. She deepened an emotional imprint on Wayne Lukas and opened the door to the acquisition of the most important client of his life, Eugene Klein, whose partnership would transform the duo into a U.S. racing powerhouse and reshape conventional paradigms of breeding, training, and racing forever. Her impression on Laffit Pincay was so great that two years later, when pressed to decide among competing Derby mounts, the jockey overrode his agent's advice and chose Swale, a son of Seattle Slew, who carried him to his first-ever blanket of roses, at least in part because the colt reminded him of Landaluce. In the next twelve seconds, she completed a performance so formidable that it elicited superlatives among veteran Hall of Fame trainers and turf writers, who compared her to Ruffian, arguably the greatest American racing filly of all time. Landaluce became the first California-based juvenile filly to inspire a national fan base, elevated

Landaluce, Laffit Pincay up, in the Winner's Circle at Hollywood Park after her spectacular twenty-one-length record-breaking win in the Lassie Stakes, July 10, 1982. Pictured are Laura Cotter (*third from left*); Jeff Lukas (*fourth from left*); Marcia Fuller French (*eighth from left*); Nancy Beal (*near flagpole*); Barry Beal (*near flagpole*); Bob French (*adjacent*); and Wayne Lukas (*far right*). (Benoit Photo)

West Coast racing in a way reminiscent of Swaps in the 1950s, and managed to break her own record, set only seven days ago in her first start, for the fastest six furlongs around a turn by any two-year-old filly in American history. Winning a six-furlong sprint by twenty-one lengths, she set a record margin of victory at Hollywood Park for any race at any distance that would never be broken there, inviting comparison with Secretariat's thirty-one-length Belmont Stakes win in a race twice as long. In the next twelve seconds, she firmly established herself as a leading contender for national championship honors and became one of the early-book favorites for the Kentucky Derby. Landaluce buoyed her trainer with so much confidence he could eschew the conventional wisdom that she must travel east to beat the best, and instead adopt the unprecedented and bold posture of daring others to travel west to confront her. Finally, and ultimately sadly, in the next twelve seconds she would find herself so inextricably bound up with the fortunes of Hollywood Park, the site of not only her debut

but also her most spectacular victory, that she would literally dissolve, along with the track itself, into the earth.

All of these events happened because Laffit Pincay decided, with an eighth of a mile left in a race he had well in hand, to tap the filly twice on the right shoulder with his whip. Wayne Lukas was bewildered. Why would Laffit, a Hall of Fame jockey, feel it was necessary to use the stick in a race he had clearly already won?

As Landaluce glided through the stretch, her rider, perhaps thinking he had nothing to lose, decided to experiment. He wanted to see how the filly would respond to the whip "in case he ever needed it." Laffit, along with the rest of the racing world, found out immediately. "She took off like a rocket ship," he told *Sports Illustrated*'s Bill Leggett after the race. "I have never been on a horse like her."

Watching trackside, Laura Cotter had a mixture of conflicting feelings. She knew Wayne didn't like anyone to use the whip on Landaluce and didn't even expect riders to carry one during morning works. "He would always tell [them] . . . you can brush her, but don't hit her. She doesn't need it,'" Cotter explained. "Nobody had to do anything to make her go. She just went." But at the same time, even Laura, knowing the filly as well as she did, was overwhelmed by the performance unfolding in front of her. "I had this wonderful feeling about her," she admitted, "but I had no idea she was going to run that fast."

Trainer Mel Stute, whose second-favorite Princess Lurullah finished fourth, had similar observations as Landaluce came down the stretch. "I've never seen anything like her in my life," he said. "I was feeling pretty good about my filly until about the quarter pole. From there on, I was humbled. . . . It looked like Landaluce opened up another length with every stride."

"When Laffit's filly went by us, it looked like her feet were floating," added jockey Frank Olivares on third-place Barzell, who wilted after her opening quarter duel with the daughter of Seattle Slew. "It didn't even look like she was running."

"I beat every horse I could see," quipped jockey Ray Sibille aboard second-place-finisher Bold Out Line. The Golden Gate Fields invader and highest price on the board finished four and one-fifth seconds behind the winner and was just at the sixteenth pole when Landaluce hit the wire.

"She's the fastest two-year-old I've ever seen," added Bold Out Line's trainer, Loren Rettele, who later told *Sports Illustrated* the race footage "looks like a trick. It was like two different races, the one with Landaluce in it, and another race." "Her hapless foes were in another zip code," wrote the *Form*. Indeed, well before the finish, the track cameraman was already having difficulty showing the field in a single shot.

In the crowd was Mickey Taylor, who watched as the daughter of his Triple Crown winner drew away. The race brought back memories of some of Slew's most dramatic finishes—the time he demolished the field at two when winning the Champagne by nearly ten lengths, his Kentucky Derby win after overcoming a slow start, and the historic meeting of two Triple Crown winners in the Marlboro Cup, in which Slew prevailed over Affirmed. None of these races overwhelmed Taylor as much as Landaluce's stretch run. "It was the most impressive, most awesome race I've ever seen," he said.

As Landaluce flashed under the wire in magnificent solitude, the Hollywood Park crowd of forty thousand erupted in a standing ovation. In a Los Angeles bar, where the race was shown on newly emerging cable television, patrons stood and applauded.

On the gallop out, Laffit Pincay stood in the irons, pulling the filly up gently and gradually as he did with all his mounts, in order to conserve strength for his remaining rides. As they came around the clubhouse turn, the mingled shadow of horse and rider hovered over a corner of the infield, a pleasant, pretty spot with a small waterfall. The sun was shining, and a gentle breeze lifted Luce's mane as she trotted back to the winner's circle, where a throng of well-wishers, including the Beal and French families, celebrated the arrival of a phenomenal filly whose racing life was just beginning.

Wayne, sporting a hunter-green blazer matching the owners' silks, seemed prepared for a victory photo this time. When Laffit dismounted, the trainer chided him briefly about the whip: "Let's just put that away until we really need it," he said. Laura Cotter and Ebaristo took hold of the filly's bridle and started hosing her down. As they all walked back to the barn to cool the filly out, Wayne couldn't help remembering his colt Stalwart, for whom he'd had such high hopes just four months ago at this same track. Since then, he'd vowed never to plan more than a race or two at a time ahead, and to keep his dreams to himself. But with each race she ran, Landaluce was making that harder and harder to do.

Sunday wasn't usually a day that Wayne Lukas's barn phone rang a lot. But while he was hand-grazing Luce at 6:00 a.m. the day after the Lassie, it was already starting to ring off the hook. When *Good Morning America* called, requesting an interview, Wayne couldn't help smiling. The filly, calm as always while horses passed by in the backstretch, had come out of the race well and seemed happy and content.

The phone at Hollywood Park's publicity department was ringing, too. Tracks from all over the country were calling, hoping to entice racing's new superstar to head their way.

Even racing connections in Europe were impressed by the race. "People were talking about it all over the world," said Mickey Taylor, whose friend and racing colleague Bert Firestone, traveling in Ireland the day after the Lassie, heard people there remarking on Landaluce's margin of victory. "I guess good news travels fast." Former Slew groom Sandy Shaw, back in Ireland as farm manager for Brownstown Stud, was following Slew's daughter with interest. The bay filly he'd hand-walked at Spendthrift as a yearling was making the dreams he cherished for his favorite stallion come true.

At home, Landaluce's triumph was still sinking in. Turf writers sought superlatives equal to the feat and scrambled to find statistics to describe it. *Sports Illustrated*'s Bill Leggett, researching margins of victory by two-year-olds, found that among colts in modern times, Seattle Slew won the Champagne, a mile race, by nearly ten lengths, and Secretariat won the Laurel Futurity at a mile and a sixteenth, by eight. Man o' War's largest juvenile margin was six. Leggett had to go back forty years to find a two-year-old who exceeded Landaluce's margin of victory: 1943 Triple Crown–winner Count Fleet won the Walden, at a mile and one-sixteenth, by thirty lengths. There was one other filly, also a dark bay, who came close to Landaluce's winning margin when she scored at five and one-half furlongs at Belmont in 1974 by fifteen lengths. Her name was Ruffian.

Four days later, turf writer Hovdey's account of the Lassie Stakes in the *Thoroughbred Record* was titled simply "Another Ruffian?" Hovdey was not alone in his assessment, presaging what would become a legion of writers and trainers who compared Landaluce to the brilliant champion, both in the immediate aftermath of her most breathtaking race and throughout the rest of her career. "Not since Ruffian's two-year-old season . . . has a thoroughbred of either sex displayed such brilliant speed and precocity," wrote Andrew Beyer in the *Washington Post*. Ruffian's fastest six furlongs at two had been the Spinaway at Saratoga, won in 1:08 3/5. Hovdey pointed out that although Ruffian's time was a full second faster than the race had ever been run at Saratoga, it was still 3/5 of a second slower than Landaluce's Lassie. While Ruffian's best time at the distance came when she was more seasoned, in the fifth and final start of her juvenile career, Landaluce had surpassed Ruffian's best in the very first start of her life. Hovdey noted that Saratoga's racing surface "most closely compared to the harder, clay-based Western courses," and Wayne Lukas recalled the Hollywood track as being faster when Terlingua set her stakes record, which Landaluce had just beaten by almost a full second.

Landaluce's two impressive scores, coming so early in the season and so close together, established her as a top two-year-old of either sex. Juvenile colts who would emerge later in the year as 1983 Classic contenders were just beginning to race, and by early July none of them had won as often or as impressively as Landaluce, and none had a graded stakes score. The road from two-year-old summer and fall prep races at shorter distances to the blanket of roses at a mile and a quarter the following May was arduous and unpredictable, but immediately after the Lassie, Landaluce appeared to be among the most impressive of that year's crop at the time. *Sports Illustrated*'s Bill Leggett, among the first to tout her as a potential Classic runner, and aware of how unseemly it might be to do so, tempered his remarks as follows: "The one certain thing about two- year-olds in July is that they should seldom be taken seriously. The rule of thumb says, wait until . . . November before getting excited about the horses that will run in the classics the following spring. But Landaluce is the exception to the rule. She took July and turned it into November."

Horsemen at Hollywood Park certainly seemed to appreciate the phenomenon in their midst, according to then racing secretary Eual Wyatt Jr., who recalled seeing Landaluce on the backstretch the week after the Lassie: "I was in the barn area for some reason, walking back to the racing office, and I heard somebody say, 'hey, there's Landaluce.' She was on her way to or from the track. There were eight or ten people there, and horses coming and going, and when that person said that, everybody stopped talking and just stopped and looked at her. It was like a wave of respect."

After the Lassie, Landaluce's fan base was already beginning to mushroom. Besides being shown on late-night news programs throughout California, the race was aired on three-year-old ESPN's *Horse Racing Weekly,* as well as the network's *Down the Stretch,* the only nationwide horse racing series in the country, which had just launched. In the weeks and months that followed, the filly received national coverage from ABC News, the *New York Times, Washington Post,* and *Sports Illustrated,* among others. Wayne Lukas began getting daily stacks of letters at his barn from fans all over the country requesting photos or locks of her mane. "I've never encountered the reaction she has generated," he said, and ordered photos to keep on hand to honor fan requests. Landaluce's fame was growing so rapidly that when one fan told turf writer Hovdey she'd just happened to be at Hollywood Park the day of the Lassie, he wrote: "That's like making your first movie 'Gone with the Wind' or your first football game the Super Bowl."

Trainers with fillies beaten in the Lassie licked their wounds back at their barns. Even if they hadn't expected to defeat Landaluce, they certainly didn't expect to lose by twenty-one lengths. It's impossible to know how many fillies' hearts were broken in the race, but some did not fare well after it. Stakes-placed Princess Lurullah bucked shins in the stretch and was never again on the board in stakes company.

Another trainer who undoubtedly found Landaluce's performance sobering was Jerry Fanning, handler of third-place Barzell, who never raced again. Fanning had a rapidly developing two-year-old colt in his barn, Desert Wine, for whom he had high hopes in next week's six-furlong Hollywood Juvenile championship, traditionally a race for colts. The bay son of Damascus had just broken his maiden at first asking at Hollywood Park in late June. Now, like other Hollywood trainers with top juvenile colts, Fanning began to worry that Wayne and his speedy bay filly might wrest the meet-ending championship trophy and its $100,000 purse from their hands as he'd done with Terlingua four years ago. "What would have happened if somebody had pressed [Landaluce]?," wondered trainer Floyd Godwin. "She'll beat the colts, too." Besides, if he could win the Juvenile, Wayne now had a real chance to finish the meet as top trainer by number of wins. Landaluce's dual scores in one week, coupled with Full Choke's Haggin victory, had put Lukas in a three-way tie for second place behind Bobby Frankel.

Wayne made bullish statements to the press immediately after the Lassie, serving notice he intended to run Landaluce against colts. Within days, he told both the *BloodHorse* and the *Daily Racing Form* her next start would likely be the Juvenile. But at the same time, the trainer told the *Thoroughbred Record:* "I really don't think we'll need to run her in the Juvenile. We may not have to fire all our bullets to win that one." Wayne had two other good colts in his barn prepping for the race—Hammond Sycamore Hill Farm's Full Choke, who was peaking at precisely the right moment, and sprinter Ft. Davis, a chestnut son of To the Quick whom Lukas owned in partnership with Beal and French. Dangling Landaluce as bait for the Juvenile would yield a shorter field for his own contenders, and indeed, three days after the Lassie, the *Form* reported that "a check with horsemen turned up very few willing to challenge . . . Landaluce in the Juvenile" and stated she would be the prohibitive favorite were she to start against colts.

Meanwhile, Wayne shrewdly underscored how little Landaluce's record-breaking win had taxed her. "She was really bucking and playing," he told reporters three days after the race, and he downplayed any ill effects of a possible third outing when he said, "I know it's three races in three weeks, but they have not been tough ones." Trainer Mel Stute, tubbing Princess Lurullah in ice back at his barn, might have felt differently.

Throughout the week, her trainer declined to commit Landaluce to the race. The official explanation for stalling was the upcoming Keeneland yearling sale, where Lukas, Beal, and French would meet in person to discuss the filly's future. Wayne left for Keeneland Wednesday morning after the Lassie, leaving son Jeff at Hollywood to deal with the press and supervise forty-nine horses stabled there, as well as ten that had already shipped to Del Mar for its upcoming meet. Although Wayne did caucus with the owners at Keeneland on Wednesday, by Thursday, only two days before the Juvenile, the *Form* reported that "it appears that . . . Landaluce . . . will not start . . . although the race still has not been completely ruled out." Back at Hollywood, Full Choke worked a sharp three furlongs in :35 4/5.

It wasn't until Friday, the day before the Juvenile, that Landaluce was officially reported out of the race. On Saturday, the *Form* reported she would be pointed to the one-mile Del Mar Debutante against fillies in early September, with one or two prep races likely leading up to it.

With Landaluce out of the way, the coast was clear for coupled entry and morning line favorites Full Choke and Ft. Davis, as well as four other starters including Fanning's Desert Wine, who went off at a respectable 5–2. Though the Lukas entry was well-placed early, Desert Wine prevailed, winning easily over a fast track by six and a half lengths in a time nearly two seconds slower than Landaluce's Lassie score. Both Lukas trainees finished on the board, collecting over a third of the purse for the $100,000 race, but Wayne was not there to see it. He was still at Keeneland, looking for future stars.

13

Her Sister's Shoes

Jim [Hill] and I can dream pretty good, but we never imagined Slew
would sire something like Landaluce.
—Mickey Taylor

"Put that filly in a corner stall," John Williams told the Spendthrift groom who led a gleaming chestnut yearling from a van in front of "Leslie's barns" at the Keeneland sales grounds on Saturday, July 17.

A week ago, Hip No. 116, the last foal of Strip Poker by Seattle Slew, wasn't supposed to be stabled in the place of honor reserved for one of the farm's expected sale-toppers. But that was before her full sister won the Hollywood Lassie Stakes in world-record time, which had the sales grounds buzzing, and muffled those who'd ridiculed the Hills and Taylors for their "all-in" approach to Slew's syndication. "Landaluce has silenced the critics," Mickey Taylor said. "We've gone from being foolish to geniuses." Landaluce's twenty-one-length victory had put her sister in this stall, and dollar signs in the eyes of anyone connected to their sire.

It was a good thing Strip Poker had passed on her unruffled disposition to Hip No. 116: besides being an indicator of expected value, a corner stall, located adjacent to the breezeway separating Spendthrift's two barns, yielded more foot traffic and activity, which would stress a high-strung yearling. As a matter of convenience, Williams put prospects he expected to be shown a lot in the corners, where it was easier to get them out into the breezeway. But he would never stable a top yearling with a nervous temperament there. He knew Strip Poker's filly had the same calm demeanor as her sister—could it be she shared her speed as well?

Before Landaluce headed postward for the Lassie, Spendthrift expected its top Slew sales yearling to be Hip No. 88, a bay filly Williams called "possibly the most attractive yearling we have ever raised," out of the Dr. Fager mare Merely, a daughter of the great handicap mare Politely. Featured prominently in magazine ads in the weeks leading up to the sale, Merely's filly romped in color in Spendthrift pastures over half a page in the farm's presale promotional brochure, while Strip Poker's filly, not pictured, earned just one simple line of text, described as a "half sister to three winners, including graded stakes winner Clout."

But soon after Landaluce crossed the finish line at Hollywood Park, advertising manager Karen Mitchell, spending her Saturday renovating a house in Lexington, found her home answering machine lit up with messages from her boss, Brownell Combs, when she checked it later in the day. "He called a bunch of times. He was all excited," she said. "It was a giant emergency." Combs told Mitchell to start work right away on splashy color ads to promote Landaluce's full sister in major racing publications prior to the Keeneland sale. There wasn't much time, as opening night was only nine days away. Mitchell put her tape measure and carpet swatches aside and hurried to the office.

This weekend, Hip No. 116 awaited inspection in the same barns where her brilliant sister had been offered for sale barely a year ago. The shapely chestnut with a coat bright and burnished as polished copper spent little time in her stall, and Williams noticed that Strip Poker's filly was attracting as much, if not more, attention, than Merely's. Among the buyers yearning to lead Strip Poker's filly back to their barn was Beverly Hills heiress Dolly Green. Her trainer, Laz Barrera, had recently campaigned back-to-back juvenile champions: 1977 two-year-old colt Affirmed and 1978 co-champion juvenile filly It's in the Air. Prior to the sale, the Hall of Famer watched videotape of Landaluce's Lassie more times than he cared to admit. "I looked at the film of the Lassie over and over again," he told *Sports Illustrated*. "It was the best performance by a two-year-old I've ever looked at." "Everyone told me not to come back home without that filly," added Green.

Ironically, Wayne Lukas, on the grounds scouting yearlings, seemed to have little interest in his superstar's sister, and John Williams thought he understood why. Although more conventionally attractive as a yearling than Landaluce, and resembling her dam more than her sire, Hip No. 116's conformation was rounder and more shapely, without her sister's ranginess, scope, or athleticism. By now Williams, like others in the business, knew Lukas scouted yearlings like a coach seeking draft prospects. If she didn't measure up as a physical specimen, Lukas was unlikely to allow the fact that Hip No. 116 was his star's full sister cloud his assessment of her racing potential. Besides, he rarely allowed himself a peek at a catalogue page until after he'd evaluated all yearlings at the sale in person. Just as his experience with Clout hadn't dictated his purchase of Landaluce, neither would her brilliance determine his selection now. If Hip No. 116 passed his conformation test, her pedigree might sway him, but it wouldn't drive his decision. Also, Lukas knew that Landaluce's superstardom might push Slew's yearling prices above his desired price range.

By this time, Wayne's picks and bids were being watched intently. His 1980 score, Blush with Pride, recent winner of the Kentucky Oaks, was on the cover for this year's sales catalogue, an accolade to the trainer's discernment. Wayne was sticking to his strategy of buying superior individuals from younger, less-established sires. Primarily because of Landaluce, and aided by fellow first-crop runners Slew Manet, Embellished, and Slewpy, all of whom had hit the board prior to this sale, Seattle Slew was about to leave those ranks for good.

Although Wayne was now among Keeneland's major buyers, its top tier was still comprised of Europeans and Arabs whose Lear Jets were once again parked across the street from Keeneland on the

Brownell Combs at Keeneland, July 1982. (Keeneland Library, Thoroughbred Times-Featherston)

tarmac of Bluegrass Airport, and they were not here primarily to buy Seattle Slew yearlings—at least not yet. Robert Sangster's BBA syndicate, Stavros Niarchos, and the sheikhs of Dubai were preparing to do battle once more for the top offspring of Northern Dancer and his son Nijinsky II. Sangster's colt Golden Fleece, a son of Nijinsky II whom BBA had purchased here at Keeneland in 1980, had just won the Epsom Derby six weeks ago, breaking a course record that had stood for nearly fifty years. Sangster's dramatic Epsom win served only to whet the appetite of foreign buying interests for the blood of Northern Dancer and his best sons at stud.

As opening night approached, Leslie and Brownell Combs had every reason to be optimistic about Spendthrift's prospects and hoped to regain their title of top Keeneland consignor after a two-year hiatus. After last year's trouncing by Windfields Farm and Northern Dancer, the Combses hoped that the new blood of Seattle Slew, J. O. Tobin, and first-year sire Affirmed would make this a banner year for the farm.

On Monday, July 19, anyone with a mare in foal to Seattle Slew or a yearling sired by the Triple Crown winner awaiting sale in Keeneland's barns, probably had a bottle or two of champagne on ice nearby. To no one's surprise, Landaluce had been named horse of the meeting at Hollywood Park, an almost unprecedented accomplishment for a two-year-old filly. Everyone knew Slew's yearlings would sell for more than last year, but the question was, just how much more?

Leslie Combs, impeccably dressed as always in a suit, tie, and pocket handkerchief, sat in his customary spot just a few rows from the auction podium, with a good view of whatever drama might unfold. He didn't have long to wait—when Hip No. 30, a dark bay Nijinsky II colt out of the stakes-winning mare Spearfish entered the ring, the fireworks began. In a matter of minutes, the striking dark bay's price reached $3.5 million, the record set last year when BBA paid that sum for the colt Ballydoyle, a full brother to Storm Bird, whom Sangster had campaigned and was now in the process of syndicating in the $30 million range. A few tense minutes moments ensued as the Spearfish colt's price climbed to $4 million, but BBA countered back at $4.25 million, and Sheikh Mohammed folded.

For this sale at least, Wayne Lukas continued to stay out of the fray at the high end of the market and focused instead on the formula that had yielded Terlingua, Blush with Pride, and Landaluce. For a half million dollars less than what BBA paid for the Nijinsky II colt alone, Wayne bought twenty-seven yearlings at this and other sales throughout the year, a group that yielded champion sprinter Mt. Livermore as well as a filly from the second crop of young stallion Cox's Ridge—eventual Breeders' Cup Distaff winner and dual champion Life's Magic. Although Wayne nearly quintupled his spending from 1982 to 1985, and was among the top American buyers during this time, his totals still paled in comparison with foreign interests.

As exciting as the sale of the record-setting Spearfish colt had been for spectators, it did not match Leslie Combs's anticipation for Hip No. 86, a Spendthrift-bred and consigned colt from the first crop of Alydar. The handsome bay now in the ring was the last foal of a great-granddaughter of Myrtlewood, Spendthrift's Masked Lady, who had died last year at the age of seventeen and was buried on the old Elmendorf land up the hill from the barn where Landaluce was foaled. Sheikh Mohammed appreciated the colt's heritage and racing potential, securing him for $2.2 million, a record for a first-year stallion, and the second-highest price of the sale. Leslie smiled broadly as the colt was led from the ring, as he would prove to be Spendthrift's sale-topper. Although her bones had long ago dissolved into the earth beneath the roses in Leslie's garden, Myrtlewood's blood coursing through her female descendants still flowed like a fountain of wealth through the farm.

Only two hips later, Leslie's smile flashed again as Hip No. 88, Merely's filly by Seattle Slew, entered the ring. The auction floor hummed as bidding quickly escalated, and the hammer fell at $1.6 million, a new world record for a filly at public auction. Spendthrift's triumph was short-lived, however, as a subsequent Northern Dancer filly sold for $1.8 million within the hour.

Shortly afterward, Strip Poker's filly entered the ring. Video cameras whirred as Hip No. 116 circled in front of the auctioneer's podium—it seemed Landaluce's star quality was already rubbing off on her younger sister. Francis Kernan and the Combses could now

Royal Strait Flush, Landaluce's only full sister and the last foal of Strip Poker, in the auction ring at Keeneland, July 19, 1982, where she sold for $1.5 million. (Lee P. Thomas)

only be overjoyed they'd decided to send Strip Poker back to Slew right after she'd foaled Landaluce, when Slew was still unproven, the only time the mare had gone back-to-back to the same sire since the beginning of her broodmare career ten years ago. Sadly, her yearling tonight was all the more valuable because there would never be another.

"This was the one I really wanted," California heiress Dolly Green would tell reporters later—but for now, she knew she had some determined bidding to do, as both Stavros Niarchos and the Taylors themselves dueled with her for Landaluce's sister. Fueled by her close personal relationship with Leslie Combs and her ties to Spendthrift, where her new stallion Premier Ministre stood at stud, Green, sitting ringside in a tailored suit next to trainer Laz Barrera and sporting huge black sunglasses, emerged victorious with a final bid of $1.5 million for the filly. "I just had to have her," she said. John Williams, observing the bidding, didn't notice Wayne Lukas participating at all.

When the hammer fell on Hip No. 116, Spendthrift had just sold two Seattle Slew fillies for over $3 million, more than his entire lot of yearlings had brought at last year's sale. Slew's top fillies were lifting Spendthrift into the heady atmosphere of Windfields sales numbers, and competing with Northern Dancer's female offspring at the very top of the select market. Landaluce's early and spectacular racing success had vaulted Slew from budding freshman sire into the stallion major leagues. It was no accident that Slew's sale-toppers this year were fillies—the market's desire to own one like Landaluce marked the first time any of his offspring topped the $1 million threshold, with none of his colts selling for anywhere near the price of these fillies throughout the rest of the year. Slew's lot of fillies offered at Keeneland would represent four of the top fifteen in the entire sale.

Although Brownell and Leslie Combs were fast becoming accustomed to multimillion-dollar yearling scores, the sale of Landaluce's sister was by far Francis Kernan's biggest accomplishment as a breeder. If he thought he'd struck gold with the sale of Landaluce, he could hardly have dreamed the sale of her sister would bring $1.5 million just twelve months later. Kernan's $70,000 purchase of Strip Poker had proven to be an investment that yielded returns many times over.

By the time the sale ended, everyone connected with Slew had reason to celebrate. The prices Slew's yearlings now commanded meant that his value as a stallion had nearly tripled since arriving at Spendthrift. The struggle to fill his book with the best-quality mares was finally over. Not only could the Slew Crew and the syndicate members heave a sigh of relief, but they could also look forward to breathing room for years to come. Slew's yearlings at this sale commanded prices behind only those of Northern Dancer, Nijinsky II, and Alydar. Thanks to Landaluce and the illustrious runners who would soon make their way postward, including Slew O' Gold, Swale, and Adored, his yearlings would be worth an average $1.7 million at Keeneland by 1984. Slew would end up producing an incredible six Grade One winners from only his first two crops to race.

Thanks to Slew, Spendthrift had reclaimed its title of number-one consignor at Keeneland, narrowly edging out Windfields Farm. In only his second year at stud, Slew enjoyed a yearling average nearly double that of Raise a Native and Exclusive Native, the former cornerstones of Spendthrift consignments. Had it not been for Slew, Spendthrift would have continued to slide down the consignor ranks, as the new blood of J. O. Tobin and Affirmed proved disappointing. While Landaluce had helped double Slew's yearling average, J. O. Tobin's failure to produce a noteworthy runner had cut his in half. The flashy champion on two continents whom Brownell once thought superior to Slew would descend through the sire ranks, whereas the dark bay with his crooked leg would become one of the top sires in the world, and arguably the best ever to stand at Spendthrift.

As he stood once more in the shedrow of "Leslie's barns," supervising the send-off of royally bred Spendthrift yearlings to farms and training facilities across the country, John Williams smiled, thinking back to all the tactics he and his staff had devised to persuade a reluctant Slew to breed in his first months at the farm. Standing beneath the magnolia tree outside the breeding shed in the rain and snow, dragging old Fleet Flight from her stall, rattling cellophane to appease Slew by feeding him after the treachery of switching mares, and even nearly getting ditched when the Triple Crown winner took off with him, had all been worth it. By the end of this year, Slew would be the only freshman among the top ten sires of two-year-olds by earnings. Williams would relish Slew's ascent through the sire ranks until the stallion claimed the top spot on the North American sires list in 1984. For the next several years, no stallion other than the great Northern Dancer would be in more demand. But for now, as he stood in front of the corner stall where Strip Poker's chestnut daughter chewed hay unaware of the new life awaiting her, Williams was simply proud of Slew for producing a runner as rare as Landaluce, and looked forward to what the future might hold for the stallion and his brilliant filly.

Sometime later, Spendthrift farrier Beach Faulkner led Dolly Green's new purchase out of her stall, and pulled her two front shoes. Hip No. 116, soon to be named Royal Strait Flush, was on her way to Spendthrift's training center to be broken before traveling west to begin her racing career with Laz Barrera. As he'd been instructed, Faulkner put the shoes aside. Someone knew that the shoes of Strip Poker's last foal and Landaluce's only full sister would have sentimental value to Williams. Even though she'd left the farm, and her marriage to Brownell was over, Linda Combs still cared deeply for the people she'd left behind, and she wanted to leave the dedicated horseman who helped rebuild Spendthrift a parting gift of thanks.

Forty years later, chrome plated and mounted on a walnut plaque, they still hang today in Williams's workshop, cherished as a reminder of his fine and loving care of Spendthrift Thoroughbreds, and the unspoken yet enduring kindness of a friend.

14

Miss California Becomes Miss America

When a beautiful woman walks into the room and all the men nudge
each other, you don't have to tell 'em all that she's pretty, and that's
the same way Landaluce is. When she walks out on the racetrack,
horsemen stop and look.
—Wayne Lukas

As he headed westward from Keeneland, Wayne's thoughts returned
to his brilliant filly waiting for him in her stall at Del Mar, where
Jeff, Laura, and Ebaristo had cared for her in his absence. The trainer
found himself getting nervous whenever he wasn't with the most
important runner in his stable. Lucky enough to have a phenom in
his barn, Lukas had to fight off a feeling of gratitude mixed with
dread that something bad was about to happen. Laffit Pincay had
that feeling too: "Normally, I'm not a superstitious man, but I walk
around these days with my fingers crossed, hoping nothing happens
to her. When I see Wayne . . . walking toward me, my instinct is to
turn away. I'm afraid he's going to tell me that something has gone
wrong." For the rest of the summer and into the fall, Wayne would
take pains to stay close to Luce. "The thought of being in a plane or
a hotel somewhere across the country and calling back here to learn
that something had gone wrong is enough to make me stay close by,"
he said.

Laura and Jeff had done a good job while Wayne was away. Landaluce and the rest of the string appeared to be thriving in the relaxed atmosphere of Del Mar, one of the nation's most beautiful tracks, with its Spanish stucco and languorous palms, so close to the ocean that patrons could often hear the surf of the Pacific Ocean "only a chip shot away." Laura reported that Landaluce was bright and healthy, cleaning up the feed tub with vigor, as she always did, and enjoying her daily afternoon grazing sessions while Wayne was gone.

As the filly neared her third start, Laura could feel Luce maturing as a racehorse. "When she went to the track it was like she knew exactly what she was going out there for," Laura observed. "I think she knew how good she was. She was not going to let anyone get in front of her. It was like she was saying, 'let me do what I'm supposed to do.'"

Laura could tell Landaluce was learning to like racing—but she liked winning even more. "Horses that run and win, they like it, and they try hard to win again. A horse that always finishes second or third, they don't know what it is to win. It's funny, horses that win the first time out, they like it."

The abundance of promising two-year-old fillies in the expansive Lukas stable meant that Wayne now had to devise ways to keep his high-quality, though second-tier juveniles learning to like winning, too. From now on, Wayne would point Landaluce to graded stakes with big purses, and run his other fillies in lesser stakes or ship them elsewhere for better spots where they could build confidence and avoid getting beaten by his own juggernaut.

Toward that end, Bobby Barnett took a group of Lukas runners on the road just a week after Landaluce's Lassie victory, including Ruth Bunn's Some Kinda Flirt. Thrashed soundly by Luce in their maiden meeting, Flirt was now a multiple stakes winner, having beaten a field of thirteen, including future Alcibiades winner Jelly Bean Holiday, in the Lady Sponsors' at Ak-Sar-Ben while setting a stakes record under Barnett's supervision, and then returning to Del Mar to follow up with a win in the Junior Miss, with her stablemate Body Talk, also owned by Bunn and trained by Wayne, finishing third. French and Beal's two-year-old filly Infantes was now stakes-placed, finishing third in the Sorrento here at Del Mar in mid-August. When he returned to Del Mar, Barnett was struck by how much Luce had grown while he'd been away. "She was awesome, strapping," he realized. "From a distance, you couldn't tell her from a stud."

Everyone, perhaps even Wayne himself, was wondering where Landaluce would run next. As the trainer considered Landaluce's next target, there was one thing he made clear from the outset: whatever happened, his filly was not going east. Immediately after the Lassie, before boarding his plane to Keeneland, Wayne had issued a salvo through turf writer Hovdey: "With the best weather and the best money in California, why should I put her on a plane . . . and run for less money against horses who haven't done half as much. . . . I'm through letting the people who vote for Eclipse Awards dictate my program. If somebody in the East thinks they have a better horse, let them get on a plane, come out here, and prove it." Hovdey's advice to connections contemplating such a move was simple: "Don't waste the plane fare."

However, there was one race Wayne would consider shipping for. The rich Arlington-Washington Futurity in late August offered a purse of more than $270,000 to the winner at a distance of seven furlongs, and would afford a chance to test Luce against colts. The cowboy wouldn't ship his star filly east for awards, but he might for money. By passing up the Hollywood Juvenile right after the Lassie, Wayne now had Luce fresh enough to beat colts for a purse worth five times more than Desert Wine had earned in the Juvenile. Of course, a win in the Grade One Arlington-Washington Futurity against colts would have the added benefit of making Luce the undisputed leader in both earnings and graded stakes wins in the entire juvenile division.

Competing trainers with promising two-year-old fillies shared Wayne's problem devising schedules that avoided Slew's speedy daughter. If Wayne ran Luce in the Futurity against colts at Arlington in late August, would he ship her back to run here at Del Mar in the Debutante for fillies just a week later? Wayne's daring and unconventional decisions about where and how often to race his top runners kept horsemen guessing.

While Wayne contemplated his next move with Luce, another milestone for the trainer was on the horizon which would shape the rest of his career. One morning in August, sixty-one-year-old San Diego Chargers owner Gene Klein, who'd already survived one heart attack and was fast becoming disillusioned with professional football, visited Del Mar with his wife, Joyce, who thought horses might provide a satisfying outlet for his considerable energies and finances. In the grandstand, Klein bumped into former Chicago Bears linebacker Dick Butkus, who also knew Wayne. "Doesn't he have Landaluce, the great filly?," said Klein. Butkus offered to introduce the two. Klein, who once called himself "Cowboy Gene" when starting out in the used-car business in the 1940s, was about to meet a kindred spirit. His partnership with another like-minded cowboy would last throughout the 1980s, creating a western-based powerhouse that the *BloodHorse* called "one of the most powerful thoroughbred empires in racing history." Remarkably, within the next six years, horses bought and trained by Wayne and owned by Klein would win eleven championships, a Kentucky Derby and a Preakness, seven Breeders' Cup races, and also a Horse of the Year title. Both gritty entrepreneurs with western roots whose success derived from risk-taking and flouting tradition, the duo formed a natural challenge to the eastern-based purview of Thoroughbred racing. As Lukas said of Klein, "he proved you don't have to belong to the Jockey Club or inherit a band of broodmares to win a lot of races."

Although there are various accounts of how Klein and Lukas met, all versions of the story mention Klein's curiosity about Landaluce as being part of it. "Landaluce broke the ice on the introduction to Klein," Lukas confirmed. The two men immediately hit it off, and within a matter of weeks Wayne would be back at the fall yearling sales, this time to buy prospects for a client with enthusiasm and pockets deep enough to take the trainer's career to the absolute pinnacle of the sport.

If the Arlington-Washington Futurity were not restricted to colts and geldings, fans in the near-record crowd of more than twenty-eight thousand, biggest of the Del Mar meet, and jammed into the stands on Sunday, September 5, over Labor Day weekend might never have had the chance to see Landaluce run at their track. Sometime in early August, Wayne had discovered to his chagrin that fillies were not eligible for the $500,000 Futurity. He was not the only one regretful about the race conditions: "I could cry," said Arlington official Tim Rivera. "We'd love to have her." "It is our loss that a filly as fine as Landaluce won't be running," added Arlington general manager Bill Thayer. "Racing fans of the Midwest would have loved to have seen her run." A few days later, Wayne announced that Luce's next start would be at Del Mar in the $125,000-added Debutante for fillies at a distance of one mile, for which 150 juveniles were still eligible. The *Daily Racing Form,* anticipating a standing-room-only crowd, called this "good news for the fans here, but bad news for the . . . other 149 fillies," and predicted if Landaluce ran as she did in the Lassie "she is liable to lap her opponents."

Here in the West, *Fast Times at Ridgemont High,* filmed at nearby Clairemont High School in San Diego, had just been released, while in the East, the Miss America pageant was about to get underway in Atlantic City, where Miss California, Debra Sue Maffett, a twenty-five-year-old strawberry blonde with dreams of becoming a celebrity, hoped to win the crown. Racing fans were grateful for the opportunity to see California's new filly superstar in her first appearance at a track outside Hollywood Park, and today's handle, bolstered by the Lukas headliner, would be an all-time record at Del Mar. Track programs sold out by the third race, and many patrons bought mutuel tickets on Luce with no intention of cashing them, simply as a souvenir of having

Cartoonist Pierre "Peb" Bellocq captured Landaluce's star quality prior to her start in the Del Mar Debutante Stakes. (Keeneland Library, Peb collection)

actually seen the great filly in person. Luce was continuing to do her part in bringing huge crowds with record handles to California tracks. Everyone wanted to see the filly *Sports Illustrated* called "the most exciting two-year-old in the country."

Although hardly the challenge or purse of the Arlington-Washington Futurity, the Debutante was still an important race for Landaluce: it would mark her first effort at a mile, and her first around two turns. A win here would cement the filly's reputation within the juvenile division, prove that she could carry her speed around two turns, and rate as she would need to win longer races in the future, establishing her as a future classic contender.

"With Landaluce starting, horsemen are expected to virtually avoid the entry box for the Debutante," reported the *Daily Racing Form*. A week before the race, Landaluce's confirmed presence yielded a meager field of only two other starters—Tom Gentry's stakes winner Issues n' Answers, ridden by Bill Shoemaker, victorious in the six-furlong Coronado here at Del Mar with an impressive time of 1:08 3/5, equaling the track record for a two-year-old filly, and Sharili Brown, recent winner of a California-bred restricted stakes.

Landaluce's most recent work a week before the race undoubtedly further discouraged entries, when she went five furlongs at Del Mar under exercise rider David Pineda in a scintillating :59 3/5. Luce's fractions were :25 and :48 2/5, meaning she covered the final eighth in a scorching :11 1/5. Laura and Wayne, watching Luce come back from the track, knew that the filly was more than ready to go.

For the first time in twenty-two years, there were no supplementary nominations to the race. No one was willing to put up $7,500 for a portion of a $180,000 purse if it meant their filly had to run against Landaluce. Eventually, the racing office managed to fill the field with three additional starters, bringing the total to six. Besides Issues n' Answers, whose connections felt she had a chance based on her maiden score, the rest of the field appeared to be hopelessly outclassed, and running only for second or third money. Trainers of other fillies in the race could only hope that Landaluce might not be able to carry the brilliant speed she showed at submile distances over more ground.

Wayne, however, already thinking ahead to longer, richer, year-end juvenile races as well as Classic races next spring, was starting to stretch Luce out in distance during works. "I could train her to be speed-crazy and go wire-to-wire all the time," the trainer pointed out. "But that wouldn't do us any good later on." He was aware there were skeptics who didn't think she could carry her speed. "There's no way she won't go a distance," he claimed, "with her attitude."

Sometime during Labor Day weekend, an ABC News crew headed by newsman Ray Gandolf arrived at Del Mar to film an extended segment about Landaluce that would air after her expected victory in the Debutante. The crew followed Wayne and his filly around the shedrow and filmed a morning work. "Unlike her daddy, Seattle Slew, who reminded some people of Buster Keaton running for a bus, Landaluce is as graceful as she is powerful," said Gandolf, who noted that her trainer was with her constantly, supervising all her activities himself instead of delegating them to others. "Is [Landaluce] the most promising horse you've ever trained?," Gandolf asked, as Wayne stood next to Luce, still bridled and standing quietly beside him back at the barn, his shoulders at her neck. "Oh, by far," Wayne replied. "I've been blessed with some nice horses, and each of them has a special place in my heart, but I don't think I've ever been around an athlete like Landaluce. When you ask her for something, she . . . responds like a good sports car. All you've got to do is step on the accelerator, and zoom, it's there." Later, as Ebaristo bathed Luce, Wayne held her by the shank in front of the camera and the filly tossed her head while the trainer smiled with genuine pleasure, pride, and an expression that looked a lot like love.

The day before the Debutante, Wayne's four-year-old Island Whirl notched another big win for the West and his trainer when he "stepped off a plane . . . to win the [Grade One] Woodward Stakes in a romp," one of the most prestigious races in the East. Such was Wayne's regard for Landaluce that he chose to stay home for the Deb instead, charging son Jeff with supervising the Belmont race. Today, in the close quarters of the paddock, Ebaristo, wearing a green Landaluce T-shirt and ball cap, calmly walked the filly as Wayne, wearing a green plaid jacket and described as "watchful as a nervous

Landaluce and her groom in the paddock at Del Mar prior to the
Debutante, September 5, 1982. (Keeneland Library, Barrett collection)

chaperone," confessed he had butterflies in his stomach. Camera-toting fans hugged the fence five deep to snap pictures of Landaluce, and Ray Gandolf's ABC News crew was again on hand, their presence a measure of what turf writer Hovdey called the growing "Landaluce craze." While noting that the television cameras were so close in the walking ring they were "almost on her saddle," the *BloodHorse* reported the filly remained unperturbed by all the attention.

This time, when Wayne gave Laffit a leg up, he told the rider to let Luce run her own race. As the field left the paddock, Laffit expected another impressive effort from his new superstar. Both of his main rivals for jockey honors had mounts in this race: Shoemaker on Issues n' Answers and McCarron on Nordic Princess. Landaluce was top weight at 119 pounds, the most she had ever carried, conceding three to six pounds to the rest of the field. As a winner of two races, Landaluce now carried more weight, which meant Laffit could make the impost.

As the field made their way postward, Landaluce was the prohibitive 3–10 favorite and had created her first minus show pool. Although Laffit gave the filly an extended warmup, she reached the starting gate without perspiring at all.

As she did before each of her filly's starts, Laura Cotter quietly slipped away to the betting window and wagered a "few dollars" across the board. She kept all Luce's winning tickets, and never cashed them.

When the field left the gate, Landaluce broke alertly, like she always did. Wayne, watching the race with Laura Cotter and Bobby Barnett, thought it was unfolding exactly as he knew it would, with Shoemaker urging Issues n' Answers from the outset, and not allowing Landaluce to take an early lead. Laffit, letting Luce relax and not asking for speed, lay two and a half lengths back from Issues n' Answers after a quarter in a blazing :22 3/5, with California-bred Granja Reina just a half length back in third. A brisk pace for horses of any age, this

Landaluce and Laffit Pincay break with the field from post position four in the Del Mar Debutante. (Keeneland Library, Barrett collection)

was the slowest opening quarter Landaluce had ever raced. Issues n' Answers did not change leads around the first turn and carried Landaluce wide. By the half pole, Landaluce had cut Issues n' Answers' lead to just a half length in :46, a brisk time for a one-mile race, with Granja Reina falling back to fourth as Nordic Princess under McCarron moved up to challenge. Laffit and Wayne both knew Landaluce could sweep by the leader anytime the rider asked her, but still he waited, and Wayne was pleased that the filly was able to rate and run slightly behind Issues n' Answers. By the three-quarter mark, Landaluce was beginning her move to take charge, "on her own," as Laffit said later, with the Hall of Famer giving her some rein and allowing her to take a narrow lead as she swept outside and headed Issues n' Answers, running six furlongs in 1:10 4/5, a time fast enough to win many sprint races, but just a breeze for Slew's speedy bay daughter. What was considered "rating" for Luce was an all-out sprint for other runners. As the two leaders rounded the second turn approaching the stretch, Landaluce switched leads perfectly, as if on cue, with the pair now three lengths ahead of the field. But into the stretch, tiring under the whip, Issues n' Answers lugged out and could no longer keep up, while Landaluce began to draw away under a hand ride, with her trademark effortless way of going. Laffit, who'd learned his lesson from the Lassie, only had to show her the whip this time. He said later that the filly's race was "methodical and businesslike" and that he never really let her run until the stretch. Clearly, Luce was learning her job, and thriving on it.

Wayne, Laura, and Bobby watched with satisfaction as Landaluce surged down the stretch. When the filly reached the wire, six lengths in front, once again without urging or extending herself, Wayne told them both, "We've got ourselves a Derby contender. If ever there was a filly that's going to win the Derby, it's gonna be her." By winning her first attempt at a mile around two turns with such ease, it was clear that Landaluce was more than a sprinter.

This time, all four members of the Slew Crew watched from the stands as their stallion's best filly flew down the stretch and became her sire's first multiple graded stakes winner. "Landaluce is awesome," said Karen Taylor. "She ran just like her old man today." Added Mickey, "This filly is more than a good horse. . . . [She's] a freak."

Luce wasn't even breathing hard as she came off the track showing not even a patch of sweat. The race had taken little out of her, and she had never really been challenged or extended. She had made her third win in a row, even by a substantial margin over a greater distance than she had ever run before, look easy. Jay Hovdey called the win "smooth, and nearly effortless." Her winning time of 1:35 3/5 was three-fifths of a second off the stakes record, and the *Racing Form* noted, "she could have gone much faster if it had been imperative." Laffit claimed the filly "was just galloping the last part. . . . [If] somebody would've come to her, she would've put out. . . . Whenever I ask for something, she gives it to me." In the winner's circle, Laura gave Luce a pat on the neck and Laffit a congratulatory hug after he dismounted. "She's the best two-year-old filly I've ever been on," the jockey said.

Wayne was pleased with the filly's effort. She had run exactly the race he'd hoped for, rating kindly, relaxing, and not extending herself. He knew this race was an important stepping-stone to the big races he had in mind for her. The next day, Lukas told reporters the filly was "extra bright. . . . It wasn't a hard race on her at all." The trainer had good reason to feel "extra bright" himself: in addition to Island Whirl's surprise score in the Woodward, his three-year-old colt Muttering had won the Del Mar Invitational Handicap against older horses the day after the Debutante. It had been a spectacular holiday weekend for the Lukas barn.

Tom Gentry, owner and breeder of second-place Issues n' Answers, was philosophical in a postrace interview: "I'm happy," he said. "She ran a helluva race, but the winner is something else. Wherever she goes, our filly will go somewhere else from now on." Bill Shoemaker, rider of Issues n' Answers, agreed: "[Landaluce] is . . . as good as I've seen."

After the Debutante, the ABC news crew accompanied Karen and Mickey Taylor to their Lexington farm, just a few miles from Spendthrift, where the couple checked on their Seattle Slew weanlings and paid Luce's sire a visit. Karen entered Slew's stall, where she patted his neck and informed him, "You sired a filly with your speed and your heart," as the Triple Crown winner tossed his head and stood nonchalantly in a corner, his nose pointed toward his hay rack.

After her third win in a row, Landaluce was already Miss America in the hearts of fans across the country, the first California juvenile filly to inspire such an ardent and widespread national following. Fan mail arrived daily in the Lukas barn from across the United States, from Virginia to Minnesota. Among the letters Wayne received was one which said, "Landaluce is as exciting to watch . . . as any horse in the country. You make sure you keep her here in California."

Another letter came from the mother of a twelve-year-old girl recovering from surgery in Texas, who read about Luce in *Sports Illustrated* and asked for her picture. Wayne sent the photo and called the family himself.

On Labor Day, just after the Debutante, Gandolf's Landaluce segment aired in prime time on ABC's national news program *World News Tonight*. Western fans were thrilled that their filly was receiving national attention, and easterners were treated to replays of the Lassie and Debutante, showing just how special Miss California really was. From the Del Mar winner's circle, Gandolf said, "It looks like [Landaluce] could be going to the prom in Kentucky . . . and if the boys want to dance, they'll have to catch her first." "As she soared higher and higher in the public's imagination, Landaluce generated a huge public response," turf writer Jay Hovdey noted: "The national media . . . whipped her into mythical proportions. The popular thing to do was to love Landaluce." By now, Landaluce's fame was worldwide. "She was an international celebrity," wrote Joe Hirsch. "Europeans coming to the United States all asked about the 'Wonder Filly of the West.'"

On the eve of the Miss America pageant in Atlantic City, real-life Miss California, Debra Maffett, readied her vocal cords and donned the same white swimsuit she'd worn in pageants for the past five years, hoping to snag the crown. Landaluce once again appeared on national television, this time the subject of a feature by ABC sportscaster Dick Schaap. "[Landaluce] is already being talked about as a possible Derby winner next year, perhaps even the first filly to win the Triple Crown," he reported. The next evening, a week after Luce's Debutante victory, Maffett strolled down the Atlantic City runway in a silver evening gown wearing the Miss America tiara.

Shortly afterward, *New York Times* turf writer Steven Crist speculated whether 1982 might also be "a West Coast year in racing's major pageants." Crist observed it was shaping up to be a banner year for western runners, and Wayne was responsible for two of the most noteworthy wins: Blush with Pride in the Kentucky Oaks, and

Island Whirl's upset in the Woodward. With Western-based Gato del Sol winning the Derby, and five-year-old gelding Perrault a virtual shoo-in for Horse of the Year if he could win the Marlboro Cup at Belmont, for which he was the odds-on favorite, Crist wondered if the best horses in the country were now located in the West.

Although Perrault already had two Grade One wins for the year at Santa Anita and Hollywood Park, and another victory in the rich but yet ungraded Budweiser Million, his connections knew that even these impressive accomplishments were unlikely to clinch a Horse of the Year title without a Grade One score in the East. Crist felt that Perrault's owners' decision to bring the grass handicapper from Europe to begin his campaign in the West was significant, and another indication of the rising importance of California racing. "Big purses are more than enough incentive for horses to be flown around the world, and simulcasting and offtrack betting are blurring regional and national boundaries," he wrote. "If the world of thoroughbred racing is becoming a global village, its capital may soon be California."

But the great gelding Perrault, injured in the race and eased by Laffit Pincay, failed in his Marlboro bid and was done for the year. The race was won by another western upstart, Lemhi Gold, a four-year-old chestnut son of Vaguely Noble trained by Laz Barrera who toted thirteen pounds fewer than Perrault and who had never won a race on dirt prior to the Marlboro. Lemhi Gold's win "will have to be regarded as clear evidence that California horses are not the patsies they used to be labeled by Eastern racing people," proclaimed the *New York Daily News,* adding, "The West Coast is truly ready to dispute Eastern supremacy in championship events." The surprising victory propelled the Aaron U. Jones runner into the championship mix within the handicap division, and according to Crist, "threw the contest for horse-of-the-year honors into chaos."

Meanwhile, a juvenile colt who had not even made his first start when Landaluce scored in the Lassie was rapidly rising to prominence on the East Coast. Fred Hooper's homebred Copelan arrived on the

Fred Hooper leads two-year-old colt Copelan, Jerry Bailey up, to the Winner's Circle after notching his third consecutive graded stakes victory in the Futurity at Belmont on September 12, 1982. (Bob Coglianese)

national scene with his score in the Sanford Stakes in mid-August, and followed it up with a win in both the Hopeful at Saratoga, and the Futurity at Belmont, becoming the only juvenile in the country with three graded stakes wins. The bay son of Tri Jet, a game, consistent colt who ran only as fast as he needed to according to trainer Mitch Griffin, seemed to be dominating the two-year-old colt division as convincingly as Landaluce controlled the fillies. With the summer season nearing its end, Copelan and Landaluce, as the only undefeated multiple graded stakes-winning two-year-olds in the country, not only were clear front-runners for juvenile division honors, but in the absence of a distinct contender among three-year-olds or older campaigners, were now also possible Horse of the Year candidates themselves.

Here at Del Mar, the fast developing and lightly raced western colt Roving Boy, a son of Olden Times trained by colorful former Charlie Whittingham assistant Joe Manzi, announced his presence with a win in the Del Mar Futurity, narrowly edging Hollywood Juvenile winner Desert Wine. Finishing eleven lengths clear of the field, Roving Boy and Desert Wine established themselves as top West Coast juveniles just three days after the Debutante.

Wayne had told *Washington Post* columnist Andrew Beyer as early as late July that he believed Landaluce was a classic distance horse, but after her victory in the Debutante, the trainer's claim had teeth. In fact, his assessment seemed almost modest in light of what Beyer himself and other journalists were already trumpeting. "[Landaluce] has the potential to be an all-time great," Beyer wrote before the Debutante. "She has the capability to make history before the year is over." Even as he continued to try to keep his dreams to himself, Wayne couldn't help thinking that Luce was his best Classic prospect so far. She was better than Codex, Partez, or Muttering, and even better than Stalwart, whom until now he'd regarded as his best chance to win the Derby. It didn't matter that Luce was a filly: physically and mentally, Wayne believed she was a match for colts.

As co-owner Marvin Warner had observed during Stalwart's juvenile campaign, Eclipse award voters remained primarily easterners. Wayne knew that prestige and awards were still in the East, but now the money was in the West. In 1982, only one race among the ten richest in the country, the Jockey Club Gold Cup at Belmont for older horses, was offered at an eastern track. Five of the top ten richest races were held in California, and two of those were for juveniles: the Hollywood Starlet for fillies and the Hollywood Futurity for colts. In 1982, winning either the Young America or the Champagne Stakes, the richest and most prestigious races in the East, would net a juvenile colt's connections $144,000 or $195,900 respectively—compared to the expected $400,000 or so the same colt could take home in the Hollywood Futurity. Even stakes races for juvenile fillies in the West paid more: $260,000 for the newly minted Grade One Oak Leaf, and $271,000 for the Hollywood Starlet. If Landaluce won either race, competing only against fillies in her own backyard, she would earn twice as much as she could bring home conquering the best colts in the East in a Grade One stakes on an unfamiliar track. Were she to compete against eastern juvenile distaffers, the disparity in earnings became even greater: the winner's share of the Grade One Sorority Stakes at Monmouth Park was $82,000, whereas the victress in Saratoga's Spinaway earned barely $50,000. Wayne, perhaps wisely, figured the risk of going east with Landaluce was no longer worth any potential reward.

Although Wayne had told the press throughout the summer that he would not travel east to seek an Eclipse for Landaluce, her convincing Debutante score made what might have been called braggadocio in July seem more like common wisdom by early September. Eastern connections with Classic prospects for next year, and even westerners pointed to the Starlet or Futurity, could now no longer persuade themselves that Wayne's brilliant filly was just a speedball, as Terlingua had been. After the Debutante, Wayne could afford to be stubborn. The upcoming Grade One Oak Leaf, along with the Hollywood Starlet and Futurity, gave him a path to achieve with

Landaluce everything he had tried and failed to do with Terlingua—
except win a major eastern stakes. And by now, Wayne cared less
about impressing the East than ever before.

But the East was impressed anyway. In a national telecast of the
Matron Stakes for two-year-old-fillies at Belmont, part of the September 18 Marlboro undercard, the subject of possible Eclipse champions came up. Trainer-commentator Frank Wright warned, "let's
not forget about a filly out west named Landaluce." Turf writer Jay
Hovdey reported: "The west was stunned. The Lassie and the Debutante have been respected races for decades, but this was the first
time a winner had been mentioned in a championship context. And
by an east coast trainer! . . . A horse of Landaluce's ability transcends
sectional bias." But even Hovdey remarked that "Tradition will get
a stern test" if Landaluce's connections sought an Eclipse Award
without going east.

To do that, the next step was for Landaluce to win a Grade One
race. The morning after the Debutante, Wayne told the *BloodHorse*
he had already received a call from New York, presumably seeking
the filly's presence in the Grade One Frizette. Wayne reiterated his
plans, leaving no room for doubt: "They forget that planes fly in
both directions. We've got all the rich races in California, so unless
New York wants to put on a $500,000 race, we're not leaving the
state." The Oak Leaf at Santa Anita would give Wayne and Luce all
they needed. Wayne was after purse money, and he wanted to win
the Derby. He said he didn't care about awards. But Miss California,
well on her way to becoming Miss America for the first time in horse
racing, might, if nothing went wrong, manage to give him all he
wanted, and more.

Much had changed in California racing in the four short years since
Terlingua's juvenile campaign, and even more was about to. In
mid-September, representatives from eight U.S. tracks arrived in
Lexington, Kentucky, to make their best case for why the inaugural

Breeders' Cup, scheduled to take place in 1984, should be held at their facility. It was a foregone conclusion that the premier event would be located in either New York or California, and the contest to host it was heated, another indicator of what turf writer Crist called an "escalating coastal rivalry."

"We have the most to lose by not getting it," claimed New York Racing Association president Gerard McKeon, exhibiting precisely the mind-set that so chafed western connections when he added, "Historically, all of the championships have been won and lost in New York." McKeon went on to point out that no western runner in history had ever won Horse of the Year without racing there, with the exception of Ack Ack in 1971.

Crist predicted that if California landed the inaugural Cup, top western runners vying for national championships "could stay on the West Coast all year and still win the title." But in the meantime, Marje Everett's inauguration of the Starlet and Futurity at Hollywood Park had in effect created the equivalent of a Breeders' Cup divisional championship in her own backyard. These year-ending races allowed top West Coast juveniles to develop without shipping east, kept fans coming to the track all year to see the best California runners, bolstering attendance and handle, with the added luster of potentially luring top eastern runners west. This year, Wayne Lukas, fortunate enough to have the right horse at the right time, was poised to take unique advantage of both races.

It was axiomatic that fillies were at a disadvantage against colts, which is why they received a weight allowance when facing them. Paradoxically, Wayne knew that Landaluce had an unprecedented opportunity precisely *because* she was a filly. What were the odds of a trainer having a juvenile filly with brilliant speed and enough staying power to prevail over her own sex at a distance of a mile and a sixteenth in a $500,000 race, and then be able to come back and do the same thing in a $750,000 race against male foes two weeks later? Further, what were the odds that these two races, the richest in the country for females, and the second-richest for males, would both be run at that filly's home track, Hollywood Park, where she had already set two records? Wayne knew Luce had what it took to win both contests, but only if he kept enough fuel in the tank of his turbo-charged high-performance racehorse at the end of the year.

If she could win both the Starlet and the Futurity, Landaluce would amass more than a million dollars in earnings, a record for a juvenile of either sex, almost double what the great Buckpasser earned at two, and more than enough to guarantee her a spot in the starting gate at Churchill Downs next year. Winning so much at two would give Wayne the luxury of running Luce at three only where and when he pleased. He could pick the races and schedule that suited her best in the months leading up to the Derby and arrive in Louisville with a fresh and supremely talented horse ready to run. How could Eastern Eclipse voters ignore such a feat? Perhaps Wayne thought that campaigning the first two-year-old filly millionaire might overcome eastern bias. But even if it didn't, he felt he had nothing to lose.

15

Pleasant Surprise

It's like she's just floating away.
—Laffit Pincay

It was late September, and a string of thirty-six Lukas runners had just arrived at Santa Anita from Del Mar. One of the first things Wayne did when he got there was knock down the wall between stalls 54 and 55 to make what he called "a master suite" for Landaluce, the only horse in the barn to enjoy such deluxe accommodations. Wayne knew Luce liked a lot of room, and whatever the filly wanted, she got. Besides, it made sense to enlarge her stall now, since the trainer planned to keep her at Santa Anita for the next six months, the longest she had ever stayed at one track since she first came to Hollywood Park as a maiden. So much had happened since then. Landaluce would soon turn three in this stall—and then it would be time to start training for the Classics.

Like many top California trainers, Wayne always stayed at Santa Anita from the conclusion of its fall meet at the end of October through the winter meet, which began the day after Christmas and ended in April. His stable was now so large he couldn't keep all his California runners at one track, so he kept a group at Santa Anita under his own supervision, with another at Hollywood Park managed by son Jeff. There had been a new wrinkle last year when Hollywood Park added its year-ending meet in the former six-week dead spot between the two Santa Anita dates. Wayne, like many trainers, vanned some runners from his Santa Anita string to Hollywood to work or race during those six weeks, since the two facilities were only thirty-four miles apart, a manageable commute in the early 1980s. Besides, Wayne by now had a beautiful home in Arcadia, just minutes from Santa Anita. This way, Landaluce would always be nearby.

Each time he passed Luce's custom-made stall, Wayne smiled and felt what he later called "boundless optimism." Wayne was once again on a winning streak, having captured seven stakes in September alone, saddling twenty-three stakes winners so far this year, and in second place nationally behind only Hall of Famer Charlie Whittingham. Things were going according to plan, as Landaluce just kept winning. She was healthy and happy and made everything she did look so easy. It was almost too good to be true.

Because Luce became more valuable with every race she won, owners Beal and French increased her insurance to $3 million, an extraordinary valuation at the time for a juvenile filly. Lukas also took the precaution of hiring a night watchman exclusively for his phenom. Wayne continued to feel that Luce's winning ways "invigorated his whole operation" and seemed to carry over to the rest of the barn, with stakes victories coming in waves. One of Wayne's core convictions in any of his life's endeavors was the importance of a positive attitude. He sensed that somehow Luce's success generated that rare and essential positive force that infused everyone in the shedrow—from hotwalkers and grooms to assistant trainers, and even himself—with an aura of belief. With Landaluce, anything was possible.

Landaluce's fans also cherished the aura of success the filly seemed to carry with her wherever she went. After the national publicity Landaluce received in her Debutante win, her fan mail increased to the point where Lukas could no longer respond personally. He ordered custom greeting cards, imprinted with an image of Luce winning at Del Mar, from an oil painting by equine artist Christine Picavet. Especially noteworthy letters received a piece of

Luce's mane along with a green-and-white ribbon that matched Beal and French's silks.

In the three months since the filly had risen from an unknown to a national star, turf writer Jay Hovdey chronicled her journey. Hovdey, a Californian, would have agreed that Ruffian was American racing's preeminent filly—until Landaluce came along. He followed Luce everywhere—from her 5:00 a.m. workouts to the winner's circle, and even her daily barn routines between races. Hovdey found himself awed by the racing record Landaluce was etching into history. In a time when only a handful of live races were ever televised, Hovdey provided a picture in words for many who would never be able to see Landaluce run. "Fans are in love with the idea of Landaluce as much as the reality," he wrote. Seen through the eyes of a Californian proud of what she meant for the West, Hovdey made Landaluce a heroine for all. His article "She Vants to Be Alone," in which he compared Luce's star quality to Greta Garbo, won the talented columnist his first-ever Eclipse Award.

In the predawn hours of September 29, Hovdey was up early to watch Luce work under exercise rider David Pineda, only her second time ever over the Santa Anita strip designated slow from recent rain. She began the work solo until she was joined by another Lukas runner, four-year-old colt Mufti under Jesse Cerillo, at the three-eighths pole, and completed five furlongs handily in 1:03 3/5. Wayne on his stable pony accompanied both runners back from the track to the paddock and observed that Luce was not in the least bit tired from her work. "Look at that," he told Hovdey. "She's not even blowing. I'll bet you the only sweat on her . . . is under the saddle." As Luce matured, the trainer noticed she was beginning to lose interest during longer works by herself, and so he decided to add the extra spice of an occasional workmate to keep her motivated. Landaluce ran better when she had someone to beat.

Landaluce worked once more on October 5, this time over a fast surface, going five furlongs in a sizzling :58 4/5. Wayne knew he could not keep Luce in the barn for another eighteen days, when the

Grade One Oak Leaf at a mile and one-sixteenth, the race he was pointing her toward, would be run. His high-performance sports car needed a tune-up. So the trainer decided at the last minute to enter Luce in the Anoakia Stakes at seven furlongs.

This was in spite of the fact that Wayne already had a runner in the race. His strategy of keeping Luce away from the barn's other juvenile fillies had reaped rewards for Ruth Bunn's Some Kinda Flirt. Over Labor Day weekend, while Luce dominated in the Debutante, Flirt finished second in the Grade One Arlington-Washington Lassie. In addition to that good result, Flirt was now a multiple stakes winner and had certainly proven her quality, but like many fillies with the misfortune of being foaled the same year as Landaluce, competing against a phenom had made her look weaker than she was. Flirt now had not raced in more than thirty days and needed to run. Wayne most likely entered Flirt in the Anoakia before he knew he would need to find a spot for Luce. He was running out of options to keep his best fillies apart.

The relative unimportance of the Anoakia and its smaller purse had persuaded rival trainers that Landaluce would not run in it. Until October 5, the race seemed a great spot for fillies like Tom Gentry's Issues n' Answers, who "ran her heart out" to finish six lengths behind Luce in the Debutante, and Hector Palma's Granja Reina, eleven lengths back in third. Both trainers scratched upon hearing of Landaluce's presence in the race. "I wouldn't have had my filly trained for this race if I'd known," lamented Gentry. "It doesn't make any sense to hook Landaluce today. We'd have no shot." The race that seemed like a perfect chance to grab part of a $60,000 purse became a looming catastrophe with Slew's daughter waiting in the starting gate. The *Los Angeles Times* called Gentry and Palma "the smartest trainers around" for scratching.

Meanwhile, it was shaping up to be a high-stakes weekend at Belmont for racing honors in several divisions as well as for Horse of the Year.

Two days before the Anoakia, both the Jockey Club Gold Cup, the richest race in the East, and the final leg of Belmont's Fall Championship series in the handicap division, as well as the Champagne Stakes for two-year-olds, would be run, with both races televised nationally. Western interloper Lemhi Gold could clinch both a divisional and Horse of the Year title with a win in the Jockey Club Gold Cup. Trainer Laz Barrera, slicing carrots on the backstretch and feeding them to his potential champion in front of the press, said, "If he wins the Gold Cup," [Lemhi Gold] should be Horse of the Year." After the son of Vaguely Noble's surprise win in the Marlboro, turf writers agreed that the older male division was in chaos but disagreed on which runner among many in contention was now favorite for Horse of the Year. Steven Crist of the *New York Times* believed that the Marlboro result returned three-year-old colt Conquistador Cielo, winner of the Belmont and Metropolitan Mile, into contention, whereas Bill Christine of the *Los Angeles Times* felt that the son of Mr. Prospector's third-place finish in the Travers and early retirement to stud eliminated him. Both writers agreed, however, that disarray within the older male division warranted new focus on both Landaluce and Copelan. "They have finished first in all eight of their combined starts," noted Christine. "Since Landaluce . . . will race the rest of the year in California, and Copelan is a colt who will apparently remain in the East, there is scant chance they will meet." Christine went so far as to suggest a match race between the dominant juveniles to decide the title.

Copelan's connections hoped that a decisive victory in the Grade One Champagne would seal juvenile colt honors for the Fred Hooper homebred and improve his chances to become the first two-year-old colt since Secretariat to be named Horse of the Year. "If Copelan wins [the] . . . Champagne," wrote columnist Luther Evans of the *Miami Herald,* "he will lock up the two-year-old championship." "If Copelan wins the Champagne big, I'm going to vote for him as Horse of the Year," claimed *Sport's Illustrated*'s Bill Leggett. "Nobody will get to the wire before Copelan in the Champagne," predicted the colt's rider, Jerry Bailey. He was right.

Copelan's six-length score in the Champagne under a hand ride prompted celebratory headlines across the nation that the son of Tri Jet had clinched two-year-old colt honors. It had been a spectacular summer for Copelan and trainer Mitch Griffin, who had campaigned the undefeated colt to three consecutive Grade One victories in a little more than six weeks. The Hooper homebred seemed invincible and was already the odds-on favorite for his last start of the year in the Young America Stakes at the Meadowlands on November 4, as well as the early book favorite for the 1983 Kentucky Derby.

In the Jockey Club Gold Cup immediately following the Champagne, Lemhi Gold emerged victorious in a race marred by tragedy, when a four-horse pileup resulted in the deaths of favored three-year-old colt Timely Writer and 50–1 shot Johnny Dance. Despite the unfortunate circumstances, the Laz Barrera trainee solidified his Horse of the Year credentials with the win. "There should be no doubt about it now," said the Hall of Famer. Lemhi Gold's score in the rich contest made him only the second runner of the year (along with Perrault) to earn more than $1 million and the first horse in history to capture both the Marlboro and the Jockey Club Gold in a single season.

So, though it was true that the Anoakia was only a Grade III race, it still had important ramifications for Landaluce, as a new challenger for two-year-old filly honors was emerging on the East Coast. Owners Jim and Paula Tucker and trainer Frank Gomez hoped that their gray daughter of Verbatim, winner of four starts against allowance and listed stakes company at Calder by a combined forty-seven lengths, would make a big splash in her first Grade One effort as the overwhelming favorite in the Frizette at Belmont, which had recruited Landaluce to no avail. A victory this weekend for Princess Rooney, the "pride of southern Florida," would make her the only undefeated Grade One juvenile winning filly in the country, and a serious challenger to Landaluce for divisional honors. Luce needed to win the Anoakia convincingly and remain undefeated to stay in contention for year-end awards. But Wayne wasn't worried. At this point in her career, as he would say later, "nobody was going to beat her . . . from the length of a corncob to a mile and a half."

Watching Landaluce win was becoming California racegoers' favorite way to spend a holiday: she ran her maiden on Fourth of July weekend, the Debutante over Labor Day, and now the Anoakia on Monday, October 11, Columbus Day. Santa Anita fans had not expected Landaluce to appear at their track for two more weeks, when they would throng to see her in the Oak Leaf near the end of the meet. Luce's entry in the Anoakia was a pleasant surprise, transforming what Jay Hovdey described as a race with no significance outside of California into "a jewel."

The afternoon of the Anoakia was hot and dry, as a record crowd of forty-eight thousand for the fall meet gathered to see Landaluce in her first start at Santa Anita. An hour prior to the race, Wayne watched Beal and French's two-year-old filly Manzanares finish second behind Sophisticated Girl, a nice Stop the Music filly trained by Gary Jones who would challenge Landaluce in the Oak Leaf in less than two weeks.

But right now, as Luce circled in the paddock, all eyes were on her—and so was nearly all the mutuel handle. Almost three-quarters of the entire amount bet on the race was on the filly's shoulders, as well as 80 percent of show money, resulting in Luce's second consecutive minus show pool. Bettors were so confident in another Landaluce score that she was bet down to 1–10 odds by post time.

Because she was already a winner of a race with a purse of at least $50,000, Landaluce was assigned top weight of 123 pounds, the most she had ever carried, and the highest impost in the history of the Anoakia. Luce conceded three pounds to Some Kinda Flirt, Sorrento Stakes–winner Time of Sale, and Sharili Brown, a distant fourth in the Debutante, while four other runners received a six-pound allowance. Laffit had no trouble making weight in today's race.

Laffit Pincay, Landaluce, and her groom prior to the start of the Anoakia Stakes at Santa Anita, October 11, 1982. (Keeneland Library, Barrett collection)

In the paddock, the Hall of Famer reflected on what had been a troubled summer; he was glad to be back in the West. After the Debutante and the close of the Del Mar meet, Laffit went east in search of more opportunities to ride. He considered taking a vacation, but "if I did that, I'd gain too much weight," he told a reporter. The East had not been kind to the Panamanian. Even before his disappointing loss on Perrault in the Marlboro Cup, where he'd expected to capture the lion's share of a $400,000 purse, Laffit endured a twelve-start winless streak and had won only five races in forty-one attempts.

Laffit's September slump had given hope to rival Angel Cordero, and the two were now locked in an earnings race for jockey of the year. Cordero, who rode primarily in the East, had never won an Eclipse Award and had been shut out of the Hall of Fame despite a career spanning more than two decades as one of the top jockeys in the country. Nearing forty, Cordero felt his time was running out. Laffit, who had already won the jockey title four times and had enjoyed seven years in the Hall of Fame, knew that Cordero was determined to surpass him. By the end of September, Cordero had closed to within $300,000 of Laffit's earnings, mostly by riding a grueling double-duty schedule of daytime races at Aqueduct followed by the Meadowlands at night. Furthermore, Laffit knew Cordero was unafraid to come west to garner more earnings: "I'll go anyplace where . . . I can earn enough purse money to give the [Eclipse] voters reason to support me," Cordero insisted.

Cordero's hopes were further bolstered when Laffit's mount Perrault, injured in the Marlboro, was declared out of racing for the year by trainer Charlie Whittingham. Laffit had hoped the gelding might recover in time for the rich Jockey Club Gold Cup this weekend. A win there would have widened the jockey's margin over Cordero with only two months left in the racing year. Laffit had lost one of his top-earning mounts, the sort every rider covets. This left him with one sure winner capable of raking in extra- large purses in the key months remaining—Landaluce.

Laffit had just flown to California from New York the day before the Anoakia to ride Landaluce in this race. Right before he left, he was offered a mount on Luce's new rival, Princess Rooney. Laffit's agent urged him to stay in New York long enough to take the mount, and the jockey was tempted, but he'd been away from his family for some time and was anxious to return to California. So here he was, hoping that his return home would rekindle his racing luck.

As the call for "riders up" came in the paddock, Wayne's instructions to Laffit were once again very simple: "Lay second or third through the first part, then chirp to her about the three-eighths [pole], and say adios."

The scratch of Hector Palma's filly Granja Reina meant Landaluce would start from the far outside post position for the first time in her career. Luce was always a good gate horse, and Laffit told the gate crew to let her leave at her own pace. The filly broke alertly, joined by 20–1 shot Kookie Kaper immediately on her inside, and those two raced briefly in front until Time of Sale under Chris McCarron rushed up from the rail to take the lead. The leaders raced together three wide on the backstretch, with Landaluce still on the far outside, third by a length after a first quarter in :22 2/5. Approaching the first turn, Landaluce and Time of Sale dispatched Kookie Kaper, who fell back, and the two leaders raced briefly just heads apart.

Rounding the turn, without appearing to accelerate, Landaluce effortlessly passed Time of Sale and was two lengths in front at the half-mile mark in a swift :45.

Jay Hovdey marveled at the fact that the filly somehow managed to change leads smoothly, round the turn, and leave the field behind all at the same time, which he described as "an amazing, balletic move." Laffit agreed: "She changes leads perfect, even before I have to ask her," he said. By the time she reached the stretch, Landaluce was well clear of the field and had extended her lead to seven lengths, completing six furlongs in a brisk 1:09. The race looked like

Landaluce still raring to go after winning the Anoakia Stakes by ten lengths. (Santa Anita Park)

a repeat of the Lassie, with riders flailing their whips to no avail behind Landaluce's wake as the filly continued to draw away, completing the final eighth in :12 4/5 and winning by ten lengths over California-bred Rare Thrill in a stakes record time of 1:21 4/5. Laffit never moved his hands or even showed the whip throughout the race, and Luce flashed under the wire with her ears pricked in what looked like a leisurely gallop. Wayne could tell Laffit knew he had the race won in the stretch: "You could see him grinning the whole last furlong," the trainer said.

It was another easy and impressive win for Slew's bay daughter. The *New York Times* called the race a paid workout. "She won by ten lengths without taking a deep breath," Jay Hovdey wrote, "and runs her final furlongs like her feet are on fire."

Watching from the Santa Anita press box, *Daily Racing Form* writer Jon White was impressed enough to believe Landaluce had the talent to win the 1983 Kentucky Derby and maybe even the Triple Crown. Thirty-six years later, White witnessed another impressive win at Santa Anita that he called "eerily similar," when a powerful chestnut with a white blaze drew off in the stretch to win a seven-furlong maiden race by the same margin of ten lengths in the exact same time of 1:21 4/5.

The chestnut's name was Justify.

In the winner's circle, Wayne was more than satisfied with Luce's effort, and called it her best race so far. No runner had managed to get within six and a half lengths of Landaluce in four starts. Sadly, this group included Ruth Bunn's Some Kinda Flirt, who ran poorly, finishing a distant sixth, and who only raced once more that year. It's possible that the multiple stakes winner, like many fillies who had to run against Luce, lost her heart for racing, for although she was sold to Wayne's new client Gene Klein and started eight times at three, she never won again.

Laffit, too, was impressed with Luce's race. "I just let her run on her own, she felt so strong," he said. "She just keeps getting better and better." "She's acting more mature now. . . . When some tougher [races] come along, maybe I'll get a chance to use her."

After four races, Laffit was most impressed with the ease with which Landaluce left the field behind, especially compared with other great runners he rode or observed. "When she starts to leave . . ., you can't really tell she's doing it. The others just seem to fall behind. With Affirmed, you could feel him grab the bit and give you something more. And horses like Spectacular Bid and Secretariat just blew other horses away. But this filly . . . it's like she's just float-ing away. You can hardly feel the difference."

Wayne, back at the barn, found himself no longer able to heed his own advice about keeping his dreams to himself. "I don't want to think too far ahead," he told the *BloodHorse,* "but the dream of every owner, trainer and jockey is to win the Kentucky Derby. I am no different. I would not hesitate to try her against colts soon."

The two-year-old gray daughter of Verbatim who stepped onto the track at Belmont for the one-mile Grade One Frizette the day before Landaluce won the Anoakia had never been tested past seven furlongs, had never raced outside of Florida, and had never run in graded stakes company. Yet the crowd on hand for the Marlboro Cup that day made Princess Rooney the overwhelming favorite. She did not disappoint them. Leading from the start, the Princess was never headed, easily handling her competition as she drew clear in the stretch and romped by eight lengths.

Suddenly, there was a legitimate challenger to Landaluce for two-year-old filly honors, and immediately after the Anoakia, a clamor in the press began for a meeting between the two undefeated juveniles. Such a meeting was unlikely, however, as Landaluce was being pointed to the Grade One Oak Leaf at Santa Anita, whereas Princess Rooney was aimed at the Grade Two Gardenia at the Meadowlands, both on October 23, and both at a distance of a mile and one-sixteenth, the longest test for either filly.

Wayne once again stood his ground, reiterating his plans to keep Landaluce in the West. "If she was just another good filly we might be taking her to Keeneland for the Alcibiades or looking around for other races," he said immediately after the Anoakia. "But we maintain that she is very, very special, maybe one in ten million, so we'll stick to our schedule and treat her like the classic filly we think she is."

Although Princess Rooney's conditioner, Frank Gomez, had trained for Wayne's mentor John Nerud during the 1970s, he and Lukas had never met. Gomez maintained that his filly's Grade One win in New York and her connections' willingness to travel outside Florida to face stiffer competition proved the Princess's record superior to Landaluce's, and he challenged Wayne to leave his home base. "I'll meet him . . . halfway anytime he wants to," Gomez said. Wayne countered by suggesting Princess Rooney come west for the Starlet in late November. Trainer Laz Barrera, one of the few present for both fillies' races, deemed Landaluce "the better filly, but not by much," then added, "you saw what I did at the [Keeneland] sales right after Landaluce won big. That should tell you what I think of her."

Leon Rasmussen of the *Daily Racing Form* cited "an intense intersectional voting rivalry . . . taking shape" between interests on both coasts, noting that "Neither [filly] has been put to the test." Were Luce to notch her first Grade One score in the upcoming Oak Leaf, "imagine the electioneering that will be going on between the East and the West," he predicted.

For the first time in history, a western juvenile filly had earned a national reputation formidable enough to make even a romp in the Frizette seem insufficient to guarantee a divisional championship. Landaluce remained the front-runner for Eclipse honors. Jay Hovdey claimed that Luce's Anoakia victory was impressive enough that it "took the wind out of the sails" of the Princess's Frizette score. Even Florida sportswriter Paul Moran admitted "[Princess Rooney's] chances are nil in light of the success and acclaim accorded to . . . Landaluce." Furthermore, the Princess's connections made it clear they had no plans or ambitions to challenge colts now or in the future, with Gomez stating that the gray would be pointed toward the filly Triple Crown next year.

As the fall racing season reached its zenith, opportunities to snare divisional honors were waning, and each remaining race became fraught with significance for Copelan, Landaluce, and Princess Rooney, the only remaining undefeated runners in the country still with a chance for a championship. Copelan's connections planned to cap off a spectacular year for the son of Tri Jet with a victory in the Young America Stakes at the Meadowlands, the richest race for two-year-old colts in the East. In existence only since 1977, the race had yielded juvenile colt champions in three of its last five runnings, most recently Deputy Minister in 1981. Owner Fred Hooper, described as "elated" after Copelan's easy win in the Champagne, was not alone in considering his homebred "a virtual lock" for two-year old-champion, with sportswriters across the nation predicting a walkover for the colt in his last race.

Meanwhile, Wayne's decision to keep Landaluce in the West meant that her lone opportunity for a Grade One score—which she needed in order to match Princess Rooney's Frizette win and make the juvenile filly championship indisputable—came very late in the year. But Wayne's confidence in Luce was boundless, and he was not afraid to wait. The upcoming Oak Leaf was just the first in a series of three races between now and mid-December that Wayne knew, if things went according to plan, would etch Landaluce's name permanently in racing history. This is why he raced her sparingly throughout the summer, only adding the Anoakia to her schedule when he felt she needed the race. He wanted his juvenile star to be well-rested and at her peak before reaching the climactic and challenging trio of races—the Oak Leaf, Hollywood Starlet, and Hollywood Futurity—that would make her the first juvenile filly millionaire. Wayne believed she could win all three.

But only three days after Landaluce won the Anoakia, rumblings percolated in the press that Copelan's connections were considering coming west for the Hollywood Futurity. "Copelan runs next in the Young America . . . then possibly in the . . . Hollywood Futurity," reported Dale Austin of the *Baltimore Sun*. The following week, the *Los Angeles Times'* Bill Christine called Hooper "noncommittal" when pressed to reveal whether or not his colt would go west. It's possible that Hooper and Griffin, who believed they already had two-year-old colt honors sewn up, were attracted by the Futurity as a way to challenge Landaluce for Horse of the Year, and to attain the unprecedented juvenile millionaire status that would accrue to whoever prevailed in the showdown. Like Wayne, Fred Hooper also had developed an early appreciation for the new year-ending races at Hollywood when he won last year's inaugural running of the Starlet with his homebred filly Skillful Joy. Hooper and Griffin were bullish on Copelan's chances for both Horse of the Year and a Futurity win—so far, he had shown them nothing to make them think otherwise. By mid-October, they were among the few eastern connections who appeared to be seriously considering a run in the Futurity to challenge top western colts as well as Landaluce. A good two months before the Futurity, turf writer Crist of the *New York Times* was already predicting it might be "the race of the year," confirming that Wayne planned to enter Luce and stating that Copelan's owner "is thinking of running him." In fact, Crist pointed out that the Eclipse Award voting deadline had already been pushed back because of the potential significance of the race.

In the West, there was at least one rival trainer who shared Fred Hooper's belief that Copelan was virtually invincible—Joe Manzi, conditioner of Del Mar Futurity–winner Roving Boy, who was prepping for his first Grade One score in the meet-ending Norfolk Stakes here at Santa Anita. Manzi found Copelan's Champagne win so impressive that he abandoned any thoughts of facing him after the Norfolk, even if the Florida-bred came west for the Futurity. Manzi said he preferred not to challenge Copelan for the two-year-old championship and to save his talented colt for the classics in the spring instead.

In the meantime, though, the undefeated eastern colt and the electrifying western filly each needed to win at least one more race in order to keep their Horse of the Year hopes alive and set up the match race at Hollywood Park that could be the decider. In mid-October of 1982, there were few in racing who would have taken the bet that either one would fail.

16

Making the Grade

She's only two, and a lot can happen in seven months.
—Wayne Lukas

Sometimes, standing outside Luce's double-wide stall, Wayne had to pause and ask himself what he was doing here. The filly needed nothing, wanted nothing. She was perfectly comfortable, calm, and content. She had plenty of room to move around, and Ebaristo, Laura, and even her own special night watchman checked her constantly, alert to any signal that something might be amiss. Still, Wayne had to be near her. He found himself coming to Luce's stall at odd times, even when there were plenty of other things for him to do. He was just looking in on her, he would tell himself. Just to be sure she was okay. And she always was.

Every morning at 6:30, he would watch as Ebaristo led her to the walking ring near the barn. He never took his eyes off her. He wanted to see how she moved, looking for the smallest change, the slightest indication something might be off. Watching her fluid motion even at a walk, Wayne often felt as if he were meditating, or in another world. Luce was so unlike any animal he'd had before. He was in awe of her, and by now she was the most important thing in his life. In the deepest part of himself lurked a fear that in spite of everything he could do to make her life perfect, something would go wrong. But whenever he passed her stall in the afternoon, she would always be

Landaluce, her groom, and Laura Cotter in the backstretch at Santa Anita. (Santa Anita Park)

looking out the window, alert and inquisitive, and Wayne would find his spirits lifted simply by the sight of her.

Lately, the weather at Santa Anita had become warmer during the day and cool at night, so that some horses, like Luce, were starting to grow their winter coats. As the fall season deepened, Landaluce, always physically precocious and unusually strong, was barrel-chested, while still growing and filling out. Although Wayne had not yet measured her, he estimated she was now about sixteen hands and approximately 1,000 pounds. Wayne knew that Luce had not yet reached her physical or mental peak—she was going to get even bigger and stronger when she turned three and became an even more experienced racehorse.

By late October, Wayne's fortunes were continuing to rise, aided by the promise and accomplishments of his superstar filly. The Lukas stable was bursting with a fall cornucopia of stakes winners, who had captured some of the top races in the country, including Santa Anita Derby and Del Mar Handicap–winner Muttering, Woodward-winner Island Whirl, Kentucky Oaks–victress Blush with Pride, and four other stakes-winning fillies—Jones Time Machine, Bara Lass, Lucky Lady Ellen, and Faneuil Lass. Most of them had important starts ahead for the rest of the year, but Wayne knew that their combined earnings in the eight weeks remaining—from mid-October to mid-December—would pale in comparison to what Landaluce could bring to the barn in her final three year-ending races. These seven proven stakes winners combined would have to earn well over $100,000 apiece to match what Luce could earn by winning the Oak Leaf, Starlet, and Futurity.

Still, even though Wayne had enormous confidence in Luce and what she could achieve in the coming months, the pressure of managing an undefeated superstar was intensifying for everyone connected to her. "Every time she runs, the tension gets worse instead of better," Wayne confessed. Each time Landaluce set foot on the track, either for a workout or a race, the pressure grew. Back in July, the filly could work in the morning nearly unobserved, like any other young racehorse just learning her job. Now, when she left the barn, throngs of admirers lined the rail to watch her. Everyone wanted a piece of Landaluce. Everyone wanted to be close to greatness. Racing neophytes and hardened veterans alike knew what they were seeing, even if they couldn't articulate it: a horse the likes of which might never come their way again. So much more was expected of her now. How many times in a row could she win? What would have to happen for another runner to reach the wire ahead of her? After four consecutive victories by incredible margins, it wasn't enough now for Landaluce simply to win—she was expected to set a record and demolish the field. Perhaps this pressure was "testimony to the flights of imagination that she inspired in those who so steadfastly believed in her and her phenomenal gifts," as William Nack once wrote about Ruffian.

Wayne Lukas ponying Landaluce and exercise rider David Pineda back to the barn after a workout at Santa Anita. (Santa Anita Park)

Landaluce's win in the Anoakia had not taken much out of her, so Wayne breezed her once at three furlongs before the Oak Leaf in :36 1/5 and was convinced she was ready to go. He was unaware that history was not on Landaluce's side—of the twelve previous Anoakia winners who started in the Oak Leaf, only two had won. Still, Santa Anita's official handicapper installed Luce as the 1–9 morning line favorite, the first horse ever in the track's history to be installed at those odds in the program.

In the days leading up to the Oak Leaf, the track at Santa Anita was hard and fast, and horses who liked to come from behind were finding it almost impossible to win. On Friday morning, the day before the race, track maintenance furrowed the track to make it deeper and more yielding, slowing times.

When race day arrived on Saturday, October 23, many of the cars pouring into Santa Anita sported "I Love Luce" bumper stickers, and some of the thirty-seven thousand fans who emerged from their vehicles in the parking lot wore green T-shirts with the same slogan.

Today was an important day for two-year-old fillies across the country. In Kentucky, the Grade Two Alcibiades offered a refuge for fillies whose trainers thought them good enough to win a stakes, but only if Landaluce were not present. Two western runners shipped east to avoid her: Wayne sent Beal and French's Manzanares to Keeneland, where she would meet Tom Gentry's Issues n' Answers, second by six lengths in Luce's Debutante score. True to his word, Gentry would never enter his filly against Landaluce again.

More important for Luce and her connections, however, was the Gardenia Stakes at the Meadowlands, where Princess Rooney would seek her sixth straight win at the same distance as today's Oak Leaf—a mile and one-sixteenth. Both the gray daughter of Verbatim and Slew's speedy bay would be stretching out past a mile for the first time. For the Princess, the Gardenia would be her first attempt around two turns, as well as her first night race. Landaluce needed a win this afternoon in California to keep the pressure on the Princess to stay undefeated when she went to the post that evening in New Jersey.

As post time for the Oak Leaf neared, Laura and Ebaristo led Landaluce from the backstretch to the paddock. Despite a temperature of nearly 95 degrees, Laura looked composed, wearing jeans, a long-sleeved white blouse with puffed sleeves, and knee-high brown boots. Landaluce walked calmly, her well-muscled shoulders and hindquarters rippling in the sun. Today was by far the warmest of any of her race days, and by the time she reached the paddock, the filly was sweating heavily. Wayne, wearing a black-and-white houndstooth jacket, stood with owner Bob French under a pepper tree in the paddock. "We get past this one and we can breathe easier," French confided as Wayne slipped on Luce's saddle cloth number six, the same number she wore in her very first race at Hollywood—except this time the cloth was black, not green. The now customary throng of photographers jostling for a good paddock shot of Luce circled around her—and for the first time, the filly seemed to notice them.

Laffit, arriving in the paddock, was hopeful that Landaluce would carry him closer to Chris McCarron's $8.3 million earnings record and widen his margin in the escalating jockey's race with Angel Cordero. The two were neck-and-neck approaching the record, trading places atop the earnings list throughout the previous week. Today, Laffit was ahead, but narrowly. He knew Cordero would be riding here tomorrow, flying west for the $300,000 Yellow Ribbon Stakes, and with three more mounts on the card. Not to be outdone, Laffit planned to match Cordero's aggressive schedule by riding day races at Santa Anita followed by evening mounts at Los Alamitos. A win by Landaluce today would extend his lead over Cordero by a welcome $150,000.

But as Laffit swung his leg over Luce's saddle and guided her toward the track, he noticed a difference in the filly's customary pre-race behavior. "She just wasn't as relaxed . . . as she usually is," he would tell reporters later. For reasons unknown to the jockey, Luce didn't have her regular stable pony to accompany her to the post today. She was sweating even more now, and fussing at the unfamiliar pony as the pair made their way to the starting gate.

High up in the announcer's booth, young track announcer Alan Buchdahl sensed the crowd's anticipation for another sensational Landaluce victory as the field paraded to the post. Even though Landaluce didn't appear to be her usual calm and collected self, and even though her official morning odds were an eye-popping 1–9, the enthusiastic crowd made her the 1–20 favorite by post time. It was apparent that the rest of the field was running for second- or even third-place money, and it made sense for them to do so. The Oak Leaf purse of more than $250,000 was rich enough to yield second-place earnings of more than $50,000—more than most fillies could earn winning an average stakes, and more than the total lifetime earnings of four of Landaluce's six opponents. Gary Jones, trainer of relative newcomer Sophisticated Girl, a Stop the Music filly making her first start in stakes company, was unabashed in his belief that the best he might hope for today was a second-place finish. "It's really not my idea to run her against Landaluce," he said. "But if she can get second . . . they're never going to remember how far she got beat." Even trainer Hector Palma, who scratched California-bred Granja Reina from the Anoakia rather than face Luce in that race, returned today with a chance to double his runner's lifetime earnings if she could manage to finish second or third. But the connections of Rare Thrill, still stung by their ten-length defeat by Landaluce in the Anoakia, and with no appetite for more of the same, actually believed their chances were better against juvenile colts, going so far as to supplement their runner to the upcoming Grade One Norfolk Stakes rather than face Landaluce again.

Luce so dominated the competition that her own lifetime earnings prior to today's start were nearly three times those of Sorrento Stakes–winner Time of Sale, also well back in the Anoakia, and the second-highest money-earning filly in the field. Double-digit odds for all her competitors reflected the crowd's belief that Luce was virtually unbeatable: as second choice, Laz Barrera–trained Lituya Bay went off at 11–1, with Sophisticated Girl under Eddie Delahoussaye installed at third choice at 17–1. So much money was bet on Landaluce that she created her third minus show pool in a row, her largest ever, more than double those seen in the Debutante and Anoakia. In all of her starts to date, Landaluce never managed to reach post time at odds less than 4–5. All fillies in the Oak Leaf were assigned 115 pounds, but Landaluce carried 117, the lowest impost Laffit could manage.

It was approaching 5:00 p.m. as the starters reached the gate, and Laffit felt Luce settling down once she arrived there. As post position six in a seven-horse field, the filly loaded next to last, and was barely in the gate before it sprang open. Luce broke well and looked as if she could easily spurt to the lead, if Laffit, who had her under a light hold, let her. But as in the Debutante, Luce's first race over a mile, Wayne and Laffit wanted to use this longer race as an opportunity to continue teaching the filly to rate behind horses and employ her speed tactically. Luce was immediately joined on her inside by both Lituya Bay, breaking from post two, and Time of Sale, from post three. Rounding the clubhouse turn, Lituya Bay swung out, forcing Landaluce wider than Laffit would have liked, with Time of Sale in front. Whatever prerace instructions Wayne might have given Laffit now appeared to be going out the window as the race began to unfold. After a quarter in :22 3/5, Time of Sale had the lead by a length over Lituya Bay, with Landaluce two lengths back in third, still running wide. Laffit asked Landaluce to move past Lituya Bay, which she did easily, and still in the three path on the outside of the leader, Time of Sale. But as Landaluce moved up to challenge Time of Sale, Lituya Bay, saving ground on the rail, moved up to match strides with the leader, while Landaluce continued on, still three wide. After a half in :45 4/5, the three front-runners were just heads apart and six lengths ahead of Sophisticated Girl in fourth.

Watching in the stands, trainer Gary Jones was satisfied with Eddie Delahoussaye's ride so far. Sophisticated Girl was well back and running easily in the clear. She was perfectly positioned to move up for second, the result he expected, when Time of Sale or Lituya Bay inevitably faltered. "I told Eddie we'd be fried if we tried to run Landaluce's race," he said.

With the three leaders still tightly bunched approaching the far turn, Laffit did not want Landaluce once again forced wide, so he asked her for a second acceleration to pass Lituya Bay and Time of Sale, and Slew's daughter quickly obliged. Time of Sale immediately dropped back, spent, and jockey Sandy Hawley on Lituya Bay went for the whip as Luce began to draw away.

Turning for home, Landaluce had opened up five lengths on Lituya Bay, and appeared on her way to another characteristic and seemingly effortless win by a significant margin, as Sophisticated Girl moved up to third, still a half length behind Lituya Bay. The crowd began to cheer, and even track announcer Alan Buchdahl seemed to have conceded the race. "Turning for home, there she goes, drawing away by five. It's Landaluce in front!," Buchdahl exclaimed. Because Luce was well clear of the field, it looked as though Laffit relaxed somewhat, no longer expecting any challenge, and no longer asking the filly to exert herself. But Sophisticated Girl, moving on the outside of Lituya Bay, and under the whip by Eddie Delahoussaye, passed that rival while Landaluce was not even under a hand ride. Her margin was now four lengths, and Laffit still appeared unaware that Sophisticated Girl was moving up. At the eighth pole, trainer Gary Jones actually thought his filly might win.

It wasn't until Laffit heard Buchdahl cry, with obvious surprise, "Sophisticated Girl closes some ground now," that he began to urge Luce, slapping her twice with the whip. The filly flicked her tail in annoyance, but sped under the wire two lengths ahead of Sophisticated Girl. Granja Reina, another eight lengths back, finished third. Even from far up in the announcer's booth, Alan Buchdahl had what he called a "gut feeling" that perhaps the brilliant young filly wasn't quite herself.

Landaluce had her first Grade One score in the very fast time of 1:41 4/5, just three-fifths off the stakes record, and the second-fastest in the fourteen-year history of the race. Back in the winner's circle, both Wayne and Laffit knew the filly was tired. "She wasn't accelerating in the stretch like she did in the other races, but she handled it like a good horse should," Laffit said. "I look for her to improve next time," he added. "She needed this one." Luce received a spray of white orchids, and a blanket of orange carnations, while actor Mickey Rooney presented the trophy to Bob French. Laura Cotter, well aware of the developing rivalry between Luce and the Princess, joked, "Maybe somebody from 'I Love Lucy' will give the trophy to Princess Rooney next time."

Today was Laffit's first-ever Oak Leaf win, and it came at a particularly good time. Smiling as he dismounted, Laffit knew Landaluce's

Laffit and Landaluce at Santa Anita on the day of the filly's victory in the Oak Leaf Stakes, October 23, 1982. (Santa Anita Park)

score in this rich race had just extended his lead over Cordero by $155,000. There were only seven remaining races anywhere in the nation that offered a larger purse than today's—and two of those were the Hollywood Starlet and Futurity, where Laffit expected to ride Landaluce. Even before today's win, Luce was already the prohibitive favorite for the Starlet, where Laffit could add another $270,000 over Cordero. Riding a superhorse who consistently won rich races made securing another Eclipse Award and breaking McCarron's earnings record much more attainable.

Back at the barn, Wayne looked on as Ebaristo gave Luce a bath and hand-walked her beneath her hunter-green cooler. Two hours later, at 10:00 p.m. on the East Coast, Princess Rooney, carrying highweight of 121 pounds, demolished her competition in the Grade

Two Gardenia Stakes, winning by eleven lengths and setting a stakes record of 1:43 for the mile and one-sixteenth contest.

The day after the Oak Leaf, Laura Cotter could tell Luce had come out of the race well and was full of energy. "She was kicking and playing in the tow-ring," she said. As they did after every race, Laura and the Lukas staff observed the filly carefully and patiently hand-walked her for a few days. Princess Rooney, however, had not fared well after the Gardenia, having cut her right foreleg at the start of the race.

In the days following both fillies' victories, reactions in the press were divided. ESPN horseracing commentator Sharon Smith pointed out that Landaluce's winning margins were decreasing as she stretched out in distance, while trainer Frank Gomez noted, "The longer Princess Rooney goes, the more lengths she seems to win by." "Princess Rooney has picked up a lot of strength among the eastern media in voting for the Eclipse Award," claimed Glen Mathes of the New York Racing Association. "Saturday's race really convinced people." Would eastern bias once again prevail in the Eclipse Award race and allow a Grade One Frizette score to overshadow the equivalent accomplishment in the West's Oak Leaf? For decades, a sweep of both the Frizette and Gardenia had been the gold standard for securing the filly juvenile championship. In any other year, the Princess's impressive double score would have clinched it. The fact that Landaluce was still widely considered the front-runner for the honor was testimony to her brilliance, and unheard of for a western filly who had never traveled east.

Not all eastern writers considered Princess Rooney a lock for the title. Steven Crist of the *New York Times* said of Landaluce, "even her worst race is a convincing one," and noted that despite the traffic problems she encountered in the Oak Leaf, she "still won with authority." In the West, the *Daily Racing Form* observed that "despite the 'relatively close' margin, Landaluce was still untested," adding that, "Pincay was not going all out at the end." The official chart for the race stated that Sophisticated Girl "did not seriously menace" Landaluce.

Gary Jones, trainer of runner-up Sophisticated Girl, was gracious in defeat, complimenting Landaluce's win. "I don't think for a minute that this race takes anything at all away from Landaluce. . . . She had to make two big moves before she even got to the stretch. And the third horse was eight lengths behind my filly at the finish. I'd say it was a super race for both horses." "This [race] only proves she's human," quipped Los Angeles sportscaster Jim Hill.

It seemed it was no longer enough for Landaluce simply to win. If she didn't score by six lengths or more, or set a record, racegoers were disappointed. Wayne, characteristically, was chagrined by press reaction to the race: "They build a horse up, just so they can tear 'em down later," he said, perhaps recalling the furor after Codex's Preakness. Wayne had just won an important race, and his filly ran well. Instead of being congratulated for five wins in a row, and a Grade One victory in near stakes-record time, the trainer was grilled about why Landaluce had won by "only" two lengths. Wayne told the *Daily Racing Form:* "The most encouraging thing . . . was her ability to adjust. . . . Laffit wanted to avoid a potential traffic problem, and when he asked her to move, she zipped right up there. We know now that when she sees a hole, she can take it. . . . She controlled the race. . . . Laffit was in charge the whole time." The trainer was impressed by Luce's ability to make two moves—one at the 3/4 pole and again at the 3/8 pole. He told turf writer Hovdey: "She won today, and that's what counts. This was a good race for her and she came back tired. She ran harder than she ever has before, and I've never said she was exempt from getting tired." Wayne also believed Laffit backed off deliberately once he thought the race was won. "When you see that level of brilliance, you don't use it all the time," the trainer explained. "There's no need to drill her." Wayne claimed that Luce "may have had trouble staying interested" near the end of the race.

Still, Princess Rooney's romp in the Gardenia on top of her impressive score in the Frizette sparked renewed interest in the press for a meeting between the two undefeated fillies. Although Wayne had no reason to alter Luce's schedule, he professed to be unintimidated by the prospect of confronting the Princess, and told the *BloodHorse,* "I hope we get a chance to run against her down the line." Unfortunately for fans on both coasts, the tantalizing matchup would not take place, as shortly after the Gardenia, the Princess's trainer, Frank Gomez, discovered a severe stone bruise in her left front foot and announced her retirement for the year.

Despite her two-length margin in the Oak Leaf, there were many ways in which Luce's record to date remained superior to Princess Rooney's. Although the Princess indeed notched six wins in a row, the first four were in maiden, allowance, and listed stakes company with negligible purses at Calder Race Course, a small and mostly local track in the suburbs of Miami. This meant that Princess Rooney had only two graded stakes wins—albeit important ones—to Landaluce's four. It could be argued that her large margins of victory were at least partially accounted for by the fact that she was not facing stakes fillies or racing at a major track for most of her two-year-old season. Although it's often unwise to compare races at different tracks, Landaluce's times were uniformly superior to the Princess's. Landaluce set records in three of her five outings, one of them a world record, whereas the Princess had only one stakes record in her final race of the year. Because she raced mainly in graded stakes, Landaluce earned $150,000 more in five wins than the Princess did in six. In fact, after only five races, Luce was just $70,000 behind the all-time earnings record for two-year-old fillies, set by champion Numbered Account, which had stood for eleven years.

The day after the Oak Leaf, Landaluce once again appeared on national television, the subject of a segment on CBS's *Sports Sunday,* with an interview with Wayne by Charlsie Cantey. Then Landaluce appeared on the cover of *BloodHorse* magazine and the front page of the *New York Times* sports section for the first time. Entitled "The

Filly Who Runs Faster Than Colts," the *Times* article also marked the first-ever front-page story for twenty-four-year-old self-described "green" sportswriter Steven Crist, a recent Harvard grad with only about a year's experience at the paper. Also on the front page was a chart comparing Landaluce's two-year-old record to Ruffian's. The comparisons to the 1974 champion that erupted immediately after the Lassie back in July by now were more substantial: Landaluce had already won three races at distances greater than Ruffian ever attempted at two, one in stakes record time. Landaluce's shortest races as a juvenile were Ruffian's longest, and she set a world record in one of them. Landaluce carried more weight in the Anoakia than Ruffian carried in her entire career. Landaluce's two-year-old campaign was designed to prepare her to meet colts, something Ruffian's connections resolved not to do. If Landaluce could defeat colts in the Hollywood Futurity, she might accomplish something even the great champion never did—become the first two-year-old filly to be named Horse of the Year.

Never before had there been a California juvenile filly with a solid chance to be Horse of the Year, much less one with so many fans across the country rooting for her. Landaluce reminded them of her sire, who himself inspired a national following as the first undefeated Triple Crown winner. With each successive win, Landaluce seemed more and more like Slew and generated more excitement as she followed in his undefeated path. Landaluce's fan base now exceeded any juvenile filly's since Ruffian, who raced exclusively in the East. With the record she'd accumulated, and bolstered by national media exposure, Landaluce by now had come to symbolize the rising importance and quality of racing in the West, perhaps best expressed by nineteen-year-old Hollywood Park employee and future California turf writer Vicky Burnham: "She was our Ruffian," she said.

After four graded stakes wins in a row, Landaluce's Horse of the Year credentials were stronger than ever. Luce and Copelan remained the only undefeated multiple graded stakes winners in the country still with important races to run. Landaluce was regarded as the de facto winner of the upcoming $500,000 Hollywood Starlet—and a win in this race, though ungraded because it was so new, would give Slew's daughter an insurmountable edge over Princess Rooney in the juvenile division. Luce now had earned more than $372,000, and a presumed win in the Starlet would not only smash Numbered Account's juvenile filly earnings record by $200,000 but would also break the glass ceiling of Buckpasser's juvenile earnings record and make Luce the top earning two-year-old of all time. This would happen even if she did not run in the Futurity or faltered against colts. A win in both races would make her the first juvenile filly millionaire. If she were to end the year undefeated and prevail against colts in the Futurity, a Horse of the Year title seemed almost assured.

In fact, Landaluce did not even need to win the Starlet to pass Numbered Account—a second-place finish would do it. But no one believed Landaluce would lose the Starlet. She was considered as much a lock for that race as Copelan was for the upcoming Young America Stakes. Luce's win in the Oak Leaf kept her undefeated streak alive, and now the pressure was back on Copelan to do the same. A win in the Young America would make him unsurpassed among juvenile colts in the East, and by far the most important challenger to Landaluce in the West.

After all his filly had already accomplished, and with her two most important races still in front of her, even Wayne, who'd mostly refrained from voicing premature hopes to the press so far, now championed Landaluce's Horse of the Year credentials. "I don't know how anyone who has seen her could not say she is the horse of the year," he told Steven Crist. "If they ran the Kentucky Derby tomorrow . . . I don't think there's a horse in the country who could beat her. Of course, she's only two and a lot can happen in seven months."

Fred Hooper and Mitch Griffin thought otherwise. As their star Copelan readied for the Young America—a race they fully expected to win—their attention would soon turn westward, where they hoped to vanquish the upstart filly and prove the son of Tri Jet indisputable Horse of the Year.

The end of October heralded the end of the Santa Anita fall meet, always punctuated by two important races—the Oak Tree Invitational Handicap on grass for older horses, and the Norfolk Stakes for juvenile colts. When Laz Barrera's Lemhi Gold finished a dull fifth in the Invitational, another potential obstacle was removed for both Landaluce and Copelan in the contest for Horse of the Year. If either juvenile could win their next race, they would remain on the path that Lemhi Gold seemed to have exited.

When Del Mar Futurity–winner Roving Boy followed up with a win in the Norfolk Stakes over a field that included fellow Kentucky Derby prospects Desert Wine, Paris Prince, and Total Departure, he established himself as the top two-year-old colt in the West, and a potential challenger to Luce and Copelan in the Futurity. In fact, regular jockey Eddie Delahoussaye believed Roving Boy superior as a two-year-old to this year's Derby winner, Gato del Sol, whom the rider had also piloted as a juvenile. But after the win, trainer Joe Manzi repeated his intention to give the son of Olden Times, who had raced six times in three months—time to mature by ending his juvenile campaign and skipping a potential engagement with either Luce or Copelan in the Futurity.

After the Norfolk, Wayne was even more optimistic about what might lie ahead for the daughter of Slew. Roving Boy had captured the race in stakes record time of 1:41 3/5—just one-fifth faster than Luce's time in the Oak Leaf—and Lukas knew the filly, even with her brilliance, was still like a budding flower that had not yet begun to unfold and bloom. "I haven't even started to train her hard yet. Haven't got anywhere near the bottom," he said. Still in the early phases of training Slew's daughter to rate and carry her speed over a distance, Wayne planned to fine-tune her for the rest of this year. Next year, he would begin toughening and extending her, as she prepped for the Classics in the spring. Who knew what she might be able to achieve? Whatever it turned out to be, Wayne knew Landaluce had potential he had not even begun to tap.

Now, the Santa Anita meet was over and Landaluce was an undefeated Grade One multiple record-setting winner. Together, Wayne and Luce were on their way back to Hollywood Park. Luce had just two races left to run, both at the track where she first became a star, and the site of Wayne's richest career victory when Stalwart captured the Futurity last year. Could Landaluce, the horse of his dreams and the best thoroughbred he'd ever trained, do the same?

17

Hurray for Hollywood

Any way you look at it, she's a star. . . . She doesn't need a script. She
makes up her own as she goes along.
—Jim Murray

The filly stretched her neck, pulling Wayne forward as she searched
for the best new grass outside the barn area at Santa Anita early Monday morning, November 1. Luce tore at the grass impatiently, the
same way she did most things—aggressively, and with flair. Wayne
liked grazing Luce. It helped them both relax. Turf writer Jon White
was here to interview the trainer about three-year-old colt Mezzo's
recent stakes win at nearby Los Alamitos, and Wayne kept a watchful eye on the filly at the end of the lead shank, her coat glossy in the
early-morning sun as he answered the writer's questions. He wanted
the filly to enjoy her time outside, but he had a lot on his mind. A day
like today was rare, with no racing at either Santa Anita or Hollywood Park. The Santa Anita meet was over, and the Hollywood Park
meet didn't start for another three days. Then Wayne would start
commuting back and forth between the two tracks, sometimes multiple times a day. Assistant trainers Bobby Barnett and Laura Cotter
would remain at Santa Anita to take care of horses stabled here, while
son Jeff was in charge of runners stabled at the Inglewood track.

Six days later, Landaluce worked at Santa Anita for the first time
since her Oak Leaf win, and once again posted a bullet—46 2/5 for
four furlongs over a fast track. This would be her last work at Santa

Anita prior to the Starlet. For the rest of the month, Wayne planned two more Sunday-morning works at Hollywood Park leading up to the $500,000 race. Because she was still stabled at Santa Anita, where she would remain for the next several months, Luce would step onto a van two more times between now and the end of November, and travel approximately forty miles to the Inglewood oval for her works. Then it would be time to aim for the filly's sixth consecutive win on a track where she had already set two records.

Landaluce was expected to win the Starlet easily, and the filly had nearly a month to prepare. The bigger prize was the $750,000 Hollywood Futurity against colts, the race that could seal her place in history. Both contests were at a mile and one-sixteenth, and Luce's Oak Leaf win had already proven she could prevail at that distance in a time competitive with the best juvenile colts. Wayne wanted the Starlet to be an easy race for Luce, so she would have plenty left for the more serious challenge of the Futurity.

Even though the Starlet and Futurity had only been run once before, Landaluce would not be the first filly to run in both races. Last year's Oak Leaf winner, Header Card, a daughter of Quack, finished second in the Starlet and third in the Futurity, accumulating half her annual earnings in those two races alone. As a brand-new race, the Starlet was still ungraded, although "it is certain that when it is, it will be Grade One," predicted Leon Rasmussen in the *Form*. In 1982, accumulated yearly earnings of $500,000 and above were enough to land a runner near racing's top ten nationally. A win in the Starlet, combined with the already impressive $372,000 Luce had banked from her five victories so far, would rank Slew's daughter among the top five earners among all U.S. runners for the year.

Hollywood fans eagerly anticipated the return of their seemingly invincible filly. No one could have dreamed in July that their Lassie superstar would now be the presumptive juvenile filly champion. Everyone was looking forward to seeing Landaluce back at Hollywood in the Starlet, where her only serious challenger was expected to be trainer Gary Jones's Sophisticated Girl. But this time,

Laffit and Landaluce would be ready for the daughter of Stop the Music—there would be no more surprising the pair from behind while Luce cruised on the lead under a hand ride.

Landaluce's expected return to Hollywood on the eve of the winter meet heralded a new era in California racing, and Marje Everett spared no expense in promoting "the richest 38-day season in thoroughbred racing history." Fans who passed through the turnstiles on opening day received a free raincoat, and a barrage of newspaper ads leading up to the meet reminded them of the potential clash between Luce and two-year-old colt Copelan, whom Marje was still doing her best to lure westward for the Futurity. "If we get lucky and attract Copelan, the Futurity could decide the two-year-old voting [for the championship]," she said, adding: "There's a growing recognition in the East of California's fall racing season that hasn't been there before. This meeting . . . will cause people to change their habits." One sign of change, and a red and blue feather in Marje's cap, was the return of Calumet Farm silks to Hollywood Park for the first time in twenty-seven years. There was even talk that Lucille Ball would make a scheduled appearance at the track on Starlet day for a photo opportunity with Hollywood's "I Love Luce" equine heroine.

Marje's strategy, begun at the onset of the first Hollywood winter meet last year, was paying off—and the eastern establishment couldn't fail to take notice. "Spectacular rises in attendance and betting have enabled the California tracks to offer the largest purses in the country and consequently attract top horses and jockeys there on a regular basis," Steven Crist pointed out. "For the last three years, Hollywood Park . . . and Santa Anita . . . have surpassed New York tracks in showing the largest daily average attendance and on-track betting handle in the country." Even better, Marje's efforts had put her track in the finals for the first Breeders' Cup scheduled for 1984, along with Santa Anita. Marje's beloved Hollywood Park could be the site of defining year-end championships both this year and in the future. For a few weeks, Hollywood Park could be the most important racetrack in the country, where the best horses would meet with the most on the line.

Perhaps the fans waiting for Luce's return to Hollywood Park sensed the importance of the occasion. No juvenile of either sex had made their debut at Hollywood and gone on to win a juvenile championship since Warfare in 1959. If she were successful, Landaluce could rival Swaps as the most well-known western horse ever to debut at Hollywood and become a champion. Luce's fans couldn't have been more proud of what their filly might achieve. No longer could it be assumed that the best horses would begin their careers in the East. Landaluce was a standard-bearer of the New West in racing—a place with more fans, better weather, bigger purses, and finally, perhaps, better horses. Things were changing. The beginning of Landaluce's juvenile campaign at Hollywood Park set the stage for future champions who would launch their racing careers at the track throughout the 1980s—including Althea, Alysheba, and Fred Hooper's own Precisionist—followed by Ghostzapper and Zenyatta at the turn of the century, both of whom would become Horse of the Year.

On Wednesday, November 3, the new Hollywood winter meet opened for only the second time, with celebrities Cary Grant, Walter Matthau, and Joe Namath on hand to see if jockey Bill Shoemaker could break the $90 million threshold in lifetime purses—only $10,000 away, the Shoe had five mounts on the opening day card. Beverly Hills heiress Dolly Green, the proud owner of Landaluce's only full sister, Royal Strait Flush, watched in the stands as Slew Manet, another Slew daughter trained by Dave Hofmans, finished a respectable third in a maiden race.

The next evening, fans in the East were eagerly anticipating Copelan's start in the Young America Stakes at the Meadowlands, where they expected the presumed two-year-old champ to score yet another victory in his first attempt around two turns and under the lights. Victory for the colt seemed assured, as he had already vanquished most of the starters in the field during his campaign. Marje Everett hoped that shortly after Copelan had his picture taken in the

Meadowlands winner's circle, he would board a plane to Hollywood for a meeting with the wonder filly and the top colts the West had to offer.

Everett was pulling out all the stops to ensure the matchup. While Copelan napped in his stall, calm as always before a race, the *New York Daily News* announced that Hollywood Park was considering boosting the purse for the Futurity to $1 million if both Landaluce and Copelan went postward.

Life had never seemed brighter or more flush with opportunity for Landaluce, who looked more and more each day as if she might become America's first two-year-old filly millionaire—and if she managed to achieve that milestone, it would happen right here in the winner's circle at Hollywood, the place where it all began.

18

Starlet

One race is all it takes to change a whole year.
—Lenny Hale

When Copelan finished a well-beaten fourth in the Young America Stakes at the Meadowlands in New Jersey at 10:15 p.m. on Saturday, November 4, the dinner hour was just beginning at Marje Everett's spacious Holmby Hills mansion in Los Angeles. Perhaps Marje lifted her glass in a toast to Hollywood Park with whomever she might have been entertaining that evening. Or maybe she asked one of her cooks to make her a chocolate soda, her favorite. In any case, she felt like celebrating—the second day of her new Hollywood Park meet had just ended, and the prospects for what might lie ahead in the remaining five weeks had become a lot more interesting. It seemed her efforts to persuade Copelan's owner, Fred Hooper, to bring his prize colt west to race at Hollywood were about to bear fruit. Before the Young America, Hooper was seriously considering coming. Now, he almost had to.

Marje was not the only one smiling after the Young America. The next morning, trainer Joe Manzi arrived at his barn at Santa Anita "with a gleam in his eye." The upset of the colt Manzi had once thought invincible meant that his two-year-old colt Roving Boy, whom he'd planned to retire for the year, now had a chance at a championship if he could win the Hollywood Futurity. "It was time to take him out of mothballs and go for it," Manzi later told turf writer Jay Hovdey.

189

Jockey Angel Cordero also had an extra spring in his step. A 28–1 longshot who had never raced at the Young America distance of a mile and one-sixteenth, and who had finished seventh in his last start, had carried Cordero to victory in the rich event, adding nearly $200,000 in unexpected purse money to the rider's total, heightening the drama in his already tense earnings race with Laffit Pincay. Fortune was smiling on Cordero this year.

Brownell Combs, the Taylors and Hills, and the rest of the Seattle Slew syndicate also had reason to celebrate. Another juvenile from Slew's first crop had captured a Grade One race. Two-year-old Slewpy, trained by Sid Watters and owned by Equusequity, a racing syndicate formed by the Taylors and Hills to campaign Slew's offspring, had augmented Landaluce's Oak Leaf score and given Slew a total of two Grade One winners in the same season from his first crop—a phenomenal accomplishment for a freshman sire. On the earnings front, Slewpy's victory in the prestigious race, combined with Landaluce's purses to date, had launched Slew on the richest start of any first-year sire in history, with Landaluce's expected earnings in the Starlet still on the horizon. Slew's early success prompted bloodstock analyst Bill Oppenheim to observe that Slew "could be the next Bold Ruler." Another Grade One winner, along with Landaluce's undefeated record, would yield rich dividends in the auction ring next summer. The Taylors and Hills had never wavered in their confidence in Slew, but these early results from first-year runners were beyond their expectations. Incredibly, Equusequity had another two-year-old just beginning to race that they thought might be even better than Slewpy. His name was Slew O' Gold.

Ironies abounded in Slewpy's win. His trainer, Sid Watters, wasn't sure he should even enter the colt in the race. Angel Cordero was less than enthusiastic about riding him, and Mickey Taylor, who missed his plane from California to view the race in person, coerced the aspiring Hall of Famer to accept the mount by threatening to take him off of the promising Slew O' Gold. Taylor, who had to call from the airport to learn the race result, was so shocked when hearing the news of Slewpy's win that his legs began to tremble. Not even Taylor could have expected one of Slew's juveniles to clear the path for another to prosper—Slewpy's surprising upset put Landaluce squarely in the forefront of the Horse of the Year contest and made the California wonder filly the only undefeated multiple graded stakes winner still in training and still in contention for the award.

Taylor had plenty of company in his shock at Slewpy's upset win. Trainer Sonny Hine, conditioner of listed stakes winner Bet Big, had never sent his runner against Copelan until the Young America. "I wasn't planning to run against Copelan until next season," Hine revealed. But his colt engaged the Hooper homebred in fast early fractions and looked like the winner at the sixteenth pole, until Slewpy came on in the stretch to prevail by four lengths. "[Slewpy] surprised me by finishing so strongly," admitted Angel Cordero. Twenty-five-year-old jockey Jerry Bailey on Copelan said the colt had "no excuses," but added that the speed duel in the early going cost his mount the race: "My horse and [Bet Big] knocked each other out. They went 1:09 3/5 going two turns. . . . That's a lot to ask of a horse going around two turns for the first time." Bailey pointed out it was Copelan's "first time under the lights and it shook him, I think."

Owner Fred Hooper and trainer Mitch Griffin likewise sought explanations for Copelan's poor performance, and both thought the colt's training schedule might have played a part. "I have to think we didn't bear down hard enough on him [between races]," said Hooper. "He wasn't entirely fit," Griffin agreed. "He was one dead horse after that race." A notoriously enthusiastic scourer of the feed tub, the colt gave another telltale sign of his condition back at the barn. "He was slow eating up afterwards," Griffin revealed. "When this colt doesn't eat, I know something's not right."

Four days after the Young America, Fred Hooper announced he was bringing Copelan to the West Coast for the Hollywood Futurity. It was now official—Marje Everett's coveted East-West showdown would take place after all. With the presence of both Copelan and Landaluce as well as the possible appearance of Roving Boy, the Futurity was shaping up to be the race of the year, and the first time in history a juvenile divisional championship and possibly Horse of the Year would be decided on a western track. Injuries and retirements among top contenders in other divisions, combined with the dominance of Copelan and Landaluce in theirs, had set up a perfect storm with Marje at the helm. Even the eastern racing press underscored the newfound importance of the Futurity, as writer Joe Hirsch noted in the *Form,* "few races have come of age faster than the Hollywood Futurity, and its dramatic timing at season's end has changed the thinking of the industry."

Copelan's surprising Young America loss, combined with Landaluce's still-undefeated record and expected presence in the Futurity, as well as the potential looming challenge of Western Grade One–winner Roving Boy, put his connections in the unheard-of position of having to go west in order to clinch the Horse of the Year award. In the years before the rich season-ending juvenile race in the West, Hooper and Griffin might have done what all eastern connections did following a disappointing year-end loss by a top divisional contender—stay in the East and hope for the best. After all, their colt had three Grade One wins to his credit, including the prestigious Champagne, a traditional championship determiner. But Copelan's Young America loss had taken the connections out of the driver's seat—if Copelan failed to contest the Futurity, and either Roving Boy or Landaluce won it, possibly the divisional title as well as any shot at Horse of the Year could be in jeopardy. The Futurity's rich purse and expected competition offered Copelan a lifeline to the juvenile title and a path to redemption for Horse of the Year—but he needed to go west to be saved. "Hooper has never given his reasons for coming West with Copelan, but it's likely he wanted to challenge Landaluce," the *Form*'s Mike Marten later wrote. Marten also credited Wayne's determination to keep his filly in the West and his refusal to chase Eclipse Awards in the East for forcing the showdown.

Besides being vital in his colt's quest for a championship, Hooper had other reasons to bring Copelan west. He and Marje had known each other since the 1940s, when Everett's father owned Arlington and Washington racetracks in Chicago, and Hooper raced horses there, including the speedy Olympia. When Marje took over Arlington Park after her father's death, Hooper became one of her favorite owners, and a regular at her evening card parties along with Jimmy Durante and Bill Shoemaker. Hooper had also raced in California since the late 1950s, employing then exercise rider Ross Fenstermaker for his homebred colt Alhambra, a son of Olympia. By the 1970s, Fenstermaker had become Hooper's primary West Coast trainer, and Hooper sometimes wintered part of his string with him in California. The octogenarian surely would have wanted to help his longtime friend and colleague promote a big race and support the track. Hooper was not shy about shipping horses cross-country if he thought he could win—in one eight-week period in 1949, his star Olympia ran in five races, shuttling back and forth between two coasts, winning three and finishing second twice.

Hooper's ties to the West and to Fenstermaker were strong enough that Copelan's trainer, Mitch Griffin, was described as "worried sick" he could lose the colt to Fenstermaker once the son of Tri Jet shipped to California to contest the Futurity. Griffin's anxiety was undoubtedly heightened by the fact that Fenstermaker had already trained two Hooper entrants in Marje's inaugural year-ending juvenile Hollywood races—the filly Skillful Joy, who won the Starlet, and the gelding Bunnell, who finished fourth in the Futurity. Hooper collected an impressive $271,000 combined from both runners' finishes. Fenstermaker, who had years of experience at Hollywood Park, also was on hand for Landaluce's Lassie victory in July and was well acquainted with what the dazzling filly could do. "She's as impressive a two-year-old filly as I've ever seen," he said, "and I saw Ruffian, too." Fortunately for Griffin, Hooper appreciated the strong bond he had developed with Copelan in his work with the colt from a yearling through his triple Grade One winning campaign, and decided that the trainer should accompany the colt west.

Meanwhile, the Wayne Lukas stable continued to thrive in the early days of Hollywood Park's new meet. Wayne was already developing a habit of winning often and early here. Last year's success with Stalwart had made him the first trainer ever to win the second-richest race in the country and the top-earning trainer for the meet. This year, he was once again off to an incredible start—in just the first five days of the meet, Wayne saddled six winners from fifteen starters, making him the leading trainer by number of wins, and ahead of Bobby Frankel, last year's top trainer in races won. But Wayne's success extended well beyond this meet: by mid-November, as the *Los Angeles Times* noted, "no trainer in the country may have accomplished what Wayne Lukas has this year—winning twenty-eight stakes races at eight different tracks with ten horses." On top of all that, Wayne still had what the *Miami News* called "the ace up his sleeve" in Landaluce, and her expected win in the Starlet.

Barely a week after his Young America loss, Copelan deplaned at Los Angeles International Airport and stepped into a waiting van to take him to Hollywood, where he would be stabled until the Futurity. Hooper and Griffin planned to get the colt accustomed to the Hollywood track with several works, then a tune-up for the Futurity in the seven-furlong Prevue Stakes the day before Landaluce went to post for the Starlet. The eastern colt and the western filly would prep for the Futurity together at the same track—Marje Everett was overjoyed.

The arrival in California of the East's star colt set off a barrage of predictable intercoastal rhetoric. Asked how he felt about the prospect of meeting the daughter of Seattle Slew in the Futurity, Hooper said, "If she's there, she's there. We're not backing off from anybody at this stage." Eastern trainer Woody Stephens, campaigning for his trainee Conquistador Cielo as Horse of the Year, and perhaps seeking to deride western runners in general, had his own opinion of Landaluce's chances against the eastern colt: "She's never crossed the Rockies, much less the Hudson River," he said acidly. "Copelan [will] . . . destroy her." "We think she's good enough to compete with anybody's racehorse," Wayne rejoined.

At the same time, trainer Joe Manzi, who was keeping his options open for Norfolk-winner Roving Boy, liberally expressed his opinion of both foes and his own colt's prospects. "There's a chance we'll run," he told the *Form*'s Jon White, who described the trainer as "not trembling with fear over the prospect of meeting Landaluce or Copelan." "I think my colt's better than either of them," Manzi said. "They're nice horses. . . . [It's] a different ballgame when a filly runs against colts. But who's to say she can't beat colts? She's . . . an exceptional filly." Manzi felt that Copelan's Young America loss proved he was vulnerable around two turns, improving Roving Boy's chances in the Futurity, also a two-turn race. Both Landaluce and Roving Boy had already scored around two turns—Luce in the Oak Leaf, and the Manzi trainee in the Norfolk. "My colt doesn't really start running until he's gone a mile," Manzi claimed. "It wouldn't take much at all to get him ready . . . two or three good works and he'd be on top of his game." Manzi generously offered to handicap the race himself, making his colt favorite at 2–1, Copelan second choice at 5–2, and Landaluce at 3–1.

A few days after Copelan arrived at Hollywood Park, both the eastern star and the western filly revved their engines at the track where their highly anticipated showdown in the Futurity would take place in less than thirty days. Landaluce vanned from her double-wide stall at Santa Anita for her first work at Hollywood prior to the Starlet. This work was her first appearance at the track since she blazed a world record and demolished the field by twenty-one lengths in the Lassie. Fans lined the rails to watch their wonder filly in her first official workout at the site of the spectacular win that had made her a national media darling. Under exercise rider Jesse Cerillo, the filly worked an easy five furlongs in 1:00 1/5. "She did it without effort, as usual," Wayne said, calling it "a good, even work," with Luce running five consecutive twelve-second panels. Wayne planned "a more serious work in six or seven days, and that should do it," he told the *Form*.

Copelan's first official work over the Hollywood strip matched Landaluce's earlier clocking of :46 2/5 for four furlongs, encouraging his connections that the colt had traveled well and settled in at Hollywood. Copelan seemed to enjoy running over the Hollywood surface "like he had trained there all his life," according to turf writer Jay Hovdey. Mitch Griffin was pleased, though unsurprised, by the way his colt was training, as Copelan had always proven adaptable to a variety of surfaces. Griffin felt that Copelan's wins in the Hopeful and Sanford at Saratoga in the summer augured well for the colt's performance here: "Of the Eastern tracks, Saratoga is the most like a fast California track," he pointed out. Meanwhile, trainer Joe Manzi continued to keep his options open with Roving Boy: "Just in case we decide to have a confrontation," Manzi said, "we're keeping him fit."

Back east, jockey Angel Cordero belatedly celebrated his fortieth birthday by surpassing Chris McCarron's single-season earnings record. Cordero was continuing to ride night and day at multiple tracks in his quest for the jockey Eclipse Award. "If I have to go to Alaska to ride, I'll go to Alaska," he declared. Determined to fend off Laffit, Cordero felt time running out in his quest for the title. "This is my last try," he confessed. "I'll never push myself again. This life is too hard on me and my family." His determination to prevail burned deeply enough that he told turf writer Jack Murray, "If I don't win the Eclipse Award this year, I'll kill myself."

With only six weeks left in the racing season, Cordero's knowledge that Laffit had the mount on Landaluce for two of the richest contests of the year further fueled his obsession. "[Laffit's] got that filly Landaluce in a $500,000 race in ten days. I've got to open up on [him] and then ride day and night until the end of the year, or he'll win the title." Cordero called Landaluce "a weapon I didn't have—a super horse. That's why I've been working so hard."

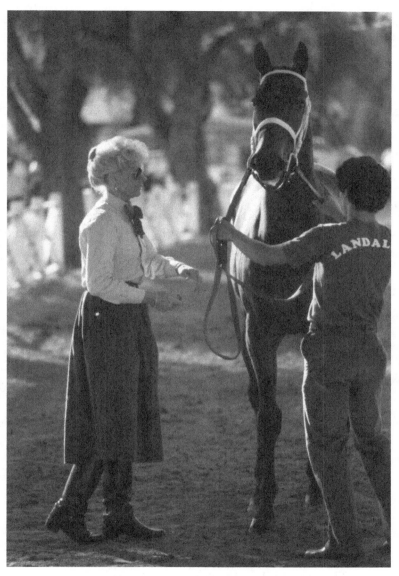

Landaluce, with Laura Cotter and groom, was the picture of health in early November, just weeks before her expected start in the rich Hollywood Starlet. (Keeneland Library, Barrett collection)

Thanks at least in part to Slewpy's unexpected score in the Young America, Cordero was now leading Laffit by about $200,000. But both riders knew the Hall of Famer could pass Cordero with Luce's expected winnings in the Starlet alone. Were she also to score in the Futurity, Cordero would have no chance. Angel's memory was long—he still remembered that sunny morning at Hollywood Park when he rode the then-unraced daughter of Slew for the first and only time, fooled by her effortless way of going into believing she wasn't running fast at all. He knew what Laffit had under him.

In the predawn hours of Sunday, November 21, Wayne once more led Luce onto a van to Hollywood for her last scheduled work prior to the race. Once there, Wayne and Luce were joined by Jeff Lukas. As Luce and rider David Pineda made their way onto the main track at Inglewood, fans who lined the rails at 7:00 a.m. for a glimpse of Slew's daughter hoped that today's five-furlong work would only increase their confidence in the filly's prospects to win the Starlet. They were not disappointed.

Landaluce covered five furlongs in :59 3/5, galloped out in 1:11 2/5, and went the final three-eighths in a sparkling :33 4/5. Wayne and Jeff could not have been more pleased with Landaluce's performance and felt her chances in the upcoming race had never been better. "I particularly liked the way she finished," Wayne told the *Form.* "This may be all she needs for the race. . . . If I feel she needs a tightener, I'll have her blow out Friday." Wayne told turf writer Hovdey he was "really confident" after the work, comparing Landaluce's current form to "a finely tuned machine." His spirits were so high that he told Laura Cotter, Bobby Barnett, Jeff, and Ebaristo that "anybody running against our filly was in big trouble."

Wayne was so convinced Landaluce would win the Starlet he later confided to the *Form*'s Joe Hirsch, "I managed her career like a young starlet of the entertainment world. I planned it so she would make a big splash in these last two races." The trainer had Luce just where he wanted her, peaking for the most important races of her young life at precisely the right time.

Things were going as Wayne had planned since as far back as July, when he realized just how brilliant Landaluce really was. After the filly was cooled out, groomed, and returned to her double-wide stall at Santa Anita by 10:00 a.m., Wayne booked a flight to Oklahoma for important dental work he'd been putting off for way too long. The man who was so attached to the filly that he found it hard to leave her, finally felt the time was right.

Sunday evening, after Wayne left the barn, Spendthrift's John Williams, on a rare vacation from the farm, stopped at Santa Anita to visit Seattle Slew's undefeated filly. In front of Luce's stall, Williams admired her appearance—well muscled, gleaming, and a picture of health. The last time he saw her, she was an unproven yearling. Now, she was a record-setting racehorse. Was it possible that Slew might already have sired a champion? After Slewpy's Young America win, and with Landaluce poised to contend for Horse of the Year, Williams once again felt the satisfaction of overcoming all the obstacles Slew had thrown in his path as a breeding stallion. It had all been worth it. Williams called Wayne, expressing how impressed he was with Landaluce.

As he hung up the phone, with Thanksgiving just around the corner, Wayne realized he had much to be grateful for—his stable was winning consistently, led by the best Thoroughbred of his life, poised on the threshold of greatness, and coming into her own.

Part Four

19

Last Race

There's nothing easy about [racing]. . . . I know
the elevator goes down, too.
—Wayne Lukas

On Monday morning, November 22, Wayne Lukas looked up at the cloudy, gray sky at Santa Anita and hoped it would clear. It had been raining for the past three days, the track was rated sloppy, and the ground was drenched. Wayne led Luce out of her double-wide stall for her regular early-morning walk and hand-graze. The trainer enjoyed these morning visits, when it was just him and Luce. Her sparkling work at Hollywood seemed to have taken little out of her. Today, just six days before the Starlet, Luce was on her toes, playful, tossing her mane, eager to run again, the muscles in her neck arched against the trainer's firm and steady hand. Wayne needed energy and concentration to keep her in line as he walked her outside the barn. "Believe me, she was a handful," he told Jay Hovdey a few days later. The only thing worrying the trainer about the race was the weather: he wanted Luce to gallop four more times before race day and hoped for a respite from the rain that had been pelting the Arcadia track.

Landaluce's dazzling final work before the Starlet only helped further diminish what already appeared to be a small field for the upcoming race, with a purse now estimated at more than $500,000. Only three definite starters had declared so far—two of whom Landaluce had already defeated in the Oak Leaf—Sophisticated Girl and Lituya Bay. Eastern shipper Gold Spruce, who finished third behind Princess Rooney in the Gardenia, was already at Hollywood training for the race. Two additional probable starters were Charlie Whittingham trainee Stephanie Bryn, and supplemental nominee O'Happy Day, both two-time winners at Hollywood in maiden and allowance company. In a six-horse field, second-place money would approach six figures, and only one starter would go home without a paycheck. The race was so rich that the fourth-place finisher would earn nearly $40,000—more than most fillies could earn winning a regular stakes. Still, in spite of the lucrative paycheck for finishing off the board, few trainers were willing to take on Luce. Jimmy Jordan, conditioner of unbeaten California-bred Fabulous Notion, had considered the Starlet for his talented filly but decided instead that the listed Courtship Stakes was a better spot, and the daughter of Secretariat's half brother Somethingfabulous was already in a van on her way to Bay Meadows for that contest. "You don't run against a horse like Landaluce unless you absolutely have to," Jordan explained.

Across town at Hollywood Park, would-be champion Copelan also logged a satisfying work in preparation for his start in the upcoming Prevue Stakes, increasing trainer Mitch Griffin's confidence after the colt's Young America loss. "I couldn't have asked for any better," he said. Back at the barn, the Hooper homebred downed a large serving of oats, then tossed his feed tub in the air and bit Griffin's hand. "He only gets this way when we feed him," the trainer said mildly. "He's acting like his old self now. . . . I'll be mighty surprised if he doesn't run his best race Saturday."

Also at Hollywood for his first work at the track was possible Futurity starter Roving Boy, who clocked seven furlongs handily in 1:26. Trainer Joe Manzi was keeping his options open for the Norfolk winner but had yet to commit to the race. Manzi and owner Bob Hibbert had a decision to make. The deadline to supplement their colt to the Futurity—at a cost of $40,000—was rapidly approaching. Pressure had been on them ever since Copelan came West to decide—were they running or not? Manzi, who postponed a ten-day vacation to Hong Kong with his wife in order to oversee Roving Boy's training for the blockbuster race, told the press he was waiting to see how Copelan performed in his first California start: "If Copelan wins the Prevue, then we might run our horse against him in the Futurity. If Copelan loses . . . we might stay in the barn and hope that we've got enough [Eclipse] votes." Excitement over the potential matchup between Copelan and Landaluce had kept the son of Olden Times somewhat under the radar, but since his Norfolk win, Roving Boy had filled out and was maturing into his large frame, putting on fifty pounds. Perhaps he was coming into his own at just the right time for the big race.

Later in the day, after Wayne left the barn, Laura Cotter was doing her afternoon rounds and noticed Landaluce had not cleaned up her morning grain. As a precaution, Laura took the filly's temperature. It was 103.

Laura immediately called veterinarian Dr. Roy Bishop. Then she tried to call Wayne. Because he was en route to Oklahoma, Laura had to page the trainer at the airport. He stiffened when he heard his name over the loudspeaker. "Any time you're paged in an airport," Wayne thought, "it's never good news."

When the trainer reached Laura and heard Landaluce had a fever, he was not too worried at first. It was not uncommon for horses stabled in close quarters to come down with mild viruses or fevers this time of year, especially with all the rain and damp weather. The trainer hoped Luce had just a minor bug that "we could knock out in twenty-four hours," allowing time if all went well to still make the starting gate for the Starlet. Dr. Bishop administered medication to bring down Luce's fever, and everyone hoped for the best.

When Wayne returned to California and the filly's temperature went down the next day, the trainer was somewhat encouraged, as Luce was well enough to be hand-walked in the shedrow. Still, from then on, the filly was never without someone in attendance at her stall. Either a veterinarian, groom, assistant trainer, night watchman, or Wayne himself was with her constantly. Wayne spent his evenings with Luce, eating dinner in her stall rather than going home. Holly-wood Park was still promoting Luce's presumed start in the Starlet, with newspaper ads exhorting fans to "watch history in the making" as the filly continued her quest to become Horse of the Year.

But when Landaluce's temperature went up again Wednesday, Wayne had to announce the filly would not run in the Starlet. "It's not like she has a crippling injury," he told the press. "She'll be back to run again. If she snaps out of this by the weekend, which the vet tells me is possible, we will still point her toward the Futurity." Wayne told reporters that Beal and French would enter Carambola in the Starlet instead. Ironically, the Alleged filly, one in the group of Keene-land yearlings purchased with Luce, occupied the stall immediately adjacent to hers and was not sick. The filly's scratch from the Starlet was a big blow for Laffit Pincay in his race for the jockey title against Angel Cordero. Neither rider had expected anything other than a win by Landaluce. Now it would be difficult for Laffit to prevail. Like Wayne, the rider held out hope Luce might recover in time to run in the Futurity.

As soon as Wayne withdrew Landaluce from the Starlet, its field began to swell. In a matter of days, the number of willing challengers nearly doubled. Eastern shipper Only Queens, winner of the Grade One Demoiselle at Aqueduct, was supplemented to the race at a cost of $20,000. Trainer Ron McAnally entered recent maiden winner Promising Girl, while Jimmy Jordan, loathe to face Landaluce just a few days ago, called his staff at Bay Meadows and told them to ship Fabulous Notion back to Hollywood. "I didn't have to think about it very long," he said. By the time entries closed, the *Form* called the Starlet "a wide open race."

After two "dark" days at Hollywood, by Wednesday it was time for racing to resume. Wayne didn't like leaving Luce, but he had a job to do. At the track, the trainer tried to put his feelings aside and con-centrate on the task at hand, but he found himself distracted by thoughts of Slew's bay daughter back in her double-wide stall at Santa Anita, still with a fever that would not subside. Another distressing development was that the filly would not eat. Although Wayne, Laura, and Dr. Bishop did all they could to coax her, she had no interest in hay or solid food, and took only small amounts of broth. After days without nourishment other than intravenous fluids, the filly was now too weak and unsteady on her feet to even leave her stall.

By Wednesday night, the mood in the Lukas barn was grim, as Landaluce's temperature soared to 104. Her condition began to worsen as her throat and chest were now infected, and she was having trouble breathing. Wayne realized that his filly would not run again for the rest of the year. Landaluce's chance to prove she could beat the best colts in the country, become the first juvenile filly millionaire, and secure Horse of the Year honors, was gone. Wayne's disappointment was bitter, but there was always next year. After she recovered, Landaluce could come back for the Classics in the spring. There was still a road ahead for a glittering career and an opportunity for his star filly to make history—but not this year. Besides robbing fans of the eagerly anticipated match race with Copelan, Landaluce's absence in the Futurity meant that Hollywood would not increase the purse to $1 million, depriving the colt of his chance to become the first juvenile millionaire. It also removed a key rival for Roving Boy in the rich contest, and made it virtually impossible for Laffit Pincay to win the jockey title.

Although veterinarian Bishop, assisted by Dr. Greg Ferraro, had started antibiotic treatment some time ago, it didn't seem to be helping. The veterinarians took cultures from Luce and sent them off for laboratory analysis to identify the cause and nature of her infection and pinpoint the best antibiotic to target it. But this took several days—time they didn't have. While they waited for lab results, the best they could do was try different antibiotics until one proved effective. Meanwhile, Wayne contacted veterinary experts around the country, hoping that someone would be able to come up with an explanation for the filly's illness and a treatment that worked. Everyone was exhausted, and no one was getting much sleep, including Wayne's Australian shepherd, Duke, who paced up and down the shedrow the whole time Landaluce was sick. Wayne, Laura, Ebaristo, the two veterinarians, Jeff Lukas, and Bobby Barnett were working around the clock. Everyone's thoughts were filled with Landaluce. Everyone hoped she could somehow find a way to shake off whatever had attacked her. But as the hours ticked by, no one seemed to have any answers.

Around the same time that Landaluce's condition became critical, another promising runner, two-year-old colt Ft. Davis, whom Wayne co-owned with Beal and French and who was also stabled at Santa Anita, spiked a fever, forcing his scratch from the Prevue Stakes. The Lukas barn couldn't help wondering if something contagious was in the air. In fact, several runners at Santa Anita were sick with what appeared to be a virus—one that seemed to threaten younger horses. Fred Hooper's three-year-old colt Art Director had died at Santa Anita in mid-October. Trainer Tom Bell's promising two-year-old colt Barberstown became seriously ill but recovered. "I've got fourteen horses at Santa Anita, and eight are coughing," he reported. California state veterinarian Roy Dillon confirmed that the timing and level of illness at the track was typical for the season. Santa Anita spokesman Larry Bortstein stated, "There is apparently some virus that has affected about ten horses," calling the situation "not unusual . . . among the six or seven hundred that we have here." Wayne, still struggling to understand what might have caused Landaluce's predicament, was baffled: "Other horses on both sides of her ate the same feed and drank the same water without becoming ill. Your mind grasps at straws and you think of everything, including foul play. But we have a day watchman and a night watchman, and we even have a special Landaluce watchman, whose job was to stay with her all the time," the trainer told Joe Hirsch.

As Thanksgiving Day dawned at Hollywood Park, a big crowd turned out for a free turkey dinner with paid admission. But back at Barn 66 at Santa Anita, there was no cause to celebrate, and Wayne overlooked the holiday altogether until someone reminded him. The trainer had forgotten to eat or shave for two days. Such things as holidays no longer occupied his thoughts. In the last twenty-four hours, he'd gone from believing Landaluce was done racing for the year to wondering if she would even survive. All he could think about was saving her life. Early Thanksgiving morning, Wayne told the *Form*'s Mike Marten, "She's certainly not any better. If anything, she's worse." When turf writer Hovdey visited the barn to check on Luce's condition, he found the trainer "haggard," and his voice "cracked and dry." Wayne told Hovdey he'd called Beal and French and "prepared them for the worst."

Meanwhile, a new and deadly challenge had come to the team caring for the filly—laminitis, or founder. Standing in her stall for days without being able to walk was reducing circulation in her legs and feet. If her hoof walls deteriorated, she would no longer be able to stand and would have to be humanely destroyed. Members of the Lukas team took turns massaging her legs, which the filly had to spread far apart just to keep her balance. She was so weak it was an effort for her to remain upright. Her breathing was becoming even more labored, and her head hung low, nearly touching the straw. Her lower lip was swollen, and her eyes were dull. Laura, Wayne, Ebaristo, and the veterinarians took turns tubbing her feet in ice all night long to keep heat from reaching her hoof walls. By now, Wayne knew that even if the filly were somehow miraculously to recover, his only hope was to save her as a broodmare. Wayne told the *Form*'s Jon White that Landaluce's illness was "definitely a life-threatening situation."

As Wayne caromed back and forth from the races at Inglewood to Landaluce's double-wide stall at Santa Anita, he bounced between one world and another—the track where healthy horses ran and either won or were defeated—and the once-large stall that now seemed small, close, and dark with frustration and diminishing hope. It was hard for the exhausted trainer to remember what life had been like on Monday, when Landaluce was still healthy and ready to run. The splendid daughter of Slew almost unable to hold her head up and wobbling in her stall was a sight the trainer could not bear to see and yet one from which he could not turn away. Still, even in her distress, Wayne could not help but admire the filly's will to live. Sometimes, he was tempted to think her stamina and spirit might even be enough to overcome what now seemed a hopeless fight. "How can she go through all these things and keep whipping 'em?" he wondered. Without any nourishment or relief from her symptoms for five days, she was still standing. "She hadn't had anything in her system, and she didn't have anything to go on and she just stood there," he said. Wayne continued to be mystified by the failure of antibiotic treatment to help Landaluce turn the corner against whatever appeared to be slowly killing her. "I gotta believe this type of virus is new, or at least one [the vets] were not familiar with," he said.

On Saturday morning, the Lukas team experienced some relief when it seemed their efforts to prevent founder had been successful. Wayne left Luce long enough to visit the nearby barn of Art Lerille, whose two-year-old gelding Male Adapter displayed symptoms similar to the filly's. The two trainers talked at length. Lerille's gelding had been sick since early November, registering a high temperature the day after he last worked, just like Landaluce. The California-bred had not left his stall for more than three weeks. His temperature fluctuated, and he couldn't breathe. "He was panting like a dog," Lerille told Wayne. "It looked like he was going to die." After hearing Wayne's description of Luce's illness, Lerille offered, "There's little doubt in my mind Male Adapter has the same thing. The symptoms are almost identical. It's just a virus that's been going around at Santa Anita." Lerille reported that veterinarians tried four different intravenous antibiotics over three weeks without success. When they switched to oral chloramphenicol, the gelding began to improve. "Maybe it's just a coincidence," Lerille speculated. "I don't know." One of the significant differences, however, between the two stricken juveniles was that the gelding never stopped eating, whereas Landaluce had been without solid food for five days.

When he returned to the barn, Wayne and Laura both thought Landaluce had perked up a little, and both hoped perhaps the filly was turning a corner. But it was not to be. "We never seemed to make any headway," Wayne said later. "Treatment seemed to do no more than mask her pain. We never seemed to pinpoint the trouble." The trainer added that he felt he was "dealing with something unknown."

Once more, Wayne returned to Hollywood Park for the races, where Saturday's headliner was the Prevue Stakes. The trainer had five runners on the card. He watched the races, but he didn't really see them. By now, word had spread around the track that Landaluce's illness was grave. Wayne shared the joyless news with the filly's Hall of Fame rider. "It's real bad, Laffit," Wayne confessed. "It's going to take a miracle to save her." It was not a good day for the Wayne Lukas stable—perhaps his runners sensed the trainer's heart was not really with them as the best horse in his stable struggled for breath back in her stall. Only one of his starters hit the board.

When Copelan won the Prevue shortly after 5:00 p.m. by a length and a half over maiden R. Awacs, Wayne realized that the Hooper homebred had come across the country for a matchup that would never take place. Watching the colt's win made the trainer more painfully aware of all he had already lost. Nothing in Copelan's performance compromised Wayne's belief in what Landaluce might have done. "I thought she could beat him," he later told Joe Hirsch.

Also watching the race, but with a lighter heart, was Joe Manzi, trainer of Roving Boy. Copelan's Prevue win clinched his decision to enter his colt in the Futurity. Like Wayne, he felt Copelan was not unbeatable in the big race, and by now it was clear Landaluce would not run. Manzi could now see a clear path to a juvenile championship were Roving Boy to defeat the best colt in the East in the Futurity.

Wayne returned to Santa Anita after the races, dreading what he might find there. Although he knew the odds were slim, he hoped, somehow, the filly might recover. Landaluce's illness had progressed so swiftly, Wayne's mind was still reeling.

By 8:30 p.m., the filly's lungs started to fill with fluid, and the outlook was dire. The morning's brief apparent victory over founder had proven cruelly irrelevant. "I was real scared," Wayne said. He stayed with the filly for much of the night but went home in the early-morning hours of Sunday, November 28, to shower, leaving her with Laura, Dr. Bishop, and assistant trainer Bobby Barnett. Returning around 4:00 a.m., the trainer saw Landaluce had deteriorated even further, and told Laura Cotter, "We're in big trouble." Around 5:00 a.m., Dr. Bishop went across the street to Arcadia Methodist Hospital to get more intravenous fluids. Shortly afterward, Wayne told Laura to summon the vet and forget about the fluids, as Landaluce's veins appeared to be collapsing. "She's not going to make it," he told her. When Laura returned with Dr. Bishop, the filly started to weave and braced herself against a stall wall. Wayne tried to hold the filly's head up so she could breathe, but she fell against him.

At 5:45 a.m., on Sunday, November 28, as Laura Cotter, Roy Bishop, and Bobby Barnett watched helplessly, Landaluce died with her head in Wayne Lukas's lap. Although he had never entered the filly's stall at any time throughout the week of her illness, Wayne's Australian shepherd, Duke, now came in and lay down next to her.

Wayne stood up and turned away, brushing back tears. He walked down the shedrow. He'd had a few days to think about what he might do if Landaluce didn't survive. He called the University of California at Davis and ordered an autopsy, hoping it would yield answers. Then he left the barn. "It was the only time I saw Wayne Lukas cry," Barnett later said.

The assistant trainer, along with Wayne's son Jeff, knew what to do. They called a truck to take the filly away, packed her body in ice, and covered it with a black tarp. "That's one thing I didn't need to see," Wayne said. "I didn't want that to be my last memory of her."

An hour and a half later, Wayne returned. There were horses waiting, and work to be done. He saddled his quarter horse pony and rode wordlessly to the track to train. The sun was coming up, but there was no warmth in Wayne's heart as he sat on the pony like a statue. His string of horses ran in and out of the lightening shadows before him, the way a once living thing was already beginning to run in and out of his memory. He couldn't help but think of them as ordinary now. His dark beauty, his brilliant comet, would never flash before his eyes again. He watched the sun squeeze itself over the horizon like a heart holding back. Already, he could feel his own hardening: he would never let himself feel this way about another horse. He would not endure this kind of pain again.

The hoofbeats of horses in the new morning half dusk of Santa Anita throbbed along with the rhythm of his heart, and they both said just one thing—*Landaluce.*

20

Grieving

Wayne Lukas has paid his dues—for the rest of his life.
—Billy Reed

When the phone rang in Laffit Pincay's East Hollywood home early Sunday morning, the jockey was prepared for bad news. At the other end of the line was his agent, Tony Matos, who told him Landaluce was gone. Laffit's first thoughts were for Wayne. "I just feel so sorry for [him]," said the Hall of Famer. "A rider has a lot more chances to get another great horse, but there aren't that many opportunities for a trainer to have one like this."

Across town, the phone at Marje Everett's Holmby Hills mansion rang early, too. When she heard the news of Landaluce's death, Marje had to scramble. She wanted to acknowledge the filly's passing on Starlet Day, which would begin in a matter of hours. A big crowd was expected. Marje offered to bury Landaluce in Hollywood Park's infield, and she arranged to have the American flag there fly at half-mast before the first race went to post. She planned a moment of silence prior to the Starlet in Luce's honor and instructed her staff to replay the filly's Lassie victory on closed-circuit television. In addition, she had a tribute to the filly printed and inserted into the Starlet program.

In the Santa Anita backstretch, calls flooded the Wayne Lukas barn. Neither the trainer nor Dr. Bishop would talk to reporters. A tearful Laura Cotter stepped in to speak with the Associated Press. The assistant trainer revealed Marje's offer to bury the filly at Holly-

214

wood but said the connections were still thinking it over. Laura understood why Wayne would not come to the phone. "It was like losing a member of the family," she said. "Literally, Wayne was broken-hearted. He loved that filly."

In Midland, Texas, Dave Feldman of the *Chicago Sun-Times* was one of the first members of the press to reach either the Beal or French residences. "We'd like to talk to you," replied Beal's wife, Nancy, "but we're all so broken up we can't talk right now." Later, Barry Beal told the *Los Angeles Times,* "The loss is devastating. It's a personal tragedy as well as a tragedy for all of racing to lose such a great horse." He explained that the Beal and French families had planned to come to California to watch Carambola in the Starlet but canceled their flight upon learning of Landaluce's death. At their Anacacho Ranch, the Bob French family received a call from Wayne breaking the news. "She was like a lightning flash in our lives—she came and went so fast," Bob's wife Marcia later recalled. "Our world just fell apart. We couldn't even talk. I cried for days. It was such a blow to all of us."

Viewers across the Greater Los Angeles metro area woke up to news about Landaluce's death on local channels; others might have heard about it on local radio. But in a predigital age, those who didn't switch on the Sunday-morning news would not have heard about the filly's passing until they arrived at the track, as daily newspapers would not carry the story until the following day. Fans who bought a copy of the *Form* at Hollywood Park's entrance gate saw a front-page article headlined "Landaluce Fighting for Her Life." For some, it was not until they passed the turnstiles and viewed the flag at half-mast that they began to understand what had happened. The mood at the track quickly turned somber as the news spread among the crowd of twenty-eight thousand. "Landaluce's death was greeted by racing fans with the shock associated with an assassination," the *Form*'s Jon White reported.

The last thing Wayne felt like doing Sunday afternoon was going to the races. But he went. He had only two runners on the Starlet card. One was two-year-old maiden filly Discreet, who'd finished seventh in her opener. Beal and French's Carambola, who stood in the stall next to Landaluce throughout her illness, was loaded on a van to Hollywood to compete in the Starlet in her stablemate's place. Although now the sentimental favorite for the race, the filly wasn't properly prepared, as Wayne had never actually pointed her to the Starlet. The dark bay daughter of Slew with a smudge of white on her forehead was supposed to win today. Just a week ago, Wayne thought this Sunday would bring one of his most satisfying victories. Instead, it had become one of the saddest days of his life. Wayne put on a dark suit and headed to the track.

It was not an easy day for the Lukas barn. Discreet finished tenth in the fourth race, and it was a long afternoon until the Starlet post at 5:00 p.m. Throughout the day, horsemen and fans approached Wayne to offer condolences, sometimes hugging him or squeezing his hand. Shortly before the headliner, Landaluce's victory in the Lassie was replayed in tribute. An announcement was made that Landaluce's connections had agreed to her burial in the Hollywood infield at a later date and that a memorial shrine would be built.

Barely twelve hours after the filly's death, Wayne held a scheduled press conference. It was obvious to those on the Hollywood grounds how much the filly's loss had overwhelmed the trainer. Described as visibly shaken, his voice cracked and choking with emotion, and often on the verge of tears, Wayne struggled to maintain his composure behind sunglasses that concealed his reddened eyes. He outlined the progression of the filly's illness and stated that he expected the cause of death would be pneumonia. "You expect the worse, but you wonder how it can still devastate you so," he confessed. "At times, almost everyone seemed about to cry," wrote the *Shreveport Journal*'s Gary West. "People openly wept," Wayne later recalled. "The two-dollar bettors in the grandstand, all of them. I knew [Landaluce] had charisma, but I didn't realize until then how many she had touched."

As a field of nine went postward for North America's richest race for females, Jay Hovdey described the Starlet as "a bloodless exercise in economics" without Landaluce present. Laffit Pincay went to the post in Beal and French's green-and-white silks—but on a different filly. His mount Carambola dueled through quick early fractions with eventual winner Fabulous Notion but tired in the stretch and finished next to last when eased by the Hall of Famer. Recent Hollywood allowance winner O'Happy Day finished second, and Charlie Whittingham–trainee Stephanie Bryn was third. California fillies swept the board, but not at all in a way anyone expected.

Wayne Lukas turned away. Copelan's Prevue win yesterday had been painful to watch, but then Landaluce was still alive, and there was still hope. Watching the Starlet today only deepened his pain. The trainer was not the only one mourning, as Gary West observed: "Some in the crowd ignored the race and stared blankly at the flag at half mast as it hung limply in the lifeless California breeze."

Sunday evening, Landaluce made national television news for the last time. Dick Schaap of ABC's *World News Tonight,* who covered the filly's blossoming career after her Del Mar Debutante win two months ago, now found himself in the unexpected position of eulogizing the filly on air the night of her death. So did Dan Rather of CBS News.

Back at Santa Anita after an emotionally wrenching day at Hollywood, Wayne found that Art Lerille's gelding Male Adapter appeared to be on the mend from the illness that seemed so similar to the one that felled the great daughter of Slew. "It looks like he's going to make it," Lerille said. Wayne's own colt Ft. Davis also appeared to have recovered. His temperature was down, and his appetite had returned. The colt's illness turned out to be as brief and mild as Wayne first thought Luce's would have been. Now, she was gone, while the son of To the Quick pulled hay from his net as if nothing had happened.

Watching him, Wayne felt his eyes well with tears again. He walked down the shedrow. Stalls 54 and 55, where the light of his life had lived for such a brief but wonderful time, were now just planks of wood in an empty space filled with straw. But Wayne didn't need a double-wide stall anymore. It was time to put some new walls up. From now on, his heart would stay behind them.

21

Getting Through

Landaluce . . . was the first thing I thought about in the morning and
the last thing at night. She was my life, for awhile.
—Wayne Lukas

The Hollywood meet still had two weeks to go before the Futurity.
While it remained an important race, and a possible determiner
for the juvenile colt championship, the contest's luster was dimmed
by Landaluce's passing. Gone was the crowd-pleasing matchup of
the wonder filly versus the colts, or a chance to see a California girl
become Horse of the Year. The winter book favorite for the Kentucky
Derby would not be a filly after all.

For the Wayne Lukas barn, the remaining weeks of the meet,
once full of hope, excitement, and anticipation, now became simply
a routine to get through. The barn would not have a starter in the big
race. Shortly after her death, one of Landaluce's grooms was found
sobbing in her stall. Wayne arranged for him to receive counseling
and sent him home for a time. The groom was not the only one suffering from Landaluce's loss. "There were a lot of sad people around
the barn after she died," said Bobby Barnett.

Perhaps the person suffering most was Wayne. "After you've been
around a horse like [Landaluce], you can't see the point in going on,"
he said. "This kind of deadens you. You lose sensitivity to everything.
You look at the horses and they're the same ones you used to be enthusiastic about, but now they're just horses."

While the Lukas barn struggled to go on without its brightest star, reaction to her death poured in from across the nation. Landaluce's widespread popularity and the shock generated by her loss made her front-page news in both the *New York Times* and *Los Angeles Times*. Sportswriter Tim Liotta was the first to call her a champion, "captivating not only the racing world, but the world of sports." "She had already become a legend," wrote the *New York Daily News'* Russ Harris. Santa Anita director of racing Frank "Jimmy" Kilroe called Landaluce "a national heroine," and turf writer Billy Reed eulogized her as possessing the "looks and heart and fire of her father." Andrew Beyer articulated the feelings of many when he wrote, "So formidable was Landaluce that it still seems inconceivable she could be struck down by what had initially seemed a routine ailment," calling her death racing's "most tragic and premature loss" since that of Ruffian. The *Hackensack (NJ) Record* reported "the filly's unbelievable speed led experts to predict the two-year-old might be the greatest ever of her sex." Tom Roach, co-breeder of rival Princess Rooney, described himself as "crushed" by Landaluce's death, adding "I doubt we'll ever see anything like her again."

Meanwhile, messages of condolence and sympathy continued to stream into the Lukas barn from racing fans. Wayne received more than five hundred letters from around the nation, including a college professor in Connecticut, a young girl in New Mexico, and a carpenter in Oregon. "All expressed a sense of personal grief," wrote Joe Hirsch. One fan in Baltimore penned an impassioned letter to the editor of the *Evening Sun* chiding the paper for its sparse coverage of Landaluce's death. In a letter to the *Los Angeles Times,* another writer confessed he "wept unashamedly" upon hearing of the filly's demise. Marcia French recalled "great big sacks of mail" arriving at the Lukas barn for months after the filly's passing. "They were three and a half feet tall and two feet thick, crammed full, and they came once or twice a week," she said.

Interspersed among the first wave of press tributes were reports of Landaluce's cause of death, even before a preliminary autopsy report was released. Indeed, headlines in the *New York Times* and *Los Angeles Times* both proclaimed the filly had succumbed to a virus. Widely syndicated in local newspapers, these accounts amplified the popular belief that a mysterious or unknown virus was the cause of the filly's death—a notion that persists to this day.

Two days after the filly's death, and after obtaining permission from her owners, Dr. Bennie Osborn of the University of California at Davis released results of a preliminary autopsy. Dr. Osborn said that blood clots on the filly's lungs as well as other organs caused her death. "There may have been pneumonia," he added. "There probably was a minor infection occurring in the lungs. We are doing continuing studies on that and we hope to be able to determine whether there was a bacteria or virus that may have caused it all." Osborn made it clear that the initial autopsy was inconclusive as to what caused the clots: "We don't know for sure it is a virus," he said. "We're just suspecting that." In order to determine the underlying cause of the fatal blood clots, veterinary pathologists cultured tissue samples in a laboratory, where they would grow for several days and then be analyzed. "Because of the widespread interest, we will make every effort to do it within a week," Osborn promised. Osborn explained that Landaluce also "had a respiratory infection early in the week, and there were also signs of mild bouts of gastrointestinal disorders which also led to her demise." The vet added: "This is not the first horse I've examined who died from similar infections after showing a history of respiratory problems. These causes of death are not common, but they do occur."

Dr. Osborn also lauded the veterinarians who attended Landaluce during her illness: "They made heroic efforts to save the horse's life. They did the best things possible under the circumstances."

After viewing his own copy of the preliminary autopsy, co-owner Barry Beal told the *Dallas Morning News* that Landaluce was the victim of a virus: "Every vital organ was infected by [it]," he said. "It was just one of those impossible things. Other horses . . . have the same thing, but they shook it. . . . Her body wouldn't reject it." And

Beal wasn't the only one who attributed Landaluce's death to a virus while awaiting final autopsy results. In spite of Osborn's comments, press reports over the next ten days continued to describe Landaluce's illness as a "mysterious virus." Meanwhile, Joe Hirsch, lamenting Landaluce's loss, pointed out a similarity between the filly's illness and one that had afflicted Seattle Slew between his three- and four-year-old campaign. Joined by *BloodHorse* editor Kent Hollingsworth, Hirsch called for more veterinary research into the filly's cause of death.

Approximately ten days after the preliminary report was released, Osborn once again took the podium to explain Landaluce's final autopsy report, which had not yielded the expected results. The pathologist revealed that the cause of Landaluce's fatal illness was a bacterial infection and that no trace of a virus was found: "We found an intestinal infection, and bacteria from the intestines invaded the blood and caused the blood clots that killed her. It doesn't mean there may not have been a virus early on to trigger these events, but all of our initial attempts to identify a virus have come up empty. There was no evidence of pneumonia, either." Osborn added that a particularly aggressive strain of hemolytic E. coli was the source of the infection that resisted antibiotic treatment. "Antibiotics obviously are not always totally effective against this particular kind of bacteria," he said, "but the treatment she received is what kept her alive as long as it did." Basically, antibiotics delayed but could not prevent the infection's spread into the filly's bloodstream.

A week later, Tracy Gantz of the *BloodHorse* reported that the University of California at Davis laboratory tested the filly's tissue samples to see what antibiotics might have proven effective against her infection and found that only gentamicin showed any potential. Dr. Osborn cautioned that this was not proof the drug would have saved Landaluce's life, calling it "hard to say." He pointed out that the presence of E. coli in the bloodstream is not common and that it is usually found more often in foals. Additionally, according to Gantz, Dr. Osborn "speculated that something such as a virus probably affected Landaluce one to two weeks before she showed signs of illness." Jim Murray of the *Los Angeles Times* suggested that Landaluce's uncharacteristic performance in the Oak Leaf might have been an indication that a virus "was already beginning to take effect." Likewise, Santa Anita track announcer Alan Buchdahl recalled his "gut feeling" that something was not quite right with Landaluce as he called the race. Still, the day after the Oak Leaf, Wayne reported the filly was in excellent condition. "She's got her head in the feed tub, right where it belongs," he told the *Form*. Landaluce also had three stellar workouts between the Oak Leaf and her illness, and according to her trainer was playful and healthy the day before she got sick. Wayne later revealed that routine blood tests taken a few days before the filly fell ill were "perfect," adding, "I don't know if this particular illness would have shown up then or not."

Another erroneous cause of death still reported today is Colitis X, a catchall term for unexplained colitis that proves fatal. However, improvements in equine veterinary diagnosis and treatment since 1982 have resulted in fewer cases of fatal unexplained colitis, and so the term Colitis X has gradually fallen out of use. It has also been suggested that Seattle Slew suffered from Colitis X while he was still racing. Whether he did or not, noted veterinarians as well as Landaluce's trainer now agree that Colitis X was not the cause of her death.

Further, antibiotic use against an infection becomes a double-edged sword when treating racehorses, as it is also the primary cause of colitis among them. Sadly, the only available treatment to wipe out her infection not only failed to help Landaluce but may have caused a secondary colitis that contributed to her death. It is also possible for a severe bacterial infection to spread into a horse's bloodstream and seed other organs, including the intestines.

Landaluce's death was "mysterious" only in the sense that no one was able to explain how she contracted the original bacterial infection that ultimately killed her, or why it failed to respond to antibiotics. Unfortunately, despite significant advances in equine veterinary medicine in the last forty years, these kinds of infections that spiral into secondary conditions and result in death still strike horses at the racetrack today.

Plans were soon finalized for a memorial service at Hollywood Park, where Landaluce would be interred in the infield on Futurity Day. "We are determined to conduct a tasteful ceremony that will honor the memory of a truly gifted racehorse . . . in the infield near our new waterfall," said Marje Everett, adding that the area "eventually will be developed into a square complete with an appropriate monument."

Clearly, it was Marje Everett's intention to provide a permanent and fitting tribute to one of the most talented and beloved fillies ever to race at Hollywood Park. When Futurity Day arrived, Landaluce would come back to the track for the last time.

22

Futurity

You point for a race, for a specific moment, with just one thing in mind. It's all you think about, and then when it happens, just the way you planned, you can hardly believe it.

—Joe Manzi

When he woke up early on the morning of Saturday, December 12, Joe Manzi hoped this would be one of the best days of his life. Today was the trainer's chance to prove that Roving Boy was not only the best juvenile colt in the West but also superior to the eastern invader who had already won three Grade One races. Manzi had not slept well for the last two nights. Owner Robert Hibbert had supplemented the son of Olden Times to the race for a stiff $40,000. Manzi hoped it would prove a sound investment. "This is a prize worth winning," he said. Manzi, who began his career as an exercise rider for Charlie Whittingham, now was the conditioner of a potential Classic winner, the first horse of his life with a chance for a national championship. The weather would be cold for California by the time his colt went to post, and it would be dark outside. Manzi donned a black suit with a red tie and a black cashmere topcoat. "You look like a banker," laughed his wife, Sandra. Leaving for Hollywood Park, the trainer knew he'd prepared his colt well, schooling him in the paddock and working him at night under the lights to accustom him to conditions at a track he'd never raced on before. There was nothing more he could do. Now it was up to Roving Boy.

Owner Fred Hooper dressed in his customary crisp suit and tie for what he hoped would be a momentous occasion and a big payday. Confident of a win for his prize colt Copelan, Hooper grabbed a pair of binoculars to keep his homebred in view as the bay flashed under the wire. The colt's namesake, veterinarian Dr. Robert Copelan, had already flown to California for the race. He wouldn't miss this one for anything and hoped to be on hand in the winner's circle to celebrate.

Just three weeks ago, turf writer Jon White thought that today he'd be covering one of the biggest races of the year at Hollywood Park. He was. But he was also going to a funeral. Invited by Laura Cotter, the writer would leave the press box shortly after the second race, and join Landaluce's connections in the infield to pay their last respects during a brief public ceremony.

Laura Cotter put on a white blouse, a long white skirt, a royal blue jacket and her brown leather boots, the same pair she wore when she and Ebaristo escorted Luce postward for the Anoakia. Bobby Barnett put on jeans like he did every day. He wouldn't be going to Hollywood Park today. Instead, he would stay behind with the Lukas string at Santa Anita. In Texas, the Beal and French families boarded a plane for California. They had always planned to be at Hollywood today—but in the winner's circle, not the infield.

In Holmby Hills, Marje Everett dressed for a big day at the track, though a sad one. All her work and planning for the Futurity had indeed made it a championship determiner, but without the western filly and fan favorite who would have made it a thrilling million-dollar race. It was a measure of the solemnity of today's occasion that Landaluce, not any of the starters in the richest race the track had ever offered, appeared on the cover of Futurity Day's racing program.

At his home in Arcadia, Wayne Lukas pulled a double-breasted navy sport coat with gold buttons from his closet and tucked his aviator sunglasses into a pocket. He surely would need them today.

As a procession of nearly thirty-five thousand fans started its stream through the turnstiles, Laffit Pincay began to dress in the jockeys' room for a mount he would not ride. He slipped an arm into the familiar sleeve of hunter green with white polka dots, even though Beal and French had no runner today. He would wear the silks briefly in memory of Landaluce. Then he would put them away for the rest of the day and try not to think of the bay filly the next time they hung waiting for him in the jockeys' room. Today would be the first and only time in his career that he would wear silks at a memorial service for a horse. It would be a busy and emotional day for the jockey—after the ceremony, Laffit had five more mounts, including Fifth Division for trainer A. T. Doyle in the Futurity. Although he was glad to have a mount in the big race, the Hall of Famer couldn't help thinking how differently today was turning out from what he had imagined. As always, he would try his best, but the loss of the filly who would have been today's overwhelming favorite was not far from his thoughts.

Shortly after two o'clock in the afternoon, Landaluce's connections, accompanied by a throng of reporters, assembled in the infield alongside its waterfall at the south end of the track. A spray of red roses and white carnations stood alongside a heart-shaped cluster of white chrysanthemums next to the waterfall. Laffit stood at the edge of the grave between Laura and Wayne. The trainer kept his hands clasped, again near tears. Exercise riders Jesse Cerillo and David Pineda, along with Jeff Lukas and Dr. Roy Bishop, lowered a plain box containing the filly's ashes into the ground. Hollywood Park announcer Alan Buchdahl provided commentary over the track's public address system, commemorating Landaluce's Lassie victory as "one of the most remarkable efforts by any athlete in any sport." Buchdahl, reading from a script written by track publicist Nat Wess, could feel waves of emotion rippling through the grandstand even from his perch high above the track in the announcer's booth. "It was an important [occasion]," Buchdahl said, "and I read from the heart." At one point, the announcer had to pause to maintain his composure before he concluded, "We'll never know the heights she might have scaled, but we do know she'll never be forgotten. She was our superstar." Laid to rest in the company of those

Landaluce's burial in the infield of Hollywood Park on Futurity Day, December 12, 1982, attended by Laura Cotter (*second from left*), Laffit Pincay, and Wayne Lukas. (Tom Abahazy, courtesy of Hollywood Park)

who loved and cared for her, Landaluce on this day resembled her sire to the end. Neither of them was ever beaten at two.

Two and a half hours later, it was nearly time for the Futurity to get underway. Jockey Eddie Delahoussaye, in the rust-and-black silks of owner Robert Hibbert, met Joe Manzi in the paddock to discuss strategy for Roving Boy, while rider Jerry Bailey in Fred Hooper's red, white, and blue silks took a leg up on the favorite, Copelan.

When the starting gate opened minutes later, the race unfolded in a way no one expected. After all the buildup, the East versus West challenge never materialized, and favored Copelan was never in contention. Edging out trainer Jerry Fanning's Desert Wine by a neck, Roving Boy won the race over a fast track in 1:41 4/5, the same time Landaluce posted in her Oak Leaf victory at Santa Anita. Copelan was humiliated, a distant fifth and sixteen lengths behind the winner.

As a jubilant Manzi and nearly forty well-wishers hurried en masse to the winner's circle, the trainer was overwhelmed with congratulations. The colt he nearly kept out of the race was now the highest-earning juvenile of all time, and perhaps a champion.

Meanwhile, jockey Jerry Bailey and trainer Mitch Griffin edged quietly past the crowd in silent disappointment while Fred Hooper graciously congratulated owner Bob Hibbert in the winner's circle. Back at the barn, Hooper, Griffin, and Dr. Robert Copelan examined the son of Tri Jet and discovered a hard piece of dirt underneath the colt's right eyelid. Around the first turn, Copelan had been hit with a dirt clod that damaged his cornea, "as if someone had taken a rasp and scraped it over the eye," the vet reported. "It would have stopped an elephant," Hooper lamented. When the vet flushed out the colt's eye, dirt streamed down his face the way the Eclipse Award and any chance for Horse of the Year had already drained away. Perhaps good luck at Hollywood Park was not in Copelan's genes—his dam Susan's Girl was ill-fated at the track, never winning a race there despite five attempts.

Fred Hooper may have consoled himself with the hope that he might still win the Derby with Copelan. But although Copelan's eye eventually healed, and he won the Fountain of Youth at three, the colt never started in any of the Classic races the following spring and was retired to stud at his birthplace on Hooper's farm. Although Hooper did win the Eclipse Award for Outstanding Breeder of 1982, he never won another Kentucky Derby. He would have gladly traded the statuette for a chance to stand in the winner's circle at Churchill one more time. "Winning Horse of the Year is not as important as winning the Kentucky Derby," he said.

Back in the jockeys' room, Laffit Pincay felt fortunate to finish third aboard Fifth Division in the Futurity after all that had happened. It was the only time he finished in the money that day. His colt ran well, especially for a juvenile in only his fourth lifetime start. Still, the Hall of Famer found it difficult to maintain the same passion and dedication for his job immediately after Landaluce's death, and he fell victim to a slump that lasted over four months. After Luce's death, the usually intense and determined Laffit started riding less. "I've been working hard all year and I'd just like to take some days off," he said. He even contemplated quitting riding completely for the rest of the Hollywood meet. By doing so, he was effectively ceding the Hollywood meet riding title to Chris McCarron and the national earnings title to his rival Angel Cordero. Laffit, like the rest of the Lukas team, knew how much the filly had meant to them all. "Wayne was distraught over the whole thing. He took it very, very bad," he later said. "We all did. We knew what we had."

On a plane back to Texas, owners Barry Beal and Bob French likewise found it hard to maintain enthusiasm for their joint enterprise following the loss of Landaluce. "She was a once in a lifetime horse," Beal said. "It will take awhile to get over this. Right now, it makes me just want to give up racing." In fact, it would be several months before the pair would attend the races again.

Relieved that the day was over, Wayne Lukas returned to Santa Anita and tried not to dwell on what might have been. Back at the barn, with his Australian shepherd, Duke, settled at his feet, he opened a box of greeting cards imprinted with an image of Luce winning the Del Mar Debutante, which he had made to answer all her fan mail. Now, he unfolded a card, opened the first envelope in a stack of condolence letters waiting on his desk, and began to write.

The holiday season came and went, but Christmas didn't seem the same without Landaluce. Last Christmas, Stalwart had just won the Futurity, and the filly had not even begun to train. To Wayne, that seemed like years ago. It was hard to remember a world without Landaluce in it. She had become the largest thing in his life, overshadowing everything else, and he still had trouble remembering she was gone. Often he felt that he was just going through the motions. He called the Pineda family's Mexican restaurant like he did every year and catered Christmas dinner for the grooms and hotwalkers, but this year he couldn't feel festive about anything at all.

Laura Cotter felt the same way. That Christmas, she unwrapped a present from Beal and French, an oil painting by the artist Christine Picavet showing Landaluce being led to the paddock by Laura herself, along with Ebaristo. They were on their way to the Anoakia Stakes, Luce's first race at Santa Anita. The artist had captured the light and shadow of that fall afternoon, the dapples on Landaluce's gleaming coat as she passed beneath the trees. The painting reminded Laura of how calm and relaxed Landaluce was that day, as if the threesome were going for a walk around the shedrow, instead of to a race. The gift had special meaning for Laura. She knew that Picavet was donating proceeds from the sale of her paintings of Landaluce to a fund the artist had created for research into the cause of the filly's illness. Thanks to the thoughtfulness of Luce's owners and Picavet herself, Laura would always be reminded of the best racing filly she had ever known. When she came home after working at the track, she would still be able to see Landaluce every day, year after year. That was something, after all.

23

Eclipse

She did just enough to raise the tantalizing possibility that she could
conceivably be the greatest filly that ever lived.
—Andrew Beyer

Roving Boy's victory over Copelan in the Futurity confounded an
already complex Horse of the Year picture, rekindling speculation
about who would win the honor. The most logical contenders—
handicappers Lemhi Gold and Perrault, Belmont Stakes–winner
Conquistador Cielo, and undefeated California superstar Landaluce
—each had legitimate claims to the title but also chinks in their
Eclipse armor. The lack of a clear front-runner inspired passionate
defenses among their respective supporters, prompting turf writer
Bill Christine to predict, "This year there may be more howling than
usual [over the results]."

Millionaire Lemhi Gold had a sensational campaign, winning
three Grade One races on turf and dirt on both Coasts, the first
horse to win both the Jockey Club Gold Cup and the Marlboro in a
single season. But after a dismal fifth in the Oak Tree Invitational,
the chestnut son of Vaguely Noble was so exhausted that his trainer,
Laz Barrera, ordered a blood test and retired him for the year. Perrault won two Grade One turf races, as well as the Arlington Budweiser Million, the richest race in the world, but ended his season
prematurely when he was eased in the Marlboro. Conquistador Cielo
won two Grade One races in the same week, capturing the Belmont

by fourteen lengths and the Metropolitan Handicap in track record time, but he ended his season earliest of the contenders following a third-place finish in the Travers Stakes in late August, after which he was retired to stud. The three-year-old's campaign provoked turf writer Andrew Beyer's defense of Landaluce as his Horse of the Year choice: "Conquistador Cielo was probably the most brilliant horse to race . . . in 1982. But . . . it would be a dangerous precedent to bestow the sport's highest honor on a horse with such limited achievements. If anything, Conquistador Cielo was the horse of the week. . . . In an era when so many good horses are campaigned conservatively to avoid defeats and are whisked off to stud prematurely, the racing industry should not give its blessing to this type of management." Steven Crist echoed this sentiment, noting "no Horse of the Year has been part of the [racing] scene for so short a time." Beyer dubbed 1982 "the year of Landaluce," calling her victory in the Hollywood Lassie "one of the outstanding performances by a two-year-old in history. . . . Purists will argue that a two-year-old should never be Horse of the Year because he or she will not have had a chance to do the things by which we judge equine greatness. . . . But in a year where there were no great horses with a great roster of achievements, nobody deserves to have her name placed in this exalted company more than Landaluce."

Beyer's comments reflected the rarity with which juveniles were ever seriously considered for the industry's highest honor. Prior to 1971, two separate entities—the Thoroughbred Racing Associations racing secretaries, and the *Daily Racing Form*—each selected their own champions without attempting to reach consensus on a unanimous choice for Horse of the Year, often resulting in shared titles. In 1952, two-year-old Native Dancer became the first juvenile champion to claim a partial Horse of the Year title when he shared it with three-year-old One Count. In 1965, two-year-old filly Moccasin shared the title with four-year-old gelding Third Brother. In 1971, three groups—The *Form,* Thoroughbred Racing Associations racing secretaries, and the National Turf Writers Association—agreed to join forces to form the Eclipse Awards, which would designate a single champion in each division as well as a unanimous choice for Horse of the Year. The first and only two-year-old to win Horse of the Year under the unified system at that time was Secretariat in 1972.

In addition, Landaluce was historically disadvantaged by virtue of her sex—in 1982, there had not been a filly or mare to win Horse of the Year outright since Busher in 1945.

Another hurdle Landaluce faced in Eclipse voting was that she never raced in the East. Wayne Lukas, stung by past experience, was well aware of Eclipse voters' preference for eastern runners. "[It's] somewhat of a popularity vote," he said, "and it's influenced by the location of the people voting." Steven Crist agreed, noting that "California is lightly represented in the Eclipse balloting. Most of the voters are based in Eastern, Southern or Middle Western states."

Still, despite these traditional obstacles, Landaluce not only captured the juvenile filly championship but also finished in a three-way tie for Horse of the Year in what Beyer called "the most hotly contested vote since the awards were established." For the first time ever, each of the voting entities selected a different runner as Horse of the Year—the racing secretaries chose Landaluce; the *Daily Racing Form* chose Lemhi Gold; and the National Turf Writers chose Conquistador Cielo. A tiebreak system had to be employed for the first time since the award's inception to ultimately name Conquistador Cielo as Horse of the Year.

It had been a spectacular year for California-based runners, who captured five of the ten Eclipse Award categories, "underscoring the growing strength of West Coast racing," according to Beyer. Landaluce's championship signaled the beginning of a trend that would debunk the long-standing stereotype that top western runners were inferior to eastern elite. In the tradition of Swaps, Warfare, and Ack Ack, and along with contemporaries Lemhi Gold, Perrault, and Roving Boy (who was named juvenile colt champion), Landaluce's 1982 campaign, as abbreviated and ultimately tragic as it was, still shone a bright light on what was already happening in the West and what might have continued, even without the supercharged Breeders' Cup races to decide championships. Wayne Lukas and Landaluce earned the championship on their own terms. In spite of the predominantly eastern voting bloc, in spite of racing only five times in barely three and a half months, in spite of a fatal illness that robbed her of the chance to win the races for which her trainer had so carefully readied her, and in spite of not even being alive when the votes were cast, Landaluce was the first California-based juvenile filly to secure a championship. In being named Horse of the Year by at least one voting group, Landaluce joined Moccasin and La Prevoyante as the only juvenile fillies ever to achieve this honor. Among this star-studded group, Landaluce is the first and only filly who earned the distinction while racing exclusively in the West. In her brilliance at two, the daughter of Seattle Slew outshone even easterner Princess Rooney, future winner of the inaugural Breeders' Cup Distaff in 1984 and Hall of Fame inductee in 1991. As turf historian Ed Bowen points out: "Landaluce had to be a virtual miracle worker to gain a national championship . . . in the face of the Frizette and Gardenia victories of the very widely respected Princess Rooney. . . . It would be difficult to exaggerate what an impression Landaluce had to have made on horsemen and media alike to win a championship staying on the West Coast against such opposition within her division back East." Indeed, eastern distaste at the precedent set by Landaluce's groundbreaking championship was eloquently rendered by Woody Stephens, trainer of Conquistador Cielo, when he said, "How could the secretaries select her? She never . . . won east of the Mississippi. The right horse got top honors."

Landaluce ended a twenty-four-year drought for Spendthrift Farm in producing a champion, its first since the filly Idun in 1958. For Leslie Combs, Landaluce's championship came near the end of his life and at the apex of his breeding empire, before it began to crumble and disappear in the throes of bankruptcy. For Francis Kernan, Landaluce fulfilled a lifetime dream to do only once what Leslie had already accomplished three times—with Myrtle Charm at the beginning of his career, Idun in its middle, and Landaluce near its end—to breed a champion. For Brownell Combs, Landaluce was first in a wave of Seattle Slew offspring who made the stallion's syndication one of the great breeding achievements in the farm's history. For Seattle Slew and his connections, producing juvenile champion Landaluce from his very first crop exceeded the syndicate's most optimistic expectations and established the stallion as one of the world's elite. For John Williams, Landaluce, the farm's most brilliant runner born and raised during his tenure at Spendthrift, was emblematic of all he achieved there.

Landaluce gave Wayne Lukas his first Eclipse Award—the one he said throughout her brief career he would not seek. There would be twenty-three more, including three runners who would become Horse of the Year. Wayne would become one of the most decorated Thoroughbred trainers of all time by winning four Eclipse Awards for Outstanding Trainer. He would be the first Thoroughbred trainer to win more than $100 million in purses in 1990 and more than $200 million by 1999, when he was inducted into the Hall of Fame.

But in January 1983, in a Thoroughbred training career that would span four more decades, Wayne surely would have traded that first Eclipse statuette for the chance to see one bay filly with a whisk broom tail and a smudge of white on her forehead standing in her double-wide stall, looking out the window—head up, eyes gleaming, and her ears pricked.

24

Legacy

Landaluce taught me not to get too close to any horse, because that
was one of the hardest things I ever had to get over.
—Wayne Lukas

In the weeks and months that followed, Wayne's heart was heavy.
With Landaluce gone, the optimism and energy in his barn van-
ished. The same string of horses that had helped propel the trainer to
the top of the national standings failed to win a race for over two
months. Wayne's slump was obvious, and the trainer was candid
about his feelings: "Don't let anyone tell you that mental attitude
and emotions don't have everything to do with racing," he told Steven Crist. "I don't let things get to me, but this did."

By spring, the Lukas stable appeared to be back on track, and
two unraced fillies occupied Landaluce's old double-wide stall. "It
took time, but now we're winning again and we're third in the country in purses this year," Wayne said. Owner Bob Spreen's Balboa
Native won the Louisiana Derby, and Beal and French returned to
the races when their promising three-year-old colt Marfa won the
Santa Anita Derby, making him the top California contender for the
Run for the Roses. Wayne sent both colts along with Total Departure to the Kentucky Derby. But the Lukas trainees did not have a
good day, finishing fifth, ninth, and nineteenth. Wayne couldn't
help feeling that this would have been his race to win with Landaluce, and evidently there were others who felt that way too, as Wayne

found out when he was pulled away from an unscheduled news conference to meet a young fan. "I'll never forget [it]," Wayne recalled. "It was cold, damp, gloomy, it fit my mood perfectly. But here came this nine-year-old. Her name was Lisa Jones. She was dressed in a rain slicker, and I had to bend down to hear what she was saying. She told me, 'I loved Landaluce just like you did.'" Wayne put his feelings aside, rallied his team, and ended the year first in the nation by purses won.

Laffit Pincay, too, was on the rebound when he again teamed with trainer Woody Stephens to win the 1983 Belmont Stakes with Caveat. In early 1984, a nice three-year-old colt by Seattle Slew came his way. Against the advice of his agent, Laffit accepted the mount on Swale in the Kentucky Derby, partly because the colt reminded him of Landaluce. Laffit's Derby drought ended when the son of Slew carried the rider to his first ever victory in the Run for the Roses after eleven tries.

Wayne's high regard for Landaluce engendered a long-standing fondness for the offspring of Seattle Slew in the auction ring— throughout the 1980s, the trainer bought more yearlings by Slew than by any other sire. In 1985, Wayne was the underbidder at Keeneland for Slew's half brother, Seattle Dancer, who sold to BBA England for a record $13.1 million. In 1990, Wayne tried unsuccessfully to buy Slew's son A. P. Indy as a yearling, this time losing out to BBA Ireland for $2.9 million. Wayne campaigned many Slew offspring throughout the 1980s and 1990s, including champions Capote and Surfside, Vagrancy Handicap–winner Le Slew, Bay Shore–winner Houston, Oaklawn Handicap–winner Slew City Slew, Jim Dandy–winner Scorpion, Santa Anita Oaks–winner Hail Atlantis, listed winner Dr. Caton, and others.

In 1986, Wayne reached another milestone when four-year-old Lady's Secret, a daughter of Secretariat, became the first American-based filly to win Horse of the Year in the Eclipse Awards era. "Yet Lady's Secret is perhaps the least gifted of four remarkable fillies to carve out brilliant careers in the country during the past two decades," wrote Neil Milbert of the *Chicago Tribune*. "The others are Genuine Risk, Ruffian and Landaluce . . . a daughter of Seattle Slew that Lukas still considers the best horse to walk into his life."

In 1988, Wayne had another star filly, this time for owner Gene Klein, a strapping gray daughter of Spendthrift sire Caro named Winning Colors. When the three-year-old beat colts in the Santa Anita Derby in the spring, she became an immediate favorite for the Kentucky Derby. Comparisons to Landaluce were inevitable. "As excited as we are about the Derby," said Wayne, "I don't know that [Winning Colors is] ever going to find a spot deep inside that Landaluce had." A few days prior to the race, turf writer James Litke described Wayne's speech to the National Turf Writers as "an emotional affair with Lukas reminiscing how the death of Landaluce . . . had steeled him for whatever disappointment lay ahead."

On the first Saturday in May, Winning Colors gave Wayne his first Derby win, becoming only the third filly in history to wear the blanket of roses. In spite of his euphoria at winning his first Derby, Landaluce was still in Wayne's thoughts. "In Lukas' mind, Winning Colors was his second filly to win the Derby," wrote Dave Anderson in the *New York Times*. "If Landaluce had run, we would have won it," Wayne insisted the day before the race.

Even Winning Color's Derby victory failed to erase the emotional scars of Landaluce's passing, as sportswriter John Eisenberg discovered when he interviewed Wayne on the eve of Winning Colors' start in the second jewel of the Triple Crown. Eisenberg asked the trainer to describe how he felt about his first Derby winner. "[I've] become a little more callous about my horses," he confessed. "I don't open up like I used to." When asked what it would take for him to have similar feelings for another horse, Wayne replied, "I don't know if it will ever happen again. After Landaluce, it almost has to be that way. . . . It's like your second love affair. You're more cautious because the end of the first one hurt so much. And mine unraveled so quickly, it left a soft spot. I don't know if it will ever go away."

In 2007, former *American Racing Manual* editor Steve Davidowitz ranked Landaluce as number two on his list of top juvenile fillies of all time, behind only Ruffian. In 2016, Bob Ehalt of *America's Best Racing* called Landaluce "one of the greatest two-year-old fillies of the twentieth century." Turf writer Jon White, who saw all of her races in person, includes Landaluce on his list of top one hundred American Thoroughbreds of all time. He points out that it may be difficult for today's fans to appreciate Landaluce's brief career. White cites her "abbreviated body of work" as the reason she is not in the Hall of Fame today.

Both Wayne Lukas and Jon White believe that perhaps Landaluce's accomplishments merit revisiting, especially in light of shorter careers among modern Thoroughbreds. The malady that killed Landaluce couldn't have been more ill-timed. An argument can be made that if she had remained healthy for just three more weeks, long enough to contest and win the important championship determiners, she might be in the Hall of Fame today as the first juvenile filly millionaire and Horse of the Year. Turf writer Jim Murray went even further, writing that if she had raced in the Classics at three, "she might not only have been Horse of the Year but Horse of the Half Century."

In 2017, the Kentucky Derby Museum at Churchill Downs unveiled its new D. Wayne Lukas exhibit, a tribute to the trainer's life and career. Included in the exhibit is a video clip in which the trainer describes his memories of Landaluce. "Every one of us in our career hopes that a Landaluce comes across our path," he begins. "You dream and want that one that is so special, that's so much better. American Pharoah with Bob [Baffert], he finally found his. I don't think you ever get over it. . . . You rub up against that greatness and it never leaves you. You think, 'what if? What could have been?'"

25

Forever a Champion

I see a horse every day, and hopefully, the last day . . . I'm here,
I'll have seen a horse.
—John Williams

Two months after the filly's passing, Marje Everett renamed the
Hollywood Lassie the Landaluce Stakes. It was fitting that the greatest performance in the race would be its last. Landaluce's time in the
contest, run until the closing of Hollywood Park in 2013, was never
equaled there. In 2014, the Landaluce Stakes moved to Santa Anita,
where it was held until 2017. Although the race is currently on hiatus, Santa Anita may revive it as part of the track's regular stakes
schedule in the future.

In February 1983, Hollywood Park was named the site of the
inaugural Breeders' Cup. "I'm thrilled, thrilled, thrilled," Marje Everett rejoiced. "In fact, it's the most thrilling day I've had in forty-two
years of racing." Marje embarked on a four-phase, $100 million reno-
vation project in anticipation of what she considered to be the most
significant event ever staged at the track. This included enlarging both
the outside dirt and inner turf tracks (which required extending the
main track to the south and adding fill dirt to a depth of twenty-five
feet over a large area), as well as construction of new tunnels from the
grandstand to the infield. In addition, a concessions area, more betting windows, and a playground were added in the infield. Marje also

built a posh new "Pavilion of the Stars" prior to the Breeders' Cup. With the exception of the construction of the Pavilion, all of these renovations would have resulted in extensive changes to the infield, some near the area where Landaluce was buried. Throughout the 1980s under Everett's tenure, "trees were uprooted, lakes were filled in, flowers were ripped out" and "general managers came and went" according to the *Racing Times*. Also during Everett's tenure at Hollywood, a simple rose-colored headstone marking Landaluce's grave was placed in the infield, but its precise location or the date it was put there is not known. Perhaps due to her preoccupation with Breeders' Cup improvements and their cost, Marje never was able to complete her planned memorial square for Landaluce.

In 1990, Great Communicator, another horse with strong ties to Hollywood Park by virtue of consecutive wins in the Hollywood Turf Handicap in the late 1980s, was interred in the infield, between its north and south tote boards. The beloved seven-year-old's gravesite was not near Landaluce's original burial site, which was south of the southernmost tote board.

The enormous cost of the unpopular new Pavilion, along with debt Everett incurred to purchase nearby Los Alamitos racetrack, were contributing factors in her ousting as chief operating officer at Hollywood Park in a hostile takeover by R. D. Hubbard in 1991. Hubbard immediately began his own extensive renovation of the infield, designed to return Hollywood to its glory days when it was known as "the track of the lakes and flowers." Two massive lakes, linked by a canal, encompassing almost a mile of shoreline, and containing 5 million gallons of water, were created in the infield. The existing north lake was enlarged to a depth of fifteen feet. Hubbard also removed the larger of two tote boards and razed at least one building in the infield. During this renovation, the infield, including those areas that contained the graves of both Landaluce and Great Communicator, was completely transformed. If Landaluce's gravesite were not moved before or during Hubbard's 1991 project, it almost certainly would have been underwater afterward.

R. D. Hubbard sold Hollywood Park in 1999, and it was sold again six years later. In 2012, track president Jack Liebau announced that the track would close and be sold for commercial real estate development. The last race ever run at the Inglewood strip on December 22, 2013, brought back memories of Landaluce when it was won by five-year-old gelding Woodman's Luck—a great-grandson of Royal Strait Flush, the filly's only full sister.

In the aftermath of the track's closure, many major news outlets, including the *BloodHorse, Daily Racing Form,* and the Associated Press, all reported plans for relocating Landaluce's remains to Spendthrift Farm, where then owner B. Wayne Hughes had graciously agreed to accept them. Wayne Lukas recalls being contacted by track management at the time and said he believes the filly's remains were recovered and sent to her birthplace. Co-owner Barry Beal says his family was never contacted, and co-owner Bob French died just months before the closing of Hollywood Park. French's son Fuller recounts the family's efforts to "get her casket shipped" to their Anacacho Ranch in Texas, where they intended to bury the filly next to 1983 Santa Anita Derby winner Marfa, who was interred there in 2001. French says the family was told that Landaluce's remains were sent to Spendthrift.

Sadly, however, it has gone unreported that Landaluce's remains were never found. Even though Landaluce and Great Communicator's gravesites were not close to one another at the time both horses were buried, their headstones were side by side at the time of the track's closing, raising the possibility that their placement by then was purely symbolic. Track officials were unsuccessful in locating either the filly's remains or those of Great Communicator, and a Spendthrift Farm spokesman confirmed that none were ever received. Construction has begun on a new facility at the farm that will include a tribute to Landaluce, its most recent champion bred by Spendthrift Farm or by Spendthrift in partnership, where fans will be able to remember her as she deserves.

Landaluce historical landmarks remain today at her foaling stall and the pastures in which she lived until she was a weanling at Stone

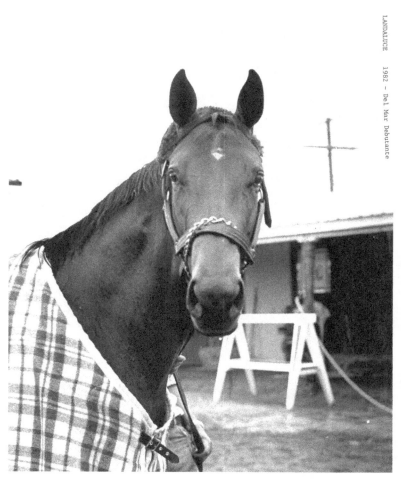

LANDALUCE   1982 – Del Mar Debutante

Forever a champion. (Del Mar Thoroughbred Club)

Columns Stables on Ironworks Pike, across the road from Spend-thrift on the old Elmendorf land so prized by Leslie Combs. Her name appears on the Honor Roll of Spendthrift-bred stakes winners in the farm's main breeding shed, and the walls of Landaluce's former double-wide stall still stand today in Barn 66 at Santa Anita. But perhaps Landaluce's most enduring legacy resides in the hearts of those privileged enough to have seen her run: for them, the dark bay daughter of Seattle Slew will remain always and forever a champion.

Epilogue

October 2019: It's a few minutes before 9:00 a.m. on a damp and soggy Sunday morning in the Wayne Lukas shedrow at Churchill Downs. The trainer has finished morning workouts, and his horses are already cooled out and back in their stalls in Barn 44. Despite the recent rain and sloppy footing, the Lukas barn is as tidy and immaculate as ever.

In a small office in the corner of the shedrow, Wayne Lukas, wearing a black windbreaker and ball cap, sits on a swivel chair in front of his desk. An orange barn cat entwines himself around Wayne's feet. With the trainer is forty-nine-year-old assistant Sebastian "Bas" Nicholl, a former tank commander and British army captain who served in Operation Desert Storm and who has been Wayne's right arm for seventeen years. When Landaluce raced, Nicholl was thirteen and riding point-to-point races in rural north England. Twenty years later, he went to work for Wayne, and he is still here, with no plans to leave.

Wayne has just turned eighty-four and is still achieving milestones. In addition to publishing *Sermon on the Mount,* a collection of memoirs, the trainer had been looking forward to contesting his first Dubai World Cup with Calumet Farm's four-year-old colt Bravazo. Still not immune to the ups and downs of racing, Wayne was disappointed when the son of Awesome Again injured his knee and was withdrawn just weeks before the race.

Wayne invites me to sit, and the orange cat prowls around his desk. On the desk is a small television. It is Arc day, and we are all rooting for the mare Enable to become the first horse in history to win the race three times in a row. The orange cat jumps onto the desk. In the stretch, it looks as though the great filly will prevail, until she is run down in the last fifty yards by eventual winner Waldgeist. The orange cat strolls across the desk in front of the television, then leaps to the floor.

We begin to talk about Landaluce. When I began the process of securing an interview with Wayne, I was told he'd been initially reluctant, and I wonder after all these years if he really wants to talk about her. But soon conversation starts to flow, and the trainer seems as though he's enjoying going back in time to remember the great filly and those early days. The orange cat springs onto Wayne's lap. As he talks, Wayne strokes the cat, who purrs in contentment.

We talk for about an hour, which goes by too quickly. I ask Wayne if he has any photos or mementos of Landaluce. He tells me he donated all his racing memorabilia, including trophies, bronzes, and artwork, to the Kentucky Derby Museum for their new exhibit. He kept just two things—a trophy he won since the exhibit's opening, and an original Christine Picavet oil portrait of Landaluce.

Wayne glances at his watch, and I get the hint. It's time for me to ask the question I came here to ask.

"After almost forty years," I begin, "after training all the great horses and champions you've had, and with the benefit of hindsight, how does Landaluce fit in now?" I ask. "How does she stack up?"

Wayne swivels in his chair, and the orange cat jumps off his lap.

"Number one," he says immediately, and without hesitation. "I've never had one like her since. Not even close."

Acknowledgments

Landaluce's power to enchant, even among horsemen who've witnessed scores of elite runners, was evident whenever her name was mentioned and eyes would still light up, forty years later. I was consistently struck by the lengths to which many in racing would go to help tell her story.

First among them is Ed Bowen, who believed in this book and its author from the beginning. There aren't sufficient words to thank him properly for his unfailing guidance and encouragement.

Then there were those from Spendthrift Farm, both past and present, who helped me understand what Landaluce's birthplace was like in the late 1970s and early 1980s. John Williams shared eloquent memories of a magical place, and Rick Nichols, Steve Johnson, Tom Riddle, Sandy Shaw, and Ann Sturgill added more. The late Karen Mitchell LaBach offered often humorous insights about life behind the scenes. Joel Cunningham, as a guide to modern-day Spendthrift, was enthusiastic about Landaluce's place in its history. Melanie Peterson Ramey of Stone Columns Stables graciously provided access to the historic Elmendorf land where Landaluce was foaled.

Of course, this book would not have been possible without the personal recollections of D. Wayne Lukas, Laffit Pincay, Laura Cotter, Bobby Barnett, Barry Beal, Fuller French, Marcia Fuller French, Dr. Robert Copelan, and Jon White. I'm grateful to all of them for spending time with me. A special thanks to the French family for sharing their extensive collection of Landaluce memorabilia. Thanks also to Brady Wayne Lukas and Christina Bossinakis for their help and support.

As curator of Hollywood Park's archives, Edward "Kip" Hannan, assisted by Roberta Weiser, Richard Walker, and Anna Armstrong, patiently dug up information relevant to the story. Special thanks to Eual Wyatt Jr., Tom Robbins, Martin Panza, Alan Buchdahl, Kenny Rice, Vicky Burnham, Mike Boatright, Nola Ferraro, and Michael Arndt for their memories of Southern California racing in the early 1980s. Dr. Rick Arthur took time from a crushing schedule to offer insight into the veterinary issues surrounding Landaluce's illness and death. Charlotte Farmer was passionate in her determination to unravel the mystery of what happened to the filly's remains.

Roda Ferraro of the Keeneland Library fulfilled hundreds of information requests over the years, including many that turned out to be more than a little off track. Like the most skilled outrider, she steered an often-wayward runner in the right direction. Later, Becky Ryder and Kelly Coffman stepped in to carry us all over the finish line.

A community of writers and editors offered support throughout the development of the manuscript, including Jamie Nicholson, Patrick O'Dowd, Peter Lee, Jennifer Kelly, and Margaret Ransom. Special thanks to Keith Banner for his friendship and honest criticism. Although not a horseman, he always knows when to give rein and when to shake the stick. Annise Montplaisir, Amy Gregory, Natalie Voss, Jen Roytz, Donna Brothers, and Michael Blowen generously shared their racing contacts.

A league of photographers and media executives helped make Landaluce's story come alive visually, including Amy Zimmerman, Tom Abahazy and Rayetta Burr of Benoit Photo, Jessica Whitehead, Mac McBride, Kate Lossen and Bobby Shifflett, Adam Coglianese, Lee Thomas, Darrin Munnerlyn, Katey Barrett and Tim Layden. Thanks also to Steve Stidham, Anne Eberhardt Keogh, and Monique Reavis Agress. Those who helped unearth video footage of Landaluce include Brien Bouyea, Bob Curran, Anthony Perrone, Mark Mandel, and Julie Townsend. A special thanks to Ric Waldman, Fabricio

Buffolo, and photographer Jordan Thomson, all of whom contributed to an in-depth understanding of Landaluce's female family, and to Roger Farrell, who still owns J. O.'s Elegance, the seventeen-year-old granddaughter of Seattle Slew's stablemate J. O. Tobin.

An entire backstretch of friends and family offered their support. For more than five years, my husband, Steve, observed his home and marriage being taken over by a dark bay filly and never complained. Cindi Weeks and a paint quarter horse named Nakoda tried to teach me dressage on many days when I'd been too long in front of a computer. Rudy Gillen and Barb Wathen offered comfortable lodging throughout the years it took to finish this race. Through it all, rescue dog Henry was a cheerful stablemate, waiting patiently as he slept in the backseat of a car or curled beneath my feet as we followed Landaluce's story wherever it took us.

Appendix A

Landaluce Pedigree

SEATTLE SLEW (USA) br. 1974	BOLD REASONING (USA) dkb/br. 1968	BOLDNESIAN (USA) b. 1963	BOLD RULER (USA) dkb/br. 1954
			ALANESIAN (USA) b. 1954
		REASON TO EARN (USA) b. 1963	HAIL TO REASON (USA) br. 1958
			SAILING HOME (USA) ch. 1948
	MY CHARMER (USA) b. 1969	POKER (USA) b. 1963	ROUND TABLE (USA) dkb/br. 1954
			GLAMOUR (USA) b. 1953
		FAIR CHARMER (USA) ch. 1959	JET ACTION (USA) ch. 1951
			MYRTLE CHARM (USA) b. 1946

STRIP POKER (USA) ch. 1967	BOLD BIDDER (USA) b. 1962	BOLD RULER (USA) dkb/br. 1954		NASRULLAH (GB) b. 1940
				MISS DISCO (USA) b. 1944
		HIGH BID (USA) b. 1956		TO MARKET (USA) ch. 1948
				STEPPING STONE (USA) b. 1950
	PANGE (GB) ch. 1955	KINGS BENCH (GB) b. 1949		COURT MARTIAL (GB) ch. 1942
				KINGS CROSS (GB) b. 1940
		YORK GALA (GB) b. 1939		HIS GRACE (GB) br. 1933
				PRINCESS GALAHAD (GB) ch. 1925

Courtesy www.pedigreequery.com

Appendix B

Landaluce Race Record

Landaluce

dkbbr. f. 1980, by Seattle Slew (Bold Reasoning)–Strip Poker, by Bold Bidder

Own.– French & Beal
Br.– Spendthrift Farm & Francis Kernan (Ky)
Tr.– D. Wayne Lukas

Lifetime record: 5 5 0 0 $372,365

23Oct82-8SA	fst 1 1/16	:23 :454 1:091 1:414	ⒻOak Leaf-G1	6 3	1hd 13 14 12	Pincay L Jr	117	*.05	92-10	Landaluce117² SophisticatedGirl115⁹ GrnjRn115½	Ridden out	7
11Oct82-8SA	fst 7f	:222 :45 1:09 1:214	ⒻAnoakia-G3	8 2	3nk 12 18 110	Pincay L Jr	123	*.10	91-15	Landaluce123¹⁰ Rare Thrill117¹½ Time of Sale120²¾	Easily	8
5Sep82-8Dmr	fst 1	:223 :46 1:104 1:353	ⒻDmr Debutante-G2	4 2	2½ 1hd 11½ 16½	Pincay L Jr	119	*.30	90-12	Landaluce119⁶½ IssuesN'Answers116⁴ GranjaReina113²	Easily	6
10Jly82-8Hol	fst 6f	:212 :434 :56 1:08	ⒻHol Lassie-G2	3 2	2½ 2½ 11½ 19	Pincay L Jr	117	*.30e	97-16	Landaluce117²¹ Bold Out Line115¹½ Barzell119½	Easy score	5
3Jly82-4Hol	fst 6f	:22 :443 :562 1:081	ⒻMd Sp Wt	6 2	11½ 13 16 17	Pincay L Jr	117	*.80	96-10	Landaluce117⁷ MidnightRapture116⁹ MissBigWig116½	Easily	7

Landaluce Race Record (*Champions: The Lives, Times, and Past Performances of America's Greatest Thoroughbreds: Champions from 1894–2015*, 4th ed. [New York: Daily Racing Form Press, 2016], 341).

Notes

Prologue

xi . . . a record twenty-four stakes races. Edward L. Bowen, *Legacies of the Turf: A Century of Great Thoroughbred Breeders,* vol. 2 (Lexington, KY: BloodHorse Publications, 2004), 71.

xi ". . . when you get a little old runt." Dr. Robert Copelan, telephone interview by the author, July 3, 2020.

xii ". . . He didn't have that big desire." Steven Crist, "Copelan Flourishes under Special Care," *New York Times,* November 4, 1982.

xii ". . . doing what he likes best." Russ Harris, "Copelan Trained Wrong," *New York Daily News,* November 6, 1982.

xii . . . usually mild-mannered. Mike Marten, "Hungry to Run," *Daily Racing Form,* November 26, 1982.

xii ". . . In his first few starts." Crist, "Copelan Flourishes."

xii . . . Keeneland's select summer sale. Keeneland's select yearling sale was held in July until 2002, after which it became a September event.

xiii . . . already third in earnings. "Money Leaders Horse Racing," *Miami News,* November 4, 1982.

xiii ". . . When you're that close to a horse." Andrew Beyer, "A Horse of a Lifetime Runs Painfully through Lukas' Dreams," *Washington Post,* January 7, 1983.

xiv ". . . wrapped his long legs around a high stool." J. A. Estes, "Five Weeks Late Kentucky Derby," *BloodHorse,* June 16, 1945.

xiv ". . . He would not hesitate." John W. Russell, "Fred Hooper: Architect of Achievement," *BloodHorse,* August 20, 2000.

xiv ". . . working high up with steel." Bowen, *Legacies of the Turf,* 65.

xiv ". . . unabashedly unsophisticated." Franz Lidz, "Breeder Goes the Distance Hanging around Horses," *Sports Illustrated,* December 1, 1997.

xiv . . . eyeballed mustangs shipped in from the Dakotas. Carlo DeVito, *D. Wayne: The High-Rolling and Fast Times of America's Premier Horse Trainer* (New York: Contemporary, 2002), 29–30.

xiv . . . broad-chested and sturdy. Anne Peters, "Pedigree Analysis: Olympia," *BloodHorse,* July 3, 2015.

xv . . . offered to boost the purse to $1 million. Russ Harris, "Copelan–Landaluce Could Be $1M Duel," *New York Daily News,* November 4, 1982.

xv . . . survived three heart attacks. Ibid.

xvi . . . never to think more than a race or two ahead. Steven Crist, "The Filly Who Runs Faster Than Colts," *New York Times,* October 25, 1982.

xvi ". . . I have had a lot of dreams." Harris, "Copelan–Landaluce."

xvi . . . the horse of his lifetime. Beyer, "A Horse of a Lifetime."

1. Leslie and Myrtlewood

Epigraph: Arnold Kirkpatrick, "He Brought Fun into the Game," *Thoroughbred Times,* April 13, 1990.

3 . . . as well as fifty-four stakes winners. Edward L. Bowen, *Legacies of the Turf: A Century of Great Thoroughbred Breeders,* vol. 2 (Lexington, KY: BloodHorse, 2004), 13.

4 . . . maintain an edge over his clients. Karen Mitchell LaBach, email to the author, September 14, 2020.

4 . . . when dealing with subordinates. Patrick Robinson, *Horsetrader: Robert Sangster and the Rise and Fall of the Sport of Kings,* with Nick Robinson (London: HarperCollins, 1993), 75.

4 . . . a dried and varnished bull penis. Henry Horenstein and Carol Flake, *Thoroughbred Kingdoms: Breeding Farms of the American Racehorse* (Boston: Bulfinch, 1990), 67.

4 ". . . knew he was a terrible rascal." Robinson, *Horsetrader,* 76.

4 . . . Kentucky Derby winner Jet Pilot. Bowen, *Legacies of the Turf,* 130.

4 . . . and dream of owning one. Joe Ward, "Leslie Combs II," *Louisville Courier-Journal,* April 27, 1980.

6 . . . first champion bred by the Combs family. Bowen, *Legacies of the Turf,* 140.

6 . . . first horse to be named champion sprinter. David L. Heckerman, Ruth Anne Carrell, and Milton C. Toby, "Fillies with Zip," *BloodHorse,* January 15, 1983.

6 . . . records at five different tracks. Bowen, *Legacies of the Turf,* 130.

6 . . . only once in her career. "Affectionately Earns Spurs among 'Amazons,'" *Paterson News,* June 29, 1965.

6 ". . . the greatest racing mare." Lewis H. Walter, "Myrtlewood Sets Mark to Win Motor City Purse," *Detroit Free Press,* August 23, 1936.

6 . . . never liked the whip. www.americanclassicpedigrees.com/myrtlewood .html.

6 . . . first champion bred in Leslie's own name. Bowen, *Legacies of the Turf,* 130.

7 . . . at age eighteen on Saint Patrick's Day. www.racingmuseum.org/hall -of-fame/myrtlewood.

8 . . . determined to buy it back someday. Robinson, *Horsetrader,* 76.

8 . . . said it was an accident. Mary Marshall, *Great Breeders and Their Methods: Leslie Combs II and Spendthrift Farm* (Neenah, WI: Russell Meerdink, 2008), 11.

8 . . . further removed from the Bluegrass. Kirkpatrick, "He Brought Fun."

8 . . . could never sit still. Sherry Hemman Hogan, "Spendthrift Then: An Interview with Leslie Combs II," *Kentucky Dossier,* May 1984.

9 . . . stood their own stallions. Advertisement in *Thoroughbred Record,* March 31, 1923.

9 . . . broodmares from England. "Foreign Horses Arrive," *Thoroughbred Record,* January 6, 1923.

9 . . . bred his first stakes winner. Bowen, *Legacies of the Turf,* 129.

9 . . . contracted malaria. Marshall, *Great Breeders,* 12.

9 . . . recovering at White Sulphur Springs. Ward, "Leslie Combs."

9 . . . Juliette loved horses. Marshall, *Great Breeders,* 14.

10 . . . she found her dead. "Cincinnati Expert Aids in Hunt to Find Killer of Huntington Resident," *Charleston Daily Mail,* October 18, 1936.

10 . . . woke Charles Baldwin. "Mrs. Enslow's Son, Charles B. Baldwin, Accused in Slaying," *Charleston Daily Mail,* October 25, 1936.

10 . . . Johnson found it odd. "Baldwin Trial Opens Monday," *Raleigh Register,* March 14, 1937.

10 . . . went to post in the Ashland Stakes. "Combs' Speedy Filly Captures $2,500 Stakes," *Louisville Courier-Journal,* October 18, 1936.

11 . . . motivated by robbery. "Hunt Clews [*sic*] in Enslow Death," *Charleston Daily Mail,* October 19, 1936.

11 . . . charged with first-degree murder. "Mrs. Enslow's Son."

11 . . . addiction to narcotics. "Baldwin Trial Opens."

11 . . . sought the death penalty. "Charles Baldwin's Trial for Slaying Mother Is Started," *Bluefield Daily Telegraph,* March 16, 1937.

11 . . . The crime was never solved. Marshall, *Great Breeders,* 15.

11 . . . By September, Leslie had moved. Sam W. Severance, "Kentucky Burgoo," *Louisville Courier-Journal,* September 3, 1937.

12 . . . availability of the old Hugh Fontaine Farm. John H. Clark, "Reminiscing with Leslie," *Thoroughbred Times,* April 8, 1988.

12 . . . gave him a toehold. W. C. Heinz and Clyde Hirt, "King of the Horse Traders," *Saturday Evening Post,* July 30, 1960.

12 ". . . One day I'm going to buy it." Robinson, *Horsetrader,* 76.

2. Cambridge Stables and the Spendthrift Connection

Epigraph: William H. Rudy, "Timbeau's Race Reminder of Coming Sales," *BloodHorse,* July 6, 1963.

13 . . . before dropping out. Mary Marshall, *Great Breeders and Their Methods: Leslie Combs II and Spendthrift Farm* (Neenah, WI: Russell Meerdink, 2008), 13.

13 . . . member of its varsity football team. John H. Clark, "Reminiscing with Leslie," *Thoroughbred Times,* April 8, 1988.

13 ". . . He is perhaps the only man." Russell Rice, "Only the Best Mares and Stallions Run on Spendthrift," *Lexington Herald-Leader,* January 15, 1967.

13 ". . . I couldn't kick, pass, or run." Clark, "Reminiscing."

13 . . . winner of the 1920 Rose Bowl. E. Benjamin Smith, "Remembering a Forgotten Upset," *Harvard Crimson,* October 28, 2011.

13 ". . . arguably the upset of the century." "David Skunks Goliath at Harvard," *New York Times,* October 29, 1921.

14 ". . . impossible formula." Smith, "Remembering."

14 . . . starting his first game. "Harvard Minus Kane Tomorrow," *Boston Globe,* October 28, 1921.

14 . . . Kernan might have faced. Royce N. Flippin III, email to the author, August 15, 2019.

14 ". . . go on down to Kentucky." Jobie Arnold, "Jobie Says," *Lexington Leader,* June 26, 1963.

14 . . . brothers who graduated from Harvard Law. "Alumni Board, Overseers Nominated," *Harvard Crimson,* January 11, 1938.

14 ". . . let himself get sidetracked." Paul Heffernan, "Personality: Builder of Pipelines in Wall Street," *New York Times,* June 9, 1957.

14 . . . would spend the next thirteen years. Ibid.

14 . . . the longest in the world. https://en.widipedia.org/wiki/TransCanada_pipeline.

14 ". . . breathing a bit easy." Heffernan, "Personality."

15 ". . . I've been interested in racing." Rudy, "Timbeau's Race."

15 ". . . quiet mannered." Heffernan, "Personality."

15 ". . . John Morris has the keenest eye." Rudy, "Timbeau's Race."

15 . . . later sold the handsome colt. Gene Wara, "Victory Morn Is Pick in Pan," *New York Daily News,* June 1, 1958.

16 ". . . We believe in going slowly." Rudy, "Timbeau's Race."

16 . . . putting himself in contention. Kent Hollingsworth, "Survey of 1958 Two-Year-Olds," *BloodHorse,* November 13, 1958.

16 . . . a filly from the first crop of Nashua. "Shuette's Liberty Belle," *Blood-Horse,* July 15, 1961.

16 ". . . a tough hussy [who] acted like a colt." "The Aiken Trials," *Blood-Horse,* March 24, 1962.

16 . . . election to the Jockey Club. Joe Nichols, "Miralgo First by Four Lengths in Rouge Dragon Hurdle at Aqueduct," *New York Times,* September 13, 1968.

16 ". . . As Cambridge has succeeded." Rudy, "Timbeau's Race."

17 ". . . a rather modest number of purchases," Ibid.

18 ". . . Strip Poker exceeded the ordinary price." Amy Gregory, "Landaluce," *Thoroughbred Record,* January 12, 1983.

18 . . . asked his brother to find a buyer. Ibid.

18 . . . a total of twelve stakes winners. Edward L. Bowen, *Legacies of the Turf: A Century of Great Thoroughbred Breeders,* vol. 2 (Lexington, KY: BloodHorse, 2004), 143–44.

19 ". . . walk away from a bright light." John Williams, interview by the author, October 3, 2019.

3. Seattle Slew Day

Epigraph: Barney Nagler, "Champion Slew Headed for Life of Luxurious Ease," *Daily Racing Form,* November 25, 1978.

20 . . . bitterly cold afternoon. Dan Mearns, *Seattle Slew* (Lexington, KY: BloodHorse, 2007), 116.

20 . . . listening to radio music. UPI, "Seattle Slew Flown into Spendthrift," *Madisonville Messenger,* November 30, 1978.

20 . . . second-highest impost. The top weight-carrying winner of the Stuyvesant was Man o' War, who toted 135 pounds in 1920. Steve Cady, "Seattle Slew Breezes to Victory as Racing Career Comes to End," *New York Times,* November 12, 1978.

21 . . . rejected from the prestigious Keeneland summer sale. Mearns, *Seattle Slew,* 12–13.

21 . . . wins in fourteen of his seventeen starts. Cady, "Seattle Slew Breezes."

21 . . . so sick he almost died. Steve Cady, "Seattle Slew Facing a Slow Recovery from Illness That Nearly Killed Colt," *New York Times,* January 18, 1978.

21 . . . at a crossroads. Mearns, *Seattle Slew,* 93.

21 . . . few horses recovered. Cady, "Seattle Slew Facing."

21 . . . a record $12 million. Mearns, *Seattle Slew,* 94.

22 . . . waited with his wife, Linda. John Williams, interview by the author, October 3, 2019.

22 . . . fed by a gold shovel. Maria Ridenour, "Big Crowd at Spendthrift, But Nashua Still King," *Lexington Herald-Leader,* November 26, 1978.

22 . . . a stakes win every two days. Steve Cady, "Slew at Stud: Courting the Big Money," *New York Times,* December 4, 1978.

22 . . . biggest rival, Gainesway. "Seattle Slew May Be Kentucky-Bound," *Lexington Herald-Leader,* January 31, 1978.

22 . . . capitalize on their uncertainty. Joe Hirsch, "Combs Group Pays $6M for Seattle Slew Half Interest," *Daily Racing Form,* February 18, 1978.

22 . . . considered conformationally superior. Mary Marshall, *Great Breeders and Their Methods: Leslie Combs II and Spendthrift Farm* (Neenah, WI: Russell Meerdink, 2008), 114.

22 . . . first breeder in history. Ed Bowen, email to the author, October 8, 2020.

22 . . . then-record $7 million. James Tuite, "$7.2-Million for 36 Shares Is Record," *New York Times,* October 5, 1975.

22 . . . monitored twenty-four hours a day. Ridenour, "Big Crowd."

23 . . . thought it was fitting. Associated Press, "Slew Settles in Spendthrift Quarters," *Paducah Sun,* November 30, 1978.

23 ". . . Welcome Home, Champ" banners. Maryjean Wall, "Horse of Dreams, Seattle Slew, Arrives in State for Stud Career," *Lexington Herald,* November 30, 1978.

24 . . . rolled in the hay. UPI, "Seattle Slew Flown."

24 ". . . Seattle Slew Day." Wall, "Horse of Dreams."

24 . . . crowd of 150. Logan Bailey, "Wooden Horse to Concentrate on Racing 'Slew' Homebreds," *Daily Racing Form,* December 4, 1978.

25 . . . paraded for the crowd. UPI, "Seattle Slew Flown."

25 . . . a private dinner. Sue Wahlgren, *Lexington Herald-Leader,* November 19, 1978.

25 . . . Fred Astaire tap-dance down the steps. Mary Marshall, *Great Breeders,* 32.

4. Slew in the Shed

Epigraph: Natalie Voss, "A Wild Ride with Seattle Slew," *Paulick Report,* October 4, 2016.

26 ". . . Mick, we have a little problem." John Williams, "Life Changer," *BloodHorse,* May 21, 2002.

26 . . . starting to turn gray. Chris McGrath, "I Had Black Hair until I Met Seattle Slew," *Thoroughbred Daily News,* April 21, 2019.

26 . . . forty-five world-class mares. All Thoroughbred matings are "live cover," meaning a physical breeding must take place, and artificial insemination is strictly prohibited. When Slew went to stud, Thoroughbred stallions customarily bred no more than forty-five mares in a single breeding season.

26 . . . qualify for fertility insurance. Steve Cady, "Slew at Stud: Courting the Big Money," *New York Times,* December 4, 1978.

26 ". . . the best guy that ever had hands." Voss, "A Wild Ride."

27 ". . . a kid in a candy shop." John Williams, interview by the author, October 3, 2019.

27 . . . one of only three horses. Dr. Patches beat Slew by a neck in the Paterson Handicap in 1978 carrying fourteen fewer pounds than the champion, and Exceller prevailed by a nose in a thrilling stretch drive in the Jockey Club Gold Cup (Bill Dwyre, "Two Horses Do Rare Feat, Then Meet," *Los Angeles Times,* September 16, 2008).

27 ". . . Without taking anything away." Billy Reed, "A Coup for Combs and Hunt," *Louisville Courier/Journal,* September 15, 1977.

27 ". . . every bit as popular." John Williams, email to the author, January 18, 2020.

27 ". . . Day after day." Cady, "Slew at Stud."

28 ". . . He lost a zest for life." Mary Marshall, *Great Breeders and Their Methods: Leslie Combs II And Spendthrift Farm,* (Neenah, WI: Russell Meerdink, 2008), 146.

28 . . . worth more than $50 million. Steve Cady, "A Team That Is Worth $100 Million," *New York Times,* December 15, 1979.

28 ". . . never been close." Marshall, *Great Breeders,* 149.

28 . . . called his father 'Mr. Combs.' Billy Reed, "World's Top Breeder, Combs, Had to Prove Himself to Dad First," *Louisville Courier-Journal,* April 8, 1979.

28 ". . . Goddammit, Brownell." Patrick Robinson, *Horsetrader: Robert Sangster and the Rise and Fall of the Sport of Kings,* with Nick Robinson (London: HarperCollins, 1993), 79.

28 . . . reached an impasse. Reed, "World's Top Breeder."

28 . . . could not have been more different. Robinson, *Horsetrader,* 79.

28 ". . . He decided to let me." Reed, "World's Top Breeder."

29 . . . initially approved of Linda. Ibid.

29 . . . all of Spendthrift's barren mares. Leon Rasmussen, "Linda Combs' Barren Mare Program Major Achievement," *Daily Racing Form,* November 11, 1976.

30 ". . . The first time I had to personally go to people." Reed, "World's Top Breeder."

30 ". . . got along famously." Williams interview.

30 . . . two out of three stallions succeeded. Cady, "Slew at Stud."

30 ". . . Instead of maneuvering." Reed, "World's Top Breeder."

30 ". . . a horse-crazy kid." McGrath, "I Had Black Hair."

30 . . . didn't think he needed a farm manager. John Williams, email to the author, February 3, 2020.

31 ". . . She was the starch." Voss, "A Wild Ride."

31 ". . . how important she was." Williams interview.

31 . . . a mare outside the shed. Virginia Anderson, "Seattle Slew: Still a Champ, and Rich, Too," *Lexington Herald-Leader,* April 1, 1985.

31 . . . mares in quick succession. Ron Mitchell, "Changed Market for Stallion Industry," *BloodHorse,* February 2, 2016.

31 ". . . at the critical moment." Williams, "Life Changer."

32 ". . . If it's too much trouble." Anderson, "Seattle Slew."

32 ". . . Old Fleet Flight." John Williams, email to the author, February 2, 2020.

32 ". . . raggedy taggedy." Anderson, "Seattle Slew."

33 ". . . He was the smartest horse." Williams interview.

33 . . . former exercise rider. Keith Chamblin, "More Than a Horse," *Blood-Horse,* April 18, 1997.

33 ". . . I turned left." Voss, "A Wild Ride."

33 ". . . I realized that it had been too long." Chamblin, "More Than a Horse."

33 ". . . He missed his job." Williams interview.

33 ". . . seemed to eat more than the others." Logan Bailey, "Hail to the Conquering Hero, Slew Returns to Kentucky," *Daily Racing Form,* November 30, 1978.

33 . . . had to occasionally muzzle him. Ed Ryan, "Bed of Roses," *Louisville Courier-Journal,* May 6, 1984.

34 ". . . all the way to Ironworks Pike." Williams interview.

34 ". . . in one hectic ninety-minute span." Cady, "Slew at Stud."

34 ". . . This is standard procedure." Andrew Beyer, "Slew Crew Went
out on a Limb and Came Back with the Goods," *Washington Post,*
May 4, 1983.

34 . . . owners kept twenty shares. Cady, "Slew at Stud."

35 . . . embarked on various partnerships. Logan Bailey, "Slew O'Gold Prod-
uct of Unusual Arrangement," *Daily Racing Form,* April 28, 1983.

35 . . . a share or 'season.' A share is a lifetime breeding right to a stallion. A
season is a single breeding opportunity in a given year. Sharehold-
ers may choose to sell a season while retaining the share.

35 ". . . short and compact." Tom Roach, owner of broodmare Parrish Princess, described her in this way, and added, "John Williams . . . has
told me . . . Strip Poker was built much the same" (Jon White,
"Ironic Match," *Daily Racing Form,* December 5, 1982).

35 ". . . She wasn't big." John Williams, telephone interview by the author,
May 31, 2019.

35 . . . caught the eye of John Gaines. Pange turned out to be an excellent
producer for Gaines. Her filly Sensibility foaled Tree of Knowledge, dam of future champion grass horse Theatrical (Ellen Parker,
"Pange," www.reines-de-course.com/pange).

36 . . . first-ever yearling consignment. Logan Bailey, "Strip Poker in Blue
Chips Now That She's Played Hand," *Daily Racing Form,* October
18, 1982.

36 . . . left her barn on the historic Elmendorf land. John Williams, email
to the author, May 23, 2020.

36 . . . the mare was scrubbed. Chris Scherf, "Where Hath Love Gone?,"
Louisville Courier-Journal, February 26, 1978.

36 ". . . hardly bigger than a one-room summer cabin." Cady, "Slew at Stud."

5. April 11, 1980

Epigraph: Mary Marshall, *Great Breeders and Their Methods: Leslie Combs II
and Spendthrift Farm* (Neenah, WI: Russell Meerdink, 2008), 120.

37 . . . won a chicken dinner. John Williams, *Spendthrift Farm Newsletter,*
February 1983.

38 . . . nearly two hundred born. Ibid.

38 . . . quiet and reserved. Nichols was so taciturn that his future boss at Shad-
well Farms, Sheikh Hamdan bin Rashid Al Maktoum, named the
stallion Quiet American after him. (Chris McGrath, "Keeneland
Life's Work Oral History Project, No. 4," *Thoroughbred Daily News,*
December 21, 2019).

38 . . . a special place in Nichols's heart. Rick Nichols, telephone interview by the author, June 4, 2019.

38 . . . more than four hundred broodmares stabled at Spendthrift. The mare count at Spendthrift in the 1970s and 1980s was as high as 600, and press reports throughout that time offer varying numbers. There were at least 425 mares at Spendthrift when Seattle Slew began his stud career, according to the *New York Times* (Steve Cady, "Slew at Stud: Courting the Big Money," *New York Times,* December 4, 1978).

39 ". . . totally dedicated to the farm." Sherry Hemman Hogan, "Spendthrift Now," *Kentucky Dossier,* May, 1984.

39 . . . attended all foalings. John Williams, interview by the author, October 3, 2019.

39 . . . Queensway drive garage. Dr. Tom Riddle, email to the author, June 10, 2019.

39 . . . lived on a third farm. Rick Nichols, telephone interview by the author, June 4, 2019; Steve Johnson, telephone interview by the author, June 13, 2019.

39 ". . . It was as good a piece of land." Williams interview.

40 . . . linden trees planted by Daniel Swigert. Joe Ward, "Leslie Combs II," *Louisville Courier-Journal,* April 27, 1980.

40 . . . sixth stall on the left. Williams interview.

40 . . . her own female line. Thoroughbred families are traced through female lines, not through sire lines. Offspring from the same broodmare are considered half siblings. Offspring from the same sire are not considered similarly related.

40 . . . survived the cut. Logan Bailey, "Spendthrift Farm Plans Broodmare Reduction," *Daily Racing Form,* June 28, 1976.

40 . . . fillies usually were quicker. Nichols interview.

41 ". . . The ones who survive." Marshall, *Great Breeders,* 120.

41 . . . the mares Ferly, Sassabunda, and Kadesh. Edward L. Bowen, *Legacies of the Turf: A Century of Great Thoroughbred Breeders,* vol. 2 (Lexington, KY: BloodHorse, 2004), 141–44.

6. Growing Up

Epigraph: Amy Gregory, "Landaluce," *Thoroughbred Record,* January 12, 1983.

42 . . . a hidden, underground river. Melanie Ramey, interview by the author, October 3, 2019.

42 . . . a group of twelve. *Spendthrift Farm Report,* September 1982.

42 . . . again traveled in a van. John Williams, email to the author, May 28, 2019.

43 . . . made a trip from New York. Rick Nichols, telephone interview by the author, June 4, 2019.

43 . . . also served as Kernan's bloodstock advisor. Gregory, "Landaluce."

43 . . . weaning took place gradually. *Spendthrift Farm Report,* October 1980.

43 . . . returned to the Bluegrass in the fall. Gregory, "Landaluce."

43 . . . left the Old Widener farm. John Williams, telephone interview by the author, May 31, 2019.

43 . . . bred in the spring. Jon White, "Hollypark Notes," *Daily Racing Form,* December 12, 1982.

45 . . . hired as a relief groom. Sandy Shaw, "A True Friend," June 1, 2004, www.seattleslew.com/articles.aspx?aid+1.

45 ". . . He could almost talk." Ibid.

45 . . . agents from Europe arrived. John Williams, email to the author, December 2, 2019.

45 . . . to keep their coats from getting sunburned. Rick Nichols, telephone interview by the author, June 13, 2019.

46 ". . . get spooked by those big, green things." John Williams, email to the author, December 2, 2019.

46 . . . measured for a custom halter. John Williams, telephone interview by the author, December 5, 2019.

46 . . . asked to help hand-walk yearlings. Shaw, "A True Friend."

46 . . . hoped that Strip Poker's filly. Sandy Shaw, email to the author, November 22, 2019.

46 . . . a severe case of colic. White, "Hollypark Notes."

46 ". . . She died the dam of Clout." John Williams, telephone interview by the author, May 31, 2019.

46 . . . Leslie's cruelty to the couple. Patrick Robinson, *Horsetrader: Robert Sangster and the Rise and Fall of the Sport of Kings,* with Nick Robinson (London: HarperCollins, 1993), 79.

47 . . . Leslie resented Brownell and Linda's success. Mary Marshall, *Great Breeders and Their Methods: Leslie Combs II and Spendthrift Farm* (Neenah, WI: Russell Meerdinck, 2008), 151.

7. Wayne and Terlingua

Epigraph: Christina Bossinakis, *Sermon on the Mount: The Wisdom and Life Experiences of Hall of Fame Trainer D. Wayne Lukas* (Lukas Enterprises, 2019), 90.

51 . . . walked out with a single horse. Ross Staaden, *Winning Trainers: Their Road to the Top* (Perth, Australia: Headway, 1991), 76.

51 . . . trainer of the year five times. Carlo DeVito, *D. Wayne: The High-Rolling and Fast Times of America's Premier Horse Trainer* (New York: Contemporary, 2002), 59.

51 . . . any kind of success worth having. Staaden, *Winning Trainers*, 40–41.

51 . . . won a Thoroughbred stakes. Neil Milbert, "It's the Ride of His Life," *Chicago Tribune*, October 20, 2002.

52 ". . . I ran myself just about ragged." DeVito, *D. Wayne*, 61.

52 . . . urging him to do just that. Ibid.

52 ". . . box office horse." Ibid., 53

52 . . . reasons for Wayne to switch. Staaden, *Winning Trainers*, 41–42

53 ". . . I'd won the NCAAs." William Nack, "While the Rest of the World Sleeps," *Sports Illustrated*, May 6, 1985.

53 ". . . All successful people." Carol Flake, "Profiles: The Intensity Factor," *New Yorker*, December 26, 1988.

53 . . . former starting gate attendant. DeVito, *D. Wayne*, 52.

53 . . . helping him make the move. Staaden, *Winning Trainers*, 42

53 ". . . to cross the barrier." Flake, "Profiles."

53 . . . steady stream of yearlings. DeVito, *D. Wayne*, 63.

53 ". . . on a whim." Staaden, *Winning Trainers*, 42.

53 ". . . oil, construction, land development and banking." Ibid., 35–36.

54 . . . longtime friend Clyde Rice. DeVito, *D. Wayne*, 29–30.

54 . . . ten-point rating system. Staaden, *Winning Trainers*, 71.

54 . . . Rod Kaufman, trained her dam. Tom Hall, "The Speedy Terlingua, Dam of Storm Cat," *BloodHorse*, February 14, 2018.

54 . . . set a track record. William Leggett, "They're Toos of a Kind," *Sports Illustrated*, September 18, 1978.

54 ". . . I always felt you had to." Demmie Stathoplos, "A Swell Dame Wins the Beldame," *Sports Illustrated*, October 20, 1986.

54 ". . . I could see her." Maryjean Wall, "Lukas, Terlingua Return to Scene of $275,000 Keeneland 'Steal,'" *Lexington Herald*, October 10, 1978.

55 . . . began to worry. Leggett, "They're Toos"

55 ". . . He had balloons." Bossinakis, *Sermon on the Mount*, 91

55 . . . even had pennies minted. Wall, "Lukas, Terlingua."

55 . . . sold on the final night. Hall, "The Speedy Terlingua."

56 . . . called Bob French. Amy Gregory, "An Encore Performance," *Thoroughbred Record*, July 21, 1982.

56 ". . . This sounds crazy." Leggett, "They're Toos."

56 . . . escorted by four Kentucky state troopers. Bossinakis, *Sermon on the Mount,* 91.

56 . . . sale average was $87,000. Staaden, *Winning Trainers,* 42.

56 ". . . I always wanted to own." Joe Hirsch, "French's '79 Derby Dream Centers on Filly Terlingua, " *Daily Racing Form,* August 12, 1978.

56 ". . . Tom Gentry never knew." DeVito, *D. Wayne,* 76.

56 ". . . You've been there long enough." Flake, "Profiles."

8. Thoroughbreds All the Way

Epigraph: William Nack, "While the Rest of the World Sleeps," *Sports Illustrated,* May 6, 1985.

57 . . . Each morning by 4:20 a.m. Lesley Visser, "Wire to Wire Winner (Almost)," *Boston Globe,* May 6, 1988.

57 . . . By 5:00 a.m., he expected. Carol Flake, "Profiles: The Intensity Factor," *New Yorker,* December 26, 1988.

57 ". . . He orders a Coke." D. Wayne Lukas Kentucky Derby Museum exhibit, viewed April 20, 2019.

57 ". . . My work is my entertainment." Alan Greenberg, "A Man in Love with His Work," *Los Angeles Times,* March 29, 1979.

57 . . . Arriving at Hollywood Park in early 1978. Ross Staaden, *Winning Trainers: Their Road to the Top* (Perth, Australia: Headway, 1991), 43.

57 . . . more than a hundred horses. Jacqueline Kiser, "Lukas' Derby Hopes Ride with Partez," *LaCrosse Tribune,* May 2, 1982.

57 . . . managed to land among the top five. Bill Christine, "Lukas Simply Ignores His Detractors," *Los Angeles Times,* July 31, 1982.

57 ". . . I still have to pinch myself." Howard Senzell, "Syndication Easy Pill for Lukas to Swallow," *Daily Racing Form,* October 23, 1980.

58 . . . he was called 'Mr. Clean.' Carlo DeVito, *D. Wayne: The High-Rolling and Fast Times of America's Premier Horse Trainer* (New York: Contemporary, 2002), 66.

58 ". . . Even the dirt . . . looks clean." Greenberg, "A Man in Love."

58 . . . bathed his favorites in Breck shampoo. https://thevaulthorseracing .wordpress.com/2011/06/04/following-terlingua.

58 ". . . Old horsemen made fun of him." John Williams, interview by the author, October 3, 2019.

58 ". . . He has a great eye." Neil Milbert, "It's the Ride of His Life," *Chicago Tribune,* October 20, 2002.

58 . . . Instead of standing at the clocker's platform. Staaden, *Winning Trainers,* 65.

58 . . . a natural development of speed. Flake, "Profiles."

58 ". . . Some of these races are won." Nack, "While the Rest."

59 ". . . Horses thrive on routine." Joe Hirsch, "Muttering at Head of Lukas' Class," *Daily Racing Form,* April 29, 1982.

59 . . . setting another record. Senzell, "Syndication."

59 . . . faster than Triple Crown–winner Affirmed. Flake, "Profiles."

59 ". . . She put us on the map." Stan Hochman, "A Most Satisfying Sunday," *Philadelphia Daily News,* May 9, 1988.

59 . . . They were hooked. Joe Hirsch, "French's '79 Derby Dream Centers on Terlingua," *Daily Racing Form,* August 12, 1978.

60 ". . . I guess I'm going to have to win." Maryjean Wall, "Lukas, Terlingua Return to Scene of $275,000 Keeneland 'Steal,'" *Lexington Herald,* October 10, 1978.

60 ". . . When a horse named Swaps." Steven Crist, "Horse Racing: An Industry Confronting Transition," *New York Times,* December 21, 1982.

61 . . . In 1959. Ron Hale, "History Challenge: Hollywood Park a Launching Point for Stars," *Daily Racing Form,* December 13, 2012.

61 ". . . The faithful at Belmont." Crist, "Horse Racing."

61 . . . two strikes against them. Steven Crist, "The Gold Rush at Belmont," *New York Times,* September 18, 1982.

61 . . . the Norfolk for colts, and the Oak Leaf for fillies. The Norfolk is now known as the American Pharoah Stakes, and the Oak Leaf was renamed the Chandelier Stakes in 2012. Both are currently Grade One races.

61 . . . not awarded Grade One status. www.toba.org/graded-stakes.

62 . . . After her score in the Hollywood Lassie. Bob Hebert, "June Darling Easy Winner of Fifth Stakes," *Los Angeles Times,* October 18, 1970.

62 . . . Injured in the barn. "Gardenia to $19 Eggy—Forward Gal Third," *New York Daily News,* November 8, 1970.

62 ". . . thus wrapped up the . . . championship." Jim McCulley, "Forward Gal Cops Frizette," *New York Daily News,* October 13, 1970.

62 ". . . It's much deeper." Joe Hirsch, "Belmont," *Daily Racing Form,* September 27, 1978.

63 ". . . The filly is much better." Jenny Kellner, UPI, "Top-Ranked Jockey Wins Less in East," *Kenosha News,* October 11, 1978.

63 ". . . Whatever wins in California." Maryjean Wall, "'Mr. Clean' Still Thinks His Filly Terlingua Can Run for the Roses," *Lexington Herald,* February 6, 1979.

63 . . . Jay Hovdey suggested. Jay Hovdey, "She Vants to Be Alone," *Horsemen's Journal,* November 1982.

63 ". . . gave him respectability." DeVito, *D. Wayne,* 79.

63 . . . ahead of veterans Charlie Whittingham. Dave Koerner, "Lukas Is Not at All Surprised by the Result in Preakness," *Louisville Courier-Journal,* May 18, 1980.

64 . . . watched the filly Genuine Risk. Staaden, *Winning Trainers,* 48.

64 ". . . had a change of heart." Dave Koerner, "Lukas Thinks Codex Set to Pluck Preakness," *Louisville Courier-Journal,* May 16, 1980.

64 . . . crates of strawberries. Koerner, "Lukas Is Not at All Surprised."

64 . . . unraced in thirty-four days. Flake, "Profiles."

64 . . . the press questioned. Barney Nagler, "Cordero, Lukas Relieve Their Tension in Different Ways," *Daily Racing Form,* June 6, 1980.

64 . . . Nerud was the one calling the shots. DeVito, *D. Wayne,* 84.

64 . . . second-fastest time in the race. Koerner, "Lukas Is Not at All Surprised."

64 . . . view of the race was blocked. Maryjean Wall, "Controversy over Preakness Stretch Haunting Trainer," *Lexington Herald,* May 19, 1980.

65 . . . attract new owners. Staaden, *Winning Trainers,* 48.

65 ". . . I'd like to wake up." Wall, "Controversy over Preakness."

65 . . . replayed seventy-eight times. DeVito, *D. Wayne,* 84.

65 . . . purchased sixteen yearlings. Joe Bagan, *Lukas at Auction* (Denver: Sachs Lawlor, 1989), 24.

65 ". . . 'a steal' at that price." Jack Murray, "West Coast Stalwart Warner's," *Cincinnati Enquirer,* December 10, 1981.

65 . . . While at Keeneland. Bobby Barnett, telephone interview by the author, April 23, 2019.

66 . . . owned a home in Arcadia. Kiser, "Lukas' Derby Hopes."

66 . . . owned in partnership. Bill Dwyre, "Partez Made the Day for an Old Man and His Trainer," *Los Angeles Times,* May 3, 1981.

66 . . . A yellow legal pad. William Leggett, "Now It's Two for the Money," *Sports Illustrated,* December 21, 1981.

66 . . . seventeenth on the entry list. Rich Suwanski, "Barrera's Steaming after Flying Nashua's Wings Clipped," *Owensboro Messenger-Inquirer,* May 1, 1981.

66 . . . first Black-owned Derby entrant. James Robert Saunders, Monica Renae Saunders, *Black Winning Jockeys in the Kentucky Derby* (Jefferson, NC: McFarland, 2003), 107. The 1962 Kentucky Derby entrant Touch Bar was partly owned by African American Tom

Harbut, but his name was omitted from the program, and he was
not even permitted to attend the race (Ed Bowen, email to the
author, October 17, 2020).

66 . . . given little chance. Dwyre, "Partez Made the Day."

67 ". . . We've either got a saint or a sinner." Murray, "West Coast."

67 ". . . He can be a handful." Jay Hovdey, "A Queen and a Stalwart," *Thoroughbred Record,* November 4, 1981.

67 ". . . throw this race out." Leggett, "Now It's Two."

67 ". . . He's got a mind of his own." Hovdey, "A Queen."

67 ". . . This year is going to enlighten people." Suwanski, "Barrera's Steaming."

9. One Bay Filly

Epigraph: Chris McGrath, "I Had Black Hair until I Met Seattle Slew," *Thoroughbred Daily News,* April 21, 2010.

69 . . . Gentry hosted a party. Susan Rhodemyre and Steve Thomas, "Sales Notes and Quotes," *Thoroughbred Record,* July 22, 1981.

69 . . . Combs held a cocktail buffet. Grace Wing Bohne, "Before Horses Go on Block, Block Goes to Parties," *Miami Herald,* July 13, 1981.

69 . . . heiress Dolly Green. Suzy, "Lexington: Blue Grass and Long Green," *New York Daily News,* July 19, 1981.

70 ". . . If I give one a six." Carlo DeVito, *D. Wayne: The High-Rolling and Fast Times of America's Premier Horse Trainer* (New York: Contemporary, 2002), 116.

70 ". . . might have to call on." Wayne Lukas, interview by the author, October 6, 2019.

70 . . . made their way through Keeneland's barns. Barry Beal, telephone interview by the author, July 26, 2021.

70 ". . . We have the same goals." Joe Hirsch, "Muttering at Head of Lukas' Class," *Daily Racing Form,* April 29, 1982.

70 . . . French usually became. Lukas interview.

71 . . . John Williams watched. John Williams, email to the author, May 23, 2020.

71 . . . Wayne preferred to see a horse. John Williams, interview by the author, October 3, 2019.

71 ". . . I'm an angles guy." Lukas interview.

72 . . . Among the twenty-four yearlings. Of the twenty-four yearlings consigned by Spendthrift at Keeneland in July 1981, four were by Seattle Slew. Of these, two were Spendthrift-bred yearlings, and

two were bred by others with Spendthrift acting as agent in their preparation and sale in return for a commission.

72 . . . focusing instead on yearlings by more established stallions. Spendthrift Farm Yearling Brochure, 1981

72 . . . darker near her neck and shoulders. Jay Hovdey, "Another Ruffian?," *Thoroughbred Record,* July 14, 1982.

72 . . . enormous heart girth. Jay Hovdey, "She Vants to Be Alone," *Horsemen's Journal,* November 1982.

72 . . . long barrel and strong hindquarters. Jon White, "Landaluce's 21-Length Lassie Score Dazzles Rival Horsemen," *Daily Racing Form,* July 15, 1982.

72 . . . she stood over more ground. Mike Martens, "Is Lukas' Latest Lassie beyond Compare?," *Daily Racing Form,* July 10, 1982.

72 ". . . if . . . you walk around a horse three times." Bill Lyon, "For Lukas, a Second Chance," *Philadelphia Inquirer,* May 19, 1988.

72 ". . . [It's] a gut reaction." Lukas interview.

72 . . . the first 'nine' he had ever seen. Carol Flake, "Profiles: The Intensity Factor," *New Yorker,* December 26, 1988.

72 . . . couldn't find a flaw. Steven Crist, "The Filly Who Runs Faster Than Colts," *New York Times,* October 25, 1982.

72 . . . careful to conceal his interest. Lukas interview.

73 . . . thought Slew was a good bet. Crist, "The Filly Who Runs."

73 ". . . Looking at that pedigree." Hovdey, "She Vants."

73 . . . anticipating a price in the millions. Billy Reed, "From Rags to Riches: A Colt by Seattle Slew Might Lure $2 Million," *Louisville Courier-Journal,* July 19, 1981.

73 . . . many were already owned in partnership. Steve Cady, "Slew at Stud: Courting the Big Money," *New York Times,* December 4, 1978.

74 ". . . [It] was a long time to wait." Jon White, "Nobody's Laughing Now," *Daily Racing Form,* August 9, 1982.

74 ". . . just another stallion." Virginia Anderson, "Seattle Slew: Still a Champ, and Rich, Too," *Lexington Herald-Leader,* April 1, 1985.

74 . . . winner of a single minor stakes. Rab Hagin, email to the author, April 23, 2020.

74 ". . . not extremely attractive." Andrew Beyer, "Slew Crew Went out on a Limb and Came Back with the Goods," *Washington Post,* May 4, 1983.

74 . . . more like Muhammad Ali. Anderson, "Seattle Slew."

75 . . . divorce proceedings with Linda. Wing Bohne, "Before Horses Go."

75 . . . resigned from his post. Gary Cohn, "Combs Won't Be Renamed to Racing Panel," *Lexington Leader,* May 2, 1981.

75 . . . known as 'Combs' night.' Arnold Kirkpatrick, "He Brought Fun into the Game," *Thoroughbred Times,* April 13, 1990.

76 ". . . There was an air of disbelief." Dan Farley, "The Northern Dancer Mystique," *Thoroughbred Record,* July 22, 1981.

76 . . . sitting on the aisle with Bob French. Lukas interview.

76 . . . once pulled off one of his boots. Seth Reichlin, "Sudden Wealth Comes to Poor Community," *Victoria Advocate,* January 3, 1982.

76 . . . Nichols led Strip Poker's filly. Rick Nichols, telephone interview by the author, June 4, 2019.

76 . . . Wayne had not seen the filly. Lukas interview.

77 ". . . the most expensive four-horse string." Logan Bailey, "The Seattle Slews Hitting Market in Time for Killing," *Daily Racing Form,* July 15, 1982.

77 . . . paled in comparison with foreign interests. Kent Hollingsworth, "Ocean of Currency," *BloodHorse,* August 1, 1981.

77 . . . the only Seattle Slew filly sold. Wooden Horse Investments, a partnership including the Taylors and Hills, paid $300,000 for the only other Seattle Slew filly sold at Keeneland from his first crop, named Sweet Slew (ibid.).

78 . . . prices that inspired incredulity. "Sires of Keeneland Yearlings," *Thoroughbred Record,* July 22, 1981.

10. Stalwart Hopes

Epigraph: Ross Staaden, *Winning Trainers: Their Road to the Top* (Perth, Australia: Headway, 1991), 81.

79 ". . . a major female force." Bill Dwyre, "Marje Everett Dies at 90," *Los Angeles Times,* March 24, 2012.

79 ". . . Iron Lady of Inglewood." Robert Henwood, "Hollywood for Sale," *BloodHorse,* December 2, 1990.

80 ". . . We wanted a natural progression." Tom Robbins, email to the author, June 24, 2020.

80 . . . crafted its Arlington-Washington Futurity." Whitney Tower, "The Racing Lady of Chicago," *Sports Illustrated,* August 20, 1962.

80 . . . simulcasting and off-track betting were not yet legal in California. Off-track betting was legalized in New York in 1971. Simulcasting in the state began on a limited basis in 1979 (Steven Crist, "Horse

Racing: An Industry in Transition," *New York Times,* December 21, 1982).

80 ". . . went on the road to New York." Tom Robbins, telephone interview by the author, February 13, 2020.

81 . . . elevated to Grade One status. Despite its large purse, the Hollywood Futurity, like all new races, could not achieve graded status until it was run under the same conditions for at least two years (www.toba.org/graded-stakes). In 1981, this meant that a win in the Norfolk—the only Grade One race in the West for two-year-old colts—would have been necessary for any California-based juvenile in order to contend for an Eclipse Award without traveling east.

81 ". . . where the most money can be made." William Leggett, "Now It's Two for the Money," *Sports Illustrated,* December 21, 1981.

81 ". . . It's been my plan all along." Bill Christine, "Stalwart's Training Plan: Up Early, Start Late," *Los Angeles Times,* February 25, 1982.

82 ". . . Laffit told me afterward." Jay Hovdey, "A Queen and a Stalwart," *Thoroughbred Record,* November 4, 1981.

82 ". . . He's a little green still." Robert Henwood, "The Yellow Ribbon," *BloodHorse,* November 7, 1981.

82 . . . around the time Wayne renewed Stalwart's campaign. Wayne Lukas, interview by the author, October 6, 2019.

82 . . . galloped every day for a mile. Staaden, *Winning Trainers,* 91.

82 . . . acted like she wanted to run. Steven Crist, "The Filly Who Runs Faster Than Colts," *New York Times,* October 25, 1982.

83 ". . . the Full Out filly." Later named Sal Si Puede and owned by Beal and French, this filly never raced (Lukas interview).

83 ". . . a big mistake." "Stalwart, and Game," *BloodHorse,* December 5, 1981.

83 ". . . I love this colt." Leggett, "Now It's Two."

83 ". . . Stalwart and Cassaleria." "Stalwart, and Game."

84 ". . . Many Californians feel." Leggett, "Now It's Two."

84 ". . . I think he deserves it." "Stalwart, and Game."

84 ". . . Horses that are exclusively in California." Jack Murray, "West Coast Stalwart's Warner's," *Cincinnati Enquirer,* December 10, 1981.

84 . . . surpassed only by the great Buckpasser. "Stalwart, and Game."

85 ". . . The bottom line is dollars." Bill Christine, "Lukas Simply Ignores His Detractors," *Los Angeles Times,* July 31, 1982.

85 . . . fourth in the nation. Billy Reed, "Firestone (D'Accord) vs. Lukas (Stalwart)?," *Louisville Courier-Journal,* January 31, 1982.

85 ". . . convinced he could win the Derby." Joe Hirsch, "Writer's Connections Hurt Deeply," *Daily Racing Form,* April 22, 1982.

85 . . . brought in veterinarians throughout the country. Billy Reed, "Stalwart, the No. 1 Prospect for Derby, Retired with Injury," *Louisville Courier-Journal,* March 19, 1982.

85 ". . . I was in a daze." Hirsch, "Writer's Connections Hurt."

85 ". . . the best horse I've ever been associated with." Jon White, "Stalwart Suffers Tendon Injury," *Daily Racing Form,* March 10, 1982.

85 . . . difficult even to walk. Billy Reed, "Muttering Aside," *Louisville Courier-Journal,* April 29, 1982.

86 ". . . big, good-looking two-year-old filly." Bobby Barnett, telephone interview by the author, April 23, 2019.

86 . . . If all went well. Staaden, *Winning Trainers,* 91.

86 ". . . publicity . . . was 'immensely greater.'" Staaden, *Winning Trainers,* 48.

87 ". . . a bull of a little man." Jay Hovdey, "She Vants to Be Alone," *Horsemen's Journal,* November 1982.

87 ". . . I must have blinked." Ibid.

87 ". . . She always did everything right." Barnett interview.

87 . . . struck by Landaluce's intelligence. Laura Cotter, telephone interview by the author, August 11, 2018.

88 . . . a horse named Landalulu. "Latest Workouts," *Daily Racing Form,* May 12, 1982.

88 ". . . the best exercise rider in California." Steven Crist, "The Filly Who Runs Faster Than Colts," *New York Times,* October 25, 1982.

88 . . . misidentified the fast filly. "Latest Workouts," *Daily Racing Form,* May 23, 1982.

88 ". . . put a good foundation on her." Jay Hovdey, "Another Ruffian?," *Thoroughbred Record,* July 14, 1982.

88 ". . . She always ate up both of them." Joe Hirsch, "Reaching out and Touching Everyone," *Daily Racing Form,* December 13, 1982.

89 ". . . a Seattle Slew filly who can really run." Mike Marten, "Is Lukas' Latest Lassie beyond Compare?," *Daily Racing Form,* July 10, 1982.

89 ". . . 'smitten' with Landaluce." Billy Reed, "Landaluce: Dream That Died, but Not Easily Forgotten," *Louisville Courier-Journal,* November 30, 1982.

90 ". . . wanted a treat." Jon White, "Streaking Comet," *BloodHorse,* October 20, 2012.

90 ". . . she's very talented." Crist, "The Filly Who Runs."

90 . . . Cordero relaxed his hold. Hovdey, "Another Ruffian?"

90 ". . . She feels real good." Lukas interview.

90 ". . . I'll ride her anywhere." Crist, "The Filly Who Runs."

90 ". . . the first significant professional rider." Lukas interview.

90 ". . . it would be a long time." Hirsch, "Reaching Out."

11. Good from the Beginning

Epigraph: Laffit: All about Winning, documentary (Six Furlongs, 2005).

93 . . . more important things on his mind. Laffit Pincay, interview by the author, January 31, 2019.

93 . . . a crowd of nearly thirty-four thousand. "Hollywood Park Notes," *Daily Racing Form,* July 7, 1982.

93 . . . ultimate goal was to surpass his idol. Laffit did eclipse Shoemaker's record on December 10, 1999, at Hollywood Park aboard Irish Nip.

94 . . . keep his weight at or near 112 pounds. Ed Golden, "Pincay Mounts up for the First Time in 15 Years," *Paulick Report,* April 5, 2018. Laffit said he needed to "weigh 112 pounds, stripped, to tack 117."

94 . . . lose six pounds in four hours. Madelyn Cain, *Laffit: Anatomy of a Winner: The Biography of Laffit Pincay, Jr.* (Pasadena, CA: Affirmed, 2008), 134.

94 . . . A typical diet. Ibid., 73.

95 . . . pulled out a single peanut. Ibid., 111.

95 ". . . I never believed." Pincay interview.

95 . . . among the premier racing facilities. "Hollywood Park Nation's Leader In July 4 Stats," *Daily Racing Form,* July 10, 1982.

95 . . . activities in the infield. Joe Hirsch, "The Promoters," *Daily Racing Form,* June 14, 1982.

95 . . . Buffets were set up. Mike Marten, "Conway on the Move," *Daily Racing Form,* December 9, 1982.

96 . . . liked to bet long shots. http://letsgototheraces.blogspot.com/2013/12/goodbye-to-hollywood-park.html.

96 . . . came out of her office. Mike Seely, "Hollywood Park Is Shutting Down: Will Horse Racing Be Next?," *LA Weekly,* December 12, 2013.

96 . . . won more races here than anywhere. John Branch, "Down to the Wire at Hollywood Park," *New York Times,* December 14, 2013.

96 . . . wore his underwear inside out. Cain, *Laffit,* 29.

96 . . . saw the dark bay daughter of Seattle Slew for the first time. Pincay interview.

97 ". . . I know he can run a quarter mile." Carlo DeVito, *D. Wayne: The High-Rolling and Fast Times of America's Premier Horse Trainer* (New York: Contemporary, 2002), 63.

97 . . . it slipped his mind. Pincay interview.

97 ". . . You're really going to enjoy this." Jon White, "Something Special," *Daily Racing Form,* July 26, 1982.

98 ". . . earmarks of a stakes filly." "Sweep's Hollywood Park Graded Handicaps," *Daily Racing Form,* July 3, 1982.

98 . . . lone holdout who preferred Flameout. "Experts' Selections," *Daily Racing Form,* July 3, 1982.

98 . . . had all finished in the money. "Inside Track," *Spendthrift Farm Newsletter,* June 1982.

100 ". . . two-year-old filly without wings." Jon White, "Hollywood Park Notes," *Daily Racing Form,* July 7, 1982.

102 . . . fastest ever recorded on any U.S. track. Leon Rasmussen, "What Landaluce, 'Tango' Have in Common," *Daily Racing Form,* July 4, 1982.

102 ". . . Nobody, not even the oldest." White, "Hollywood Park."

102 . . . current world record-holder. Mike Marten, "Why Should He Sit on Bomb That Is About to Explode?," *Daily Racing Form,* July 3, 1982.

102 . . . might see another record-breaking performance. "11 Enter Saturday's Express Cap Renewal," *Daily Racing Form,* July 5, 1982.

102 . . . met twice before. Marten, "Why Should He Sit."

12. "She Just Went"

Epigraph: Carol Flake, "Profiles: The Intensity Factor," *New Yorker,* December 26, 1988.

104 . . . mane was too short. Jay Hovdey, "Another Ruffian?," *Thoroughbred Record,* July 14, 1982.

104 . . . front page of the *Daily Racing Form.* Jon White, "Landaluce Tops Lassie Stakes Line-up; Dash for Cash Derby on Alamitos Bill," *Daily Racing Form,* July 10, 1982.

104 . . . already predicting she'd win. Jon White, "Hollywood Park Notes," *Daily Racing Form,* July 7, 1982.

104 . . . Laura was responsible. Wayne Lukas, interview by the author, October 6, 2019.

105 ". . . You're my girl everything." Laura Cotter, telephone interview by the author, August 11, 2018.

106 . . . Barn 65 North. Mike Marten, "Lukas Dips into All-Star Line-up," *Daily Racing Form,* July 17, 1982.

106 . . . more nervous than the filly. Hovdey, "Another Ruffian?"

106 . . . track record for a two-year-old filly. Jon White, "'Princess' Gets Chance to Prove Herself," *Daily Racing Form,* June 30, 1982.

106 . . . potential starters against colts. Mike Marten, "Mulhall Has Some Nice Juveniles in Barn," *Daily Racing Form,* July 2, 1982.

106 . . . boarded mares at his Hedgewood farm. Logan Bailey, "Hedgewood Holds West Connection," *Daily Racing Form,* July 8, 1982.

106 . . . Barzell and Landaluce would hook up. Andrew Beyer, "Filly Appears History Bound," *Washington Post,* July 29, 1982.

107 . . . virtually no chance. Hovdey, "Another Ruffian?"

107 . . . crowd of more than forty thousand. Beyer, "Filly Appears."

107 . . . a tote-bag giveaway. Joe Hirsch, "The Promoters," *Daily Racing Form,* June 14, 1982.

107 . . . record for a nonholiday weekend. Mike Marten, "Landaluce May Be Racing's E.T. (Equestrian Turbojet)," *Daily Racing Form,* July 14, 1982.

107 . . . distributed the tote bags. Hirsch, "The Promoters."

107 ". . . like perfect ladies." Hovdey, "Another Ruffian?"

108 . . . would never miss another. Jay Hovdey, "She Vants to Be Alone," *Horsemen's Journal,* November 1982.

108 . . . managed to angle her out. Mike Marten, "Pincay Adds Finishing Touch," *Daily Racing Form,* July 7, 1982.

108 . . . leading jockey in the country. William Leggett, "Just Like Dear Old Dad," *Sports Illustrated,* August 9, 1982.

108 . . . unable ever to duplicate it. Laffit Pincay, interview by the author, January 31, 2019.

108 . . . eleven had returned winners. Steven Crist, "Trainer Relying on Quality," *New York Times,* April 10, 1983.

108 . . . with eighty-two horses in training. Bill Christine, "Trainer Lukas Simply Ignores His Detractors," *Los Angeles Times,* July 31, 1982.

108 ". . . sunlight made [her] dapples dance." Hovdey, "Another Ruffian?"

109 ". . . Bust her out of the gate." Ibid.

109 . . . the crowd gasped. Ibid.

110 . . . appeared to be anybody's race. David Schmitz, "Slew in the Breeding Shed," *BloodHorse,* May 14, 2002.

110 . . . anticipating another record. Hovdey, "Another Ruffian?"

110 . . . the colt reminded him of Landaluce. Madelyn Cain, *Laffit: Anat-
    omy of a Winner: The Biography of Laffit Pincay, Jr.* (Pasadena, CA:
    Affirmed, 2008), 168.
111 . . . would never be broken there. Landaluce's stakes record and margin
    of victory stood for thirty-one years, until Hollywood Park was
    shuttered in 2013. Her margin of victory was never exceeded at
    Hollywood, except in a 1974 match race between fillies Chris
    Evert and Miss Musket when the latter was eased, ironically, by
    Laffit Pincay (Leonard Koppett, "Chris Evert Victor," *New York
    Times,* July 21, 1974).
111 . . . inviting comparison with Secretariat's . . . Belmont Stakes win. Jon
    White, "Landaluce's 21-Length Lassie Score Dazzles Rival Horse-
    men," *Daily Racing Form,* July 15, 1982.
112 ". . . took off like a rocket ship." Leggett, "Just Like."
112 . . . didn't like anyone to use the whip. Cotter interview.
112 ". . . never seen anything like her." White, "Landaluce's 21-Length Lassie."
112 ". . . like her feet were floating." Marten, "Landaluce May Be."
113 . . . four and one-fifth seconds. Steven Crist, "The Filly Who Runs
    Faster Than Colts," *New York Times,* October 25, 1982.
113 . . . at the sixteenth pole. Marten, "Landaluce May Be."
113 ". . . fastest two-year-old I've ever seen." Leggett, "Just Like."
113 ". . . in another zip code." Jon White, "Hollywood Park Notes," *Daily
    Racing Form,* July 15, 1982.
113 . . . Mickey Taylor, who watched. Leggett, "Just Like."
113 ". . . It was the most impressive." Jon White, "Nobody's Laughing
    Now," *Daily Racing Form,* August 9, 1982.
113 . . . erupted in a standing ovation. Beyer, "Filly Appears."
113 . . . as he did with all his mounts. Lukas interview.
114 ". . . Let's just put that away." Hovdey, "Another Ruffian?"
114 . . . and to keep his dreams to himself. Crist, "The Filly Who Runs."
114 . . . calm as always while horses passed. White, "Landaluce's 21-Length
    Lassie."
114 . . . Tracks from all over the country. Jon White, "Hollywood Park
    Notes," *Daily Racing Form,* July 19, 1982.
114 ". . . People were talking about it." White, "Nobody's Laughing Now."
114 . . . Sandy Shaw, back in Ireland. Sandy Shaw, email to the author,
    December 13, 2019.
115 . . . Leggett, researching margins of victory. Leggett, "Just Like."
115 . . . a legion of writers and trainers. Hollywood Park trainers who com-
    pared Landaluce to Ruffian included John Sadler, who said, "she

might be one of the best fillies . . . in a generation . . . one of the best
of all time—another Ruffian," and Dave Vance, who noted, "I saw
Ruffian win the Sorority. . . . This filly does remind me of Ruffian."
Darrell Vienna went even further: "She might be the best horse
we've ever laid eyes on" (White, "Landaluce's 21-Length Lassie").

115 ". . . Not since Ruffian's two-year-old season." Beyer, "Filly Appears."

115 . . . Hovdey pointed out. Hovdey, "Another Ruffian?"

115 . . . surpassed Ruffian's best. Crist, "The Filly Who Runs."

115 ". . . most closely compared." Hovdey, "Another Ruffian?"

116 ". . . The one certain thing." Leggett, "Just Like."

116 ". . . a wave of respect." Eual Wyatt Jr., telephone interview by the
author, November 1, 2019.

116 . . . shown on late-night news. Leggett, "Just Like."

116 . . . *Down the Stretch.* "ESPN (National) and ON-TV (Local) Win
Eclipse Awards for Television," *Daily Racing Form,* December 15,
1982.

116 . . . received national coverage. Hovdey, "She Vants."

116 ". . . I've never encountered the reaction." Leggett, "Just Like."

117 ". . . making your first movie 'Gone With the Wind.'" Jay Hovdey,
"She, Too, Left Us Too Soon," *Spur,* February, 1983.

117 . . . Princess Lurullah bucked shins. White, "Landaluce 21-Length Lassie."

117 ". . . What would have happened?" Ibid.

117 . . . three-way tie for second place. "Hollypark Trainers' Race Begins
Week in 3-Way Tie," *Daily Racing Form,* July 14, 1982.

117 . . . told both the *BloodHorse* and the *Daily Racing Form.* Robert Hen-
wood, "Sangue Takes the Track," *BloodHorse,* July 17, 1982; Mike
Marten, "Short Fields for Trio of Stakes Likely This Weekend at
Hollypark," *Daily Racing Form,* July 13, 1982.

117 ". . . I really don't think." Hovdey, "Another Ruffian?"

118 ". . . a check with horsemen." Marten, "Short Fields."

118 ". . . She was really bucking." Jon White, "Landaluce 'On Hold' for
Juvenile; Erins Isle May Run in Sunset 'Cap," *Daily Racing Form,*
July 14, 1982.

118 ". . . I know it's three races." Henwood, "Sangue."

118 . . . left for Keeneland Wednesday. Mike Marten, "Lukas Dips into All
Star Lineup," *Daily Racing Form,* July 17, 1982.

118 ". . . it appears that . . . Landaluce . . . will not start." Jon White, "Landaluce Unlikely Starter For Juvenile Championship," *Daily Racing
Form,* July 15, 1982.

118 . . . On Saturday, the *Form* reported. Marten, "Lukas Dips."

13. Her Sister's Shoes

Epigraph: Jon White, "Nobody's Laughing Now," *Daily Racing Form,* August 9, 1982.

120 ". . . Leslie's barns." John Williams, *Spendthrift Farm Report,* August 1982.

120 ". . . Landaluce has silenced the critics." White, "Nobody's Laughing Now."

121 . . . he would never stable. John Williams, email to the author, November 18, 2019.

121 ". . . possibly the most attractive yearling." Williams, *Spendthrift Farm Report.*

121 ". . . He called a bunch of times." Karen Mitchell LaBach, email to the author, November 21, 2019.

121 . . . as much, if not more, attention than Merely's. Williams, *Spendthrift Farm Report.*

122 ". . . I looked at the film." William Leggett, "Just Like Dear Old Dad," *Sports Illustrated,* August 9, 1982.

122 ". . . Everyone told me." Jay Hovdey, "She Vants to Be Alone," *Horsemen's Journal,* November 1982.

122 . . . scouted yearlings like a coach. John Williams, interview by the author, October 3, 2019.

122 . . . was on the cover. Maryjean Wall, "During Sales, Dollars and Sense Are Equal to Lukas," *Lexington Herald,* July 21, 1982.

122 . . . top tier was still comprised of Europeans and Arabs. In 1981 and 1982, Lukas spent $6 million combined at Keeneland July, and was one of the sale's top American buyers. Although it's difficult to know exactly how much was spent by foreign interests, as they often bought through agents, conservative estimates put their totals in the neighborhood of $63 million during the same time period ("Top Spenders, Foreign Touch," *BloodHorse,* July 24, 1982; "Buyers at Keeneland," *Thoroughbred Record,* July 22, 1981).

124 . . . stood for nearly fifty years. "Golden Fleece by 3 Lengths," *New Straits Times,* June 3, 1982.

124 . . . appetite of foreign buying interests. This is not to say that foreign interests ignored Slew's bloodlines or offspring entirely. BBA privately bought Lomond, a half brother to Slew by Northern Dancer, in 1981 to avoid dueling with the Arabs at public auction (Patrick Robinson, *Horse Trader: Robert Sangster and the Rise and Fall of the Sport of Kings,* with Nick Robinson [London: Harper-

Collins, 1993], 200). BBA also bought an Affirmed colt at Keene-land in 1982 out of Slew's dam My Charmer as well as two Seattle Slew fillies ("Top Spenders," *BloodHorse*). Arab interests also pur-chased a Seattle Slew filly in 1982 for $800,000. Niarchos bought Seattle Song from Slew's second crop for the bargain price of $320,000. But in 1981 and 1982, while the three foreign buying groups spent a minimum of nearly $33 million combined on Northern Dancer–line yearlings at Keeneland's July select sale, they spent only approximately $2 million on Seattle Slew's.

124 . . . regain their title. "Spendthrift, Top Seller," *BloodHorse*, July 24, 1982.

124 . . . named horse of the meeting. "Drill Has Landaluce Honed for Debutante," *Daily Racing Form*, September 1, 1982.

124 . . . sat in his customary spot. John Williams, *Spendthrift Farm Report*, July 1982.

124 . . . the fireworks began. Kent Hollingsworth, "Exotic Prices, and Also Buyers," *BloodHorse*, July 24, 1982.

124 . . . syndicating in the $30 million range. Kent Hollingsworth, "Ocean of Currency," *BloodHorse*, August 1, 1981.

124 . . . Sheikh Mohammed folded. Logan Bailey, "Sangster and Partners Bid Record $4.25 Million for Nijinsky Yearling," *Daily Racing Form*, July 20, 1982.

125 . . . bought twenty-seven yearlings. Joe Bagan, *Lukas at Auction* (Den-ver: Sachs-Lawlor, 1989), 57–58.

125 . . . still paled in comparison. Lukas's total yearling purchases at public auction went from $3.6M in 1982 to $9.4M just a year later. By 1985, Lukas spent a total of $17 million (Ibid., 288). But during this same time, foreign spending at Keeneland alone increased from $56 million in 1983 ("Foreign Investors Dominant," *Blood-Horse*, July 23, 1983) to $77 million in 1984 ("Keeneland Buy-ers," *BloodHorse*, July 28, 1984).

125 . . . buried on the old Elmendorf land. www.tbheritage.com/ TurfHallmarks/Graves/cem/GraveMattersGreenGates.html.

125 . . . record for a first-year stallion. Hollingsworth, "Exotic Prices."

125 . . . Spendthrift's sale-topper. Williams, *Spendthrift Farm Report*.

125 . . . new world record. "Highest Priced Yearlings," *Daily Racing Form*, December 10, 1982.

126 ". . . the one I really wanted." Susan Rhodemyre, "Sales Notes," *Thor-oughbred Record*, July 21, 1982.

126 . . . her close personal relationship. Hollingsworth, "Exotic Prices."

127 ". . . I just had to have her." Hovdey, "She Vants."

127 . . . Williams, observing the bidding. Williams interview.

127 . . . topped the $1 million threshold. "Highest Priced Yearlings."

127 . . . four of the top fifteen. Hollingsworth, "Exotic Prices."

127 . . . could hardly have dreamed. John Williams, telephone interview by the author, May 31, 2019.

127 . . . prices behind only those of Northern Dancer. "The Dancer's Lure," *BloodHorse,* July 24, 1982.

128 . . . average $1.7 million. "Keeneland Sires," *BloodHorse,* July 28, 1984.

128 . . . six Grade One winners. Jana Nemeckova, "Seattle Slew," Horse Racing Library, www.racing-library.org/sires-seattle-slew.html.

128 . . . reclaimed its title. "Spendthrift, Top Seller."

128 . . . yearling average nearly double. "The Dancer's Lure."

128 . . . cut his in half. Ibid.

128 . . . For the next several years. John Williams, "Life Changer," *Blood-Horse,* May 21, 2002.

129 . . . farrier Beach Faulkner. John Williams, email to the author, November 18, 2019.

14. Miss California Becomes Miss America

Epigraph: *World News Tonight,* courtesy of ABC News archives, featuring Ray Gandolf, aired September 6, 1982.

130 ". . . I'm not a superstitious man." William Leggett, "Just Like Dear Old Dad," *Sports Illustrated,* August 9, 1982.

130 ". . . The thought of being in a plane." Jay Hovdey, "Like Ruffian, in the Worst Way," *Thoroughbred Record,* December 1, 1982.

131 ". . . only a chip shot away." 2019 Del Mar Media Guide, dmtc.com /media/guides.

131 ". . . When she went to the track." Laura Cotter, telephone interview by the author, August 11, 2018.

131 . . . Barnett took a group of Lukas runners. Bobby Barnett, telephone interview by the author, April 23, 2019.

131 . . . while setting a stakes record. Jon White, "Attention Getter," *Daily Racing Form,* August 16, 1982.

132 ". . . With the best weather." Jay Hovdey, "Another Ruffian?," *Thoroughbred Record,* July 14, 1982.

133 . . . In the grandstand, Klein bumped into. William Nack, "Another View from the Top," *Sports Illustrated,* May 9, 1988.

133 . . . starting out in the used-car business. Carlo DeVito, *D. Wayne: The High-Rolling and Fast Times of America's Premier Horse Trainer* (New York: Contemporary, 2002), 97.

133 ". . . one of the most powerful." Steve Thomas, "Death of Eugene Klein," *BloodHorse,* March 17, 1990.

133 . . . within the next six years. Jay Hovdey, "Gene Klein Getting out of Racing," *Los Angeles Times,* June 10, 1989.

133 ". . . he proved you don't have to belong." Barry M. Horstman and Dave Distel, "Ex-Charger Owner Klein Dead at 69," *Los Angeles Times,* March 13, 1990.

133 ". . . Landaluce broke the ice." Wayne Lukas, interview by the author, October 6, 2019.

134 . . . near-record crowd. Jon White, "Landaluce, Muttering, Rock Softly Star in Weekend Action at Del Mar," *Daily Racing Form,* September 8, 1982.

134 ". . . I could cry." Bill Christine, "The Wrong Sex," *Los Angeles Times,* August 11, 1982.

134 ". . . It is our loss." "Landaluce Scheduled to Compete in Rich Del Mar Debutante Sunday," *Daily Racing Form,* September 1, 1982.

134 ". . . good news for the fans." Jon White, "Lukas Hoping This Will Be Beginning of Lucky Streak," *Daily Racing Form,* September 4, 1982.

134 ". . . liable to lap her opponents." Jon White, "Nobody's Laughing Now," *Daily Racing Form,* August 9, 1982.

134 . . . a twenty-five-year-old strawberry blonde. Louis Toscano, "Miss California, Debra Sue Maffett, a blond Texan Who . . .," UPI Archives, September 12, 1982.

134 . . . all-time record at Del Mar. White, "Landaluce, Muttering."

134 . . . programs sold out. Bill Christine, "Landaluce Has It All Her Way," *Los Angeles Times,* September 6, 1982.

134 . . . no intention of cashing them. Jon White, "Graceful Landaluce Remains the Perfect Lady in Victory," *Daily Racing Form,* September 8, 1982.

135 ". . . the most exciting two-year-old." Leggett, "Just Like Dear Old Dad."

136 ". . . With Landaluce starting." "Drill Has Landaluce Honed for Debutante," *Daily Racing Form,* September 1, 1982.

136 ". . . She went five furlongs. Ibid. At least one of these fractions were erroneous, as they do not add up to the correct final workout time. Assuming the first three mentioned are correct, Landaluce had to have run the final furlong in 11 1/5.

136 . . . no supplementary nominations. Robert Henwood, "At Del Mar: A Weekend Double," *BloodHorse*, September 11, 1982.

137 ". . . train her to be speed-crazy." Jay Hovdey, "She Vants to Be Alone," *Horsemen's Journal*, November 1982.

137 ". . . Unlike her daddy." *World News Tonight* video.

137 ". . . stepped off a plane." Steven Crist, "The Gold Rush at Belmont," *New York Times*, September 18, 1982.

137 . . . Such was Wayne's regard. Steven Crist, "Island Whirl in Belmont Upset," *New York Times*, September 5, 1982.

137 ". . . watchful as a nervous chaperone." *World News Tonight* video.

139 . . . confessed he had butterflies. Jon White, "She Slew Them Again," *Thoroughbred Record*, September 8, 1982.

139 ". . . Landaluce craze." Hovdey, "She Vants."

139 ". . . almost on her saddle." Robert Henwood, "At Del Mar: A Weekend Double," *BloodHorse*, September 11, 1982.

139 . . . let Luce run her own race. White, "Graceful Landaluce."

139 . . . prohibitive 3–10 favorite. White, "Landaluce, Muttering."

139 . . . first minus show pool. Most states require a minimum payout of five percent on a show wager. A minus show pool is created when so much money is bet on a favorite to show that the track must pay out more than it received to "cover" the bets at the guaranteed minimum (Scott Jagow, "'Show Us the Money?' The Plight of a Simple Wager," *Paulick Report*, July 12, 2017).

139 . . . without perspiring at all. Henwood, "At Del Mar."

139 ". . . few dollars." Cotter interview

140 . . . did not change leads. Henwood, "At Del Mar."

140 . . . pleased that the filly was able to rate. Hovdey, "She Vants."

140 ". . . on her own." White, "Graceful Landaluce."

141 . . . switched leads perfectly. Ibid.

141 . . . only had to show her the whip. White, "Landaluce, Muttering."

141 ". . . methodical and businesslike." Henwood, "At Del Mar."

141 ". . . a Derby contender." Bobby Barnett, interview by the author, October 6, 2019.

141 ". . . If ever there was a filly." Cotter interview.

141 ". . . Landaluce is awesome." *World News Tonight*, courtesy of ABC News archives, featuring Dick Schaap, aired September 12, 1982.

141 . . . wasn't even breathing hard. Hovdey, "She Vants."

141 . . . not even a patch of sweat. Henwood, "At Del Mar."

141 ". . . smooth, and nearly effortless." Hovdey, "Like Ruffian."

141 ". . . she could have gone much faster." White, "Graceful Landaluce."

141 ". . . was just galloping." "Landaluce Lives up to Reputation," *Miami Herald,* September 7, 1982.

141 . . . In the winner's circle. *World News Tonight* video, September 6, 1982.

142 ". . . She's the best." Henwood, "At Del Mar."

142 ". . . extra bright. . . . It wasn't a hard race." White, "Graceful Landaluce."

142 ". . . as good as I've seen." Christine, "Landaluce Has It All."

142 . . . checked on their Seattle Slew weanlings. *World News Tonight* video, September 12, 1982.

142 . . . Fan mail arrived daily. Jay Hovdey, "She, Too, Left Us Too Soon," *Spur,* February 1983.

143 ". . . going to the prom." *World News Tonight* video, September 12, 1982.

143 ". . . As she soared higher." Jay Hovdey, "Like Ruffian."

143 ". . . an international celebrity." Joe Hirsch, "1982 Racing in Review," *American Racing Manual* (Daily Racing Form, 1983 ed.), 66.

143 . . . the same white swimsuit. Toscano, "Miss California."

143 ". . . possible Derby winner." *World News Tonight* video, September 12, 1982.

143 . . . a silver evening gown. Toscano, "Miss California."

143 ". . . a West Coast year." Crist, "The Gold Rush."

144 ". . . California horses are not the patsies." Russ Harris, "California Based Horses Seek N.Y. Crown," *New York Daily News,* September 16, 1982.

144 ". . . threw the contest." Steven Crist, "Lemhi Gold Scores Upset in Marlboro," *New York Times,* September 19, 1982.

146 . . . only as fast as he needed to. Steven Crist, "Copelan Flourishes under Special Care," *New York Times,* November 4, 1982.

146 . . . the only undefeated multiple graded stakes-winning two-year-olds. Copelan crossed the wire in front in his second start, an allowance at Belmont, but was later disqualified due to a drug overage.

146 ". . . potential to be an all-time great." Andrew Beyer, "Filly Appears History-Bound," *Washington Post,* July 29, 1982.

146 . . . best Classic prospect so far. "She's a better horse than Ruffian. At the same age, she's a better horse than Stalwart" (Richard Sowers, "Even if Blush Fails in Spinster, Lukas Can Take Pride," *Louisville Courier/ Journal,* October 30, 1982). Also, "I've had a lot of good ones— Stalwart, Codex, Blush with Pride, Terlingua—but I'd have to say Landaluce is the best, no question about it" (Jon White, "Landaluce Tops $259,850 Oak Leaf," *Daily Racing Form,* October 23, 1982).

147 . . . five of the top ten richest races. "Richest North America Races of 1982," *The American Racing Manual* (Daily Racing Form, 1983 ed.), 78.

147 . . . just a speedball. "This race dismissed any thoughts of her not being able to go a mile and a quarter," wrote the *Form's* Jon White ("Graceful Landaluce").

148 ". . . let's not forget." Hovdey, "She Vants."

148 . . . morning after the Debutante. Henwood, "At Del Mar."

149 ". . . escalating coastal rivalry." Crist, "The Gold Rush."

149 . . . created the equivalent of a Breeders' Cup. It was no surprise to anyone that Marje Everett, displaying the same tenacity that won Hollywood's new dates and the resultant Starlet and Futurity, was vigorously lobbying for her track to host the inaugural Cup.

15. Pleasant Surprise

Epigraph: Jay Hovdey, "She Vants to Be Alone," *Horsemen's Journal,* November 1982.

151 . . . stalls 54 and 55. Steven Crist, "The Filly Who Runs Faster Than Colts," *New York Times,* October 25, 1982.

151 ". . . a master suite." Andrew Beyer, "A Horse of a Lifetime Runs Painfully through Lukas' Dreams," *Washington Post,* January 7, 1983.

152 . . . vanned some runners. Wayne Lukas, interview by the author, October 6, 2019.

152 . . . home in Arcadia. Jon White, telephone interview by the author, June 9, 2020.

152 ". . . boundless optimism." Beyer, "A Horse of a Lifetime."

152 . . . seven stakes in September alone. Bill Christine, "Opening Session at Oak Tree Finds a Familiar Face in Winner's Circle," *Los Angeles Times,* September 30, 1982.

152 . . . increased her insurance. Randy Galloway, "Horse Fans Drape '82 in Black," *Dallas Morning News,* November 30, 1982.

152 ". . . invigorated his whole operation." Beyer, "A Horse of a Lifetime."

152 . . . ordered custom greeting cards. Jay Hovdey, "She, Too, Left Us Too Soon," *Spur,* February 1983.

153 ". . . Fans are in love." Hovdey, "She Vants."

153 ". . . Look at that." Ibid.

154 . . . decided at the last minute. Jay Hovdey, "The Time Was Ripe," *Thoroughbred Record,* October 13, 1982.

154 ". . . ran her heart out." Ibid.

154 ". . . smartest trainers around." Bill Christine, "Landaluce Outruns the Brave Ones," *Los Angeles Times,* October 12, 1982.

155 . . . slicing carrots on the backstretch. Russ Harris, "Lemhi Gold Hungry for Horse of the Year Honors," *New York Daily News,* October 9, 1982.

155 . . . Crist of the *New York Times* believed. Steven Crist, "Lemhi Gold Scores," *New York Times,* September 19, 1982.

155 . . . retirement to stud eliminated him. Bill Christine, "2-Year-Olds in Horse of the Year Race," *Los Angeles Times,* September 24, 1982.

155 ". . . They have finished first." Ibid.

155 ". . . If Copelan wins." Luther Evans, "Horse of Year Honors on the Line," *Miami Herald,* October 8, 1982.

155 ". . . I'm going to vote for him." Ibid.

155 ". . . Nobody will get to the wire." Ibid.

156 . . . early book favorite. "Copelan Revels in Champagne," *Louisville Courier-Journal,* October 10, 1982.

156 . . . race marred by tragedy. Vincent Perrone, "Timely Writer Breaks Leg at Belmont," *Washington Post,* October 10, 1982.

156 ". . . There should be no doubt." Bee News Services, "Timely Writer Destroyed after Spill," *Sacramento Bee,* October 10, 1982.

156 . . . second runner of the year. Perrone, "Timely Writer."

156 . . . first horse in history. Steven Crist, "Race Still on for Horse of the Year," *New York Times,* October 18, 1982.

156 ". . . pride of southern Florida." Paul Moran, "El Kaiser Chases Stallion Stakes," *South Florida Sun Sentinel,* September 23, 1982.

157 ". . . nobody was going to beat her." Lukas interview.

157 ". . . a jewel." Hovdey, "The Time Was Ripe."

157 . . . record crowd of forty-eight thousand. Ibid.

157 . . . on the filly's shoulders. Ibid.

157 . . . second consecutive minus show pool. Christine, "Landaluce Outruns."

157 . . . highest impost in the history of the Anoakia. Landaluce's weight assignment in the Anoakia is still the highest ever carried in the race, matched by just four others: B. Thoughtful in 1977, Skillful Joy and Belle of Rainier in 1981, and Lukas-trained Althea in 1983. Only Landaluce and B. Thoughtful won the race (2018 Santa Anita media file, www.santaanita.com/wp-content/uploads/2018/10/SAA18_MediaGuide_Web.pdf, 20).

159 ". . . I'd gain too much weight." Bill Christine, "Pincay Follows the Sum," *Los Angeles Times,* August 21, 1982.

159 . . . twelve-start winless streak. Bill Christine, "2-Year-Olds in Horse of Year Race," *Los Angeles Times,* September 24, 1982.

159 . . . never won an Eclipse Award. Carmine Bilotti, "Cordero Racing toward His First Eclipse Award," *Passaic (NJ) Herald-News,* November 3, 1982.

159 . . . spanning more than two decades. Jack Murray, "Bartons Will Ride at Latonia," *Cincinnati Enquirer,* November 19, 1982. It was widely assumed in racing circles that the reason for Cordero's snub was his rough riding style, resulting in 220 infractions throughout his career, "believed to be a record," according to sportswriter Murray.

159 . . . won the jockey title four times. ntra.com/eclipse-awards/history /records.

159 . . . closed to within $300,000. Bill Christine, "It's Not So Easy for Landaluce," *Los Angeles Times,* October 24, 1982.

159 ". . . I'll go anyplace." Christine, "Pincay Follows."

160 . . . offered a mount. Laffit Pincay, interview by the author, January 31, 2019. Princess Rooney ran in the Frizette on October 10, and Landaluce's Anoakia was October 11. Presumably, the jockey could have ridden both fillies if he stayed in New York just one more day.

160 ". . . Lay second or third." Hovdey, "The Time Was Ripe."

160 ". . . say adios." Hovdey, "She Vants."

160 . . . start from the far outside. Christine, "Landaluce Outruns."

160 . . . told the gate crew. Jay Hovdey, "Living in a Pressure Cooker," *Thoroughbred Record,* October 27, 1982.

160 ". . . an amazing, balletic move." Hovdey, "She Vants."

161 . . . a paid workout. Crist, "The Filly Who Runs."

161 ". . . without taking a deep breath." Hovdey, "Like Ruffian."

161 ". . . like her feet are on fire." Hovdey, "The Time Was Ripe."

162 ". . . eerily similar." Jon White, "When Triple Crown Winners Clashed," October 18, 2018, Xpressbet.com/component/content/article/11 -xb360/xb-blog/3375-when-triple-crown-winners-clashed.

162 . . . No runner had managed. "John Henry's Trainer Ponders Whither Anita, Aqueduct Races," *Cincinnati Enquirer,* October 13, 1982.

162 ". . . I just let her run." "Like Father, Like Daughter: Landaluce Wins Again," *Miami News,* October 12, 1982.

162 ". . . just keeps getting better." Robert Henwood, "Soaring at Oak Tree," *BloodHorse,* October 16, 1982.

162 ". . . acting more mature." Christine, "Landaluce Outruns."

162 ". . . just floating away." Hovdey, "She Vants."

162 ". . . I don't want to think too far ahead." Henwood, "Soaring at Oak Tree."

163 . . . made Princess Rooney the overwhelming favorite. "Princess Rooney Heads Gardenia at Meadowlands," *Daily Racing Form,* October 23, 1982.

163 ". . . just another good filly." Hovdey, "The Time Was Ripe."

163 . . . proved the Princess's record superior. Bill Christine, "A Princess May Eclipse Landaluce," *Los Angeles Times,* October 22, 1982.

164 ". . . I'll meet him." Luther Evans, "Unbeatens Race 2,800 Miles Apart," *Miami Herald,* October 15, 1982.

164 ". . . the better filly." Christine, "A Princess."

164 ". . . intersectional voting rivalry." Leon Rasmussen, "Suddenly There Is Someone to Give Landaluce a Tussle," *Daily Racing Form,* October 14, 1982.

164 ". . . wind out of the sails." Hovdey, "The Time Was Ripe."

164 ". . . chances are nil." Paul Moran, "Awards Races are Off and Running," *Fort Lauderdale News,* October 8, 1982.

164 . . . pointed toward the filly Triple Crown. Don Zamarelli, "Princess Rooney Wins Gardenia Stakes Race," *Morristown (NJ) Daily Record,* October 24, 1982.

164 . . . richest race for two-year-old colts. "Richest North American Races of 1982," *American Racing Manual* (Daily Racing Form, 1983 ed.), 78.

164 . . . three of its last five runnings. Other Young America winners who went on to become juvenile champions were Spectacular Bid in 1978 and Lord Avie in 1980.

165 . . . described as 'elated.' Dale Austin, "Bad Step, Not Track, Blamed at Belmont," *Baltimore Sun,* October 11, 1982.

165 . . . predicting a walkover. Russ Harris, "Bet Big Takes Aim at Copelan," *New York Daily News,* November 3, 1982.

165 . . . upcoming Oak Leaf. The Oak Leaf became the Chandelier Stakes in 2012 and is now a Breeders' Cup "Win and You're In" race for juvenile fillies.

165 ". . . Copelan runs next." Dale Austin, "Coveted Lemhi Gold Might Skip Laurel," *Baltimore Sun,* October 14, 1982.

165 ". . . noncommittal." Bill Christine, "Flying Partner, A Top Filly, Is Being Retired," *Los Angeles Times,* October 21, 1982.

166 . . . among the few eastern connections. The connections of eastern colt Total Departure, winner of the Grade One Arlington Washington Futurity but fifth to Copelan in the Champagne, also reportedly were still considering a run in the Futurity at this time but did not enter the race (Bill Christine, "It's an Early Arrival for Total Departure," *Los Angeles Times,* October 29, 1982).

166 ". . . the race of the year." Steven Crist, "Race Still on for Horse of the Year," *New York Times,* October 18, 1982.
166 . . . abandoned any thoughts. Mike Marten, "Eye on Kentucky," *Daily Racing Form,* December 14, 1982.
166 . . . save his talented colt. Mike Marten, "Fight for Top Billing," *Daily Racing Form,* November 1, 1982.

16. Making the Grade

Epigraph: Steven Crist, "The Filly Who Runs Faster Than Colts," *New York Times,* October 25, 1982.
167 . . . lurked a fear. Ibid.
167 . . . whenever he passed her stall. Andrew Beyer, "A Horse of a Lifetime Runs Painfully through Lukas' Dreams," *Washington Post,* January 7, 1983.
168 . . . warmer during the day. Jay Hovdey, "Living in a Pressure Cooker," *Thoroughbred Record,* October 27, 1982.
168 . . . barrel-chested. Jay Hovdey, "She Vants to Be Alone, *Horsemen's Journal,* November, 1982.
168 . . . had not yet reached. Crist, "The Filly Who Runs."
169 . . . captured some of the top races. Hovdey, "She Vants."
169 ". . . Every time she runs." Hovdey, "Living."
169 . . . admirers lined the rail. UPI, "Precocious Filly Landaluce Has Shot at Horse of the Year," *New York Daily News,* October 23, 1982.
169 ". . . testimony to the flights of imagination." William Nack, "Ruffian: A Racetrack Romance" (New York: ESPN Books, 2007), 80.
170 . . . only two had won. Bill Christine, "Flying Partner, a Top Filly, Retired," *Los Angeles Times,* October 21, 1982.
170 . . . the first horse ever. Jon White, "When Triple Crown Winners Clashed," October 18, 2018, Xpressbet.com/component/content/article/11-xb360/xb-blog/3375-when-triple-crown-winners-clashed.
170 . . . track maintenance furrowed the track. Hovdey, "Living."
171 ". . . I Love Luce." Hovdey, "She Vants."
171 . . . only if Landaluce were not present. "Great Hunter Triumphs at Keeneland," *Louisville Courier/Journal,* October 22, 1982.
171 . . . filly was sweating heavily. Hovdey, "Living."
172 . . . were neck-and-neck. Bill Christine, "It's Not So Easy for Landaluce," *Los Angeles Times,* October 24, 1982.

172 ". . . wasn't as relaxed." Mike Marten, "Margin Not the Whole Story," *Daily Racing Form,* October 27, 1982.

172 . . . didn't have her regular stable pony. Hovdey, "Living."

172 . . . sensed the crowd's anticipation. Alan Buchdahl, email to the author, September 22, 2020.

172 . . . 1–20 favorite. White, "When Triple Crown Winners."

173 ". . . really not my idea." Hovdey, "Living."

173 . . . odds less than 4–5. Bob Mieszerski, "Landaluce Stakes a Special Race for Lukas," *Los Angeles Times,* July 3, 1999.

173 . . . felt Luce settling. Marten, "Margin Not the Whole."

174 ". . . I told Eddie." Hovdey, "Living."

175 . . . crowd began to cheer. Ibid.

175 ". . . Turning for home." Buchdahl email.

175 . . . thought his filly might win. Jon White, "Hollypark Notes," *Daily Racing Form,* November 11, 1982.

175 ". . . Sophisticated Girl closes." Christine, "It's Not So Easy."

175 ". . . gut feeling." Buchdahl email.

175 . . . three-fifths off the stakes record. Hovdey, "Living."

175 . . . second-fastest in the fourteen-year history. The Oak Leaf stakes record was held by champion filly It's in the Air, who won the race in 1:41 1/5 when she shipped in from the East on her way to her own Eclipse Award in 1978. It would be eleven years before Luce's Oak Leaf time would be bettered—by two one-hundredths of a second—by Phone Chatter, the only other filly to this day to run faster in the race ("Santa Anita Fall 2019 Media Guide," santaanita.com/wp-content/uploads/2019/09/SAA19_MediaGuide-web.pdf).

175 ". . . She wasn't accelerating." Christine, "It's Not So Easy."

175 ". . . look for her to improve." Robert Henwood, "The Fillies of Youth," *BloodHorse,* October 30, 1982.

175 ". . . somebody from 'I Love Lucy.'" Hovdey, "Living."

175 . . . first-ever Oak Leaf win. Madelyn Cain, *Laffit: Anatomy of a Winner: The Biography of Laffit Pincay, Jr.* (Pasadena: Affirmed, 2008), 338.

176 . . . only seven remaining races. "Richest North American Races of 1982," *The American Racing Manual* (Daily Racing Form, 1983 ed.), 78.

177 . . . setting a stakes record. Don Zamarelli, "Princess Rooney Wins Gardenia," *Morristown (NJ) Daily Record,* October 24, 1982.

177 ". . . She was kicking." Laura Cotter, telephone interview by the author, August 11, 2018.

177 . . . cut her right foreleg. Zamarelli, "Princess Rooney Wins."
177 ". . . The longer Princess Rooney goes." Luther Evans, "Rooney Plays Hurt Like a Princess," *Miami Herald,* October 26, 1982.
177 ". . . even her worst race." Crist, "The Filly Who Runs."
177 ". . . despite the 'relatively close' margin." Marten, "Margin Not the Whole."
178 ". . . I don't think for a minute." Hovdey, "Living."
178 ". . . only proves she's human." "Quotable Quotes," *LaCrosse Tribune,* November 28, 1982.
178 ". . . They build a horse up." Wayne Lukas, interview by the author, October 6, 2019.
178 ". . . the most encouraging thing." Marten, "Margin Not the Whole."
178 . . . ability to make two moves. Henwood, "Fillies of Youth."
178 ". . . She won today." Hovdey, "Living."
178 ". . . that level of brilliance." Lukas interview.
178 ". . . trouble staying interested." Christine, "It's Not So Easy."
179 ". . . hope we get a chance." Henwood, "Fillies of Youth."
178 . . . severe stone bruise. Art Grace, "Gardenia Means a Million for Trainer Frank Gomez," *Miami News,* November 17, 1982.
179 . . . Calder Race Course. Today, the track is known as Gulfstream Park West (americasbestracing.net/tracks/gulfstream-park-west). Florida turf writer Paul Moran said the track's stars "carried the stigma of the *Calder horse,* a designation which served to lessen the importance of whatever they may have accomplished" (Moran, "Stallion Stakes May Change Calder's Unstable Rep," *Fort Lauderdale News,* September 25, 1982).
179 . . . set by champion Numbered Account. Christine, "It's Not So Easy."
179 . . . The day after the Oak Leaf. "Landaluce in Excellent Condition after Oak Leaf," *Daily Racing Form,* October 26, 1982.
180 . . . first-ever front-page story. Craig Lambert, "Horseplayer Extraordinaire," *Harvard Magazine,* March/April, 2010.
180 . . . only about a year's experience. "Steven Crist, Longtime Daily Racing Form Executive & Columnist, Retires," press release, *Paulick Report,* July 20, 2016.
180 . . . even the great champion never did. William Nack suggests that had Ruffian defeated colts at two, she almost certainly would have been Horse of the Year (Nack, *Ruffian: A Racetrack Romance* [New York: ESPN Books], 69).
180 ". . . She was our Ruffian." Vicky Burnham, telephone interview by the author, February 23, 2019.
181 ". . . I don't know how anyone." Crist, "The Filly Who Runs."

182 . . . believed Roving Boy superior. Mike Marten, "Eye on Kentucky," *Daily Racing Form,* December 14, 1982.

182 . . . raced six times in three months. Mike Marten, "Fight for Top Billing," *Daily Racing Form,* November 1, 1982.

182 . . . stakes record time. Bill Christine, "Roving Boy Wins Norfolk Stakes by 4½ Lengths with Record Time," *Los Angeles Times,* October 31, 1982.

182 ". . . haven't even started." Hovdey, "Living."

17. Hurray for Hollywood

Epigraph: "She's Far Ahead of All the Boys," *Los Angeles Times*, November 2, 1982.

184 . . . White was here. Jon White, "Los Alamitos," *Daily Racing Form,* November 3, 1982.

184 . . . remain at Santa Anita. Wayne Lukas, interview by the author, October 6, 2019.

184 . . . posted a bullet. "Corrected Workouts," *Daily Racing Form,* November 10, 1982.

184 . . . her last work at Santa Anita. Lukas interview.

185 ". . . it is certain." Leon Rasmussen, "From This Family You Would Expect Something Fabulous," *Daily Racing Form,* December 11, 1982.

185 . . . near racing's top ten. "Leading Money-Winning Horses of 1982," *American Racing Manual* (Daily Racing Form, 1983 ed.), 288.

186 ". . . richest 38-day season." Hollywood Park print ad, *Los Angeles Times,* October 27, 1982.

186 ". . . If we get lucky." Mike Marten, "Fight for Top Billing," *Daily Racing Form,* November 1, 1982.

186 . . . return of Calumet Farm. "Calumet Colors Come West after Long Absence," *Daily Racing Form,* November 14, 1982.

186 . . . there was even talk. Fuller French, telephone interview by the author, August 3, 2021.

186 ". . . Spectacular rises in attendance." Steven Crist, "Horse Racing: An Industry Confronting Transition," *New York Times,* December 12, 1982.

186 . . . in the finals. Logan Bailey, "Breeders' Cup on Schedule; Some Changes," *Daily Racing Form,* October 22, 1982. After its board named Santa Anita and Hollywood Park as finalists, Everett made a $200,000 personal contribution to the Breeders' Cup. The inaugural Cup was held at Hollywood (Bill Dwyre, "Marje Everett Dies at 90," *Los Angeles Times,* March 24, 2012).

187 . . . No juvenile of either sex. Ron Hale, "History Challenge: Hollywood a Launching Point for Stars," *Daily Racing Form,* December 13, 2012.

187 . . . set the stage for future champions. Ibid.

187 . . . only $10,000 away. "'Shoe' near $90 Million," *Daily Racing Form,* November 4, 1982.

187 . . . heiress Dolly Green. "Celebrities Attend Opener of Hollywood Fall Meeting," *Daily Racing Form,* November 5, 1982.

187 . . . already vanquished most. Don Zamarelli, "Unbeaten Copelan Ready for Big M's Young America," *Paterson News,* November 4, 1982.

188 . . . boosting the purse. Russ Harris, "Copelan-Landaluce Could Be $1 Million Deal," *New York Daily News,* November 4, 1982.

18. Starlet

Epigraph: David Dink, "Experimental Free Handicap for Three-Year-Olds of 1983," *Thoroughbred Record,* January 12, 1983.

189 . . . Holmby Hills mansion. Ray Paulick, "Former Hollywood Park Owner Marje Everett Dead: 'She Saw the Best Days in Racing,'" *Paulick Report,* March 23, 2012.

189 . . . a chocolate soda. Whitney Tower, "The Racing Lady of Chicago," *Sports Illustrated,* August 20, 1962.

189 ". . . with a gleam in his eye." Jay Hovdey, "A Boy with a Bright Future," *Thoroughbred Record,* December 1, 1982.

190 . . . never raced at the Young America distance. Russ Harris, "28–1 Slewpy Wins Young America," *New York Daily News,* November 5, 1982.

190 . . . richest start of any first-year sire. Steven Crist, "Seattle Slew Finds Success as Sire," *New York Times,* November 6, 1982.

190 . . . wasn't sure he should even enter Harris, "28–1 Slewpy."

190 . . . had to call from the airport. Ruth Bonapace, "Slewpy Wins 'Young America,'" *Miami News,* November 5, 1982.

191 ". . . I wasn't planning." Russ Harris, "Bet Big Takes Aim at Copelan," *New York Daily News,* November 3, 1982.

191 ". . . surprised me by finishing so strongly." Harris, "28–1 Slewpy."

191 ". . . knocked each other out." "Copelan Coming West to Race in $750,000 Hollywood Futurity, *Daily Racing Form,* November 10, 1982.

191 ". . . first time under the lights." Shirley Povich, "Copelan Class of the Cast," *Washington Post,* March 5, 1983.

191 ". . . I have to think." Russ Harris, "Copelan Trained Wrong," *New York Daily News,* November 6, 1982.

191 ". . . He wasn't entirely fit." Mike Marten, "Hungry to Run," *Daily Racing Form,* November 26, 1982.

191 . . . bringing Copelan to the West Coast. Russ Harris, "Copelan, Landaluce Vie in Hollywood Futurity," *New York Daily News,* November 8, 1982.

192 . . . first time in history. Joe Hirsch, "Classic Confrontation Puts Young Futurity on the Map," *Daily Racing Form,* December 10, 1982.

192 ". . . has never given his reasons." Mike Marten, "Nailing Down the Big Guns for an Important Payday," *Daily Racing Form,* December 12, 1982.

193 . . . since the 1940s. Bill Dwyre, "Marje Everett Dies at 90; Legendary Figure in Horse Racing," *Los Angeles Times,* March 24, 2012.

193 . . . one of her favorite owners. Jim O'Donnell, "First Stop: Arlington Park," *Chicago Sun-Times,* December 10, 1999.

193 . . . since the late 1950s. Paul Lowry, "Fifteen Race in Juvenile Stakes Today," *Los Angeles Times,* July 18, 1959.

193 . . . primary West Coast trainer. "Special Goddess Captures California Oaks," *Fremont Argus,* March 24, 1974.

193 . . . wintered part of his string. Steven Crist, "Copelan Flourishes under Special Care," *New York Times,* November 4, 1982.

193 . . . not shy about shipping horses. After beating quarter horse Stella Moore in a January match race, Olympia finished second in Florida's Hibiscus Stakes, won the San Felipe Stakes at Santa Anita in mid-February and finished second in the Santa Anita Derby four days later. The colt then shipped back to Florida to win the Flamingo Stakes March 3 ("[Santa Anita] Derby Becomes Jockey Battle; Olympia Choice," *Bakersfield Californian,* February 16, 1949; Paul Lowry, "Old Rockport Outruns Olympia in Stretch to Capture Derby," *Los Angeles Times,* February 20, 1949; George Swift, "Hooper's Olympia Takes Flamingo; Sneak Second," *Miami Herald,* March 4, 1949).

193 ". . . worried sick." Crist, "Copelan Flourishes."

193 ". . . She's as impressive." Jon White, "Landaluce's 21-Length Lassie Score Dazzles Rival Horsemen," *Daily Racing Form,* July 15, 1982.

193 . . . strong bond he had developed. Crist, "Copelan Flourishes."

194 . . . trainer should accompany the colt. Mike Marten, "Championship Season," *Daily Racing Form,* November 13, 1982.

194 . . . top earning trainer for the meet. "Lukas off to Fast Start with Six Hollypark Winners," *Daily Racing Form,* November 10, 1982.

194 . . . six winners from fifteen starters. Ibid.

194 ". . . no trainer in the country." Bill Christine, "Cordero Passes McCarron as Pincay Closes In," *Los Angeles Times,* November 19, 1982.

194 ". . . the ace up his sleeve." Jim Milner, "Angel Cordero Jr. Chasing Laffit Pincay in Competition for Coveted Eclipse Award," *Miami News,* October 1, 1982.

194 . . . deplaned at Los Angeles. Jon White, "Three's No Crowd," *Daily Racing Form,* November 14, 1982.

194 ". . . If she's there, she's there." Bill Christine, "Copelan Is Shipped West after Poor Showing. . .," *Los Angeles Times,* November 9, 1982.

195 ". . . She's never crossed the Rockies." Billy Reed, "Stephens Says 'Cielo' Merits Horse of the Year," *Louisville Courier-Journal,* November 10, 1982.

195 ". . . We think she's good enough." Luther Evans, "Copelan Poised for Florida Derby," *Miami Herald,* November 18, 1982.

195 ". . . There's a chance we'll run." White, "Three's No Crowd."

195 . . . handicap the race himself. Bill Christine, "Manzi May Let His Roving Boy out of Barn after All," *Los Angeles Times,* November 23, 1982.

195 ". . . She did it without effort." Jon White, "Hollypark Notes," *Daily Racing Form,* November 17, 1982.

196 . . . matched Landaluce's earlier clocking. "Copelan in Half-Mile Workout at Hollypark," *Daily Racing Form,* November 17, 1982.

196 ". . . like he had trained there all his life." Jay Hovdey, "Like Ruffian, in the Worst Way," *Thoroughbred Record,* December 1, 1982.

196 ". . . Just in case we decide." "Roving Boy Drills Five Panels for Possible Futurity Try," *Daily Racing Form,* November 18, 1982.

196 . . . surpassing Chris McCarron's. Steven Crist, "Earnings Mark for Cordero," *New York Times,* November 18, 1982.

196 ". . . If I have to go to Alaska." Bob Raimonto, "Cordero Wants His Just Due," *Hackensack (NJ) Record,* November 7, 1982.

196 ". . . This is my last try." Luther Evans, "Cordero Winning Duel with Pincay for Riding Title," *Miami Herald,* December 4, 1982.

196 ". . . If I don't win." Jack Murray, "Bartons Will Ride at Latonia," *Cincinnati Enquirer,* November 19, 1982.

196 ". . . got that filly Landaluce." Crist, "Earnings Mark."

196 ". . . a weapon I didn't have." Evans, "Cordero Winning Duel."

198 . . . leading Laffit by about $200,000. Crist, "Earnings Mark."

198 . . . joined by Jeff Lukas. Hovdey, "Like Ruffian."

198 . . . covered five furlongs. Jon White, "Fever Leaves Landaluce Starlet Status Uncertain," *Daily Racing Form,* November 24, 1982.

198 ". . . I particularly liked." Mike Marten, "Copelan, Landaluce Prepare for Hollypark Engagements," *Daily Racing Form,* November 23, 1982.

198 ". . . really confident." Hovdey, "Like Ruffian."

198 ". . . I managed her career." Joe Hirsch, "Reaching out and Touching Someone," *Daily Racing Form,* December 13, 1982.

199 . . . important dental work. Hovdey, "Like Ruffian."

199 . . . stopped at Santa Anita. Hirsch, "Reaching Out."

19. Last Race

Epigraph: Jon White, "She Slew Them Again," *Thoroughbred Record,* September 8, 1982.

203 ". . . Believe me, she was a handful." Jay Hovdey, "Like Ruffian, in the Worst Way," *Thoroughbred Record,* December 1, 1982.

203 . . . three definite starters. Mike Marten, "Copelan, Landaluce Work for Weekend Hollywood Stakes," *Daily Racing Form,* November 23, 1982.

204 . . . had considered the Starlet. Hovdey, "Like Ruffian."

204 . . . logged a satisfying work. Marten, "Copelan, Landaluce Work."

204 . . . a large serving of oats. Mike Marten, "Hungry to Run," *Daily Racing Form,* November 26, 1982.

204 . . . postponed a ten-day vacation. Bill Christine, "Manzi May Let His Roving Boy out of the Barn after All," *Los Angeles Times,* November 23, 1982.

205 . . . Roving Boy had filled out. Jay Hovdey, "A Boy with a Bright Future," *Thoroughbred Record,* December 15, 1982.

205 . . . doing her afternoon rounds. Jon White, "Persistent Fever Leaves Landaluce Starlet Status Uncertain," *Daily Racing Form,* November 23, 1982.

205 . . . stiffened when he heard. Bill Lyon, "For Lukas, a Second Chance," *Philadelphia Inquirer,* May 19, 1988.

205 ". . . we could knock out." Hovdey, "Like Ruffian."

205 . . . hand-walked in the shedrow. Jon White, "Fever Leaves Landaluce's Status Uncertain," *Daily Racing Form,* November 24, 1982.

206 ". . . watch history in the making." *Los Angeles Times* print ad, November 23, 1982.

206 . . . filly would not run. White, "Persistent Fever."

206 ". . . If she snaps out of this." "Ailing Landaluce Is out of Starlet," *New York Times,* November 25, 1982.

206 . . . field began to swell. White, "Persistent Fever."

206 . . . called his staff. Mike Marten, "The Right Call," *Daily Racing Form,* December 1, 1982.

206 ". . . a wide open race." Jon White, "Juvenile Filly Test Is Wide Open with Nine Entrants," *Daily Racing Form,* November 28, 1982.

207 . . . days without nourishment. Bill Christine, "Lukas Was Afraid Something Might Happen," *Los Angeles Times,* November 29, 1982.

207 . . . soared to 104. Mike Marten, "Starlet Field Swells, Landaluce Still Sick," *Daily Racing Form,* November 26, 1982.

207 . . . throat and chest were now infected. Hovdey, "Like Ruffian."

207 . . . come back for the Classics. Ibid.

207 . . . veterinarians took cultures. Laura Cotter, telephone interview by the author, August 11, 2018.

207 . . . contacted veterinary experts. Russ Harris, "Landaluce, Unbeaten Filly, Dies of Virus," *New York Daily News,* November 29, 1982.

207 . . . paced up and down. Bobby Barnett, text message to the author, August 2, 2020.

208 . . . spiked a fever, forcing his scratch. Christine, "Lukas Was Afraid."

208 . . . runners at Santa Anita were sick. Hovdey, "A Boy."

208 . . . colt Art Director had died. Mike Marten, "Autopsy Expected to Reveal Landaluce Died of Pneumonia," *Daily Racing Form,* November 30, 1982.

208 . . . Barberstown became seriously ill. Jon White, "A Close Call," *Daily Racing Form,* December 2, 1982.

208 . . . typical for the season. Hovdey, "A Boy."

208 ". . . There is apparently." "Clots Led to Death of Filly," *New York Times,* November 30, 1982.

208 ". . . Other horses on both sides." Joe Hirsch, "Reaching out and Touching Someone," *Daily Racing Form,* December 13, 1982.

208 . . . free turkey dinner. "Landaluce Continuing Bid for Championship in Starlet on Sunday," *Daily Racing Form,* November 22, 1982.

208 . . . overlooked the holiday. Hovdey, "Like Ruffian."

209 ". . . She's certainly not any better." Marten, "Starlet Field Swells."

209 ". . . haggard." Hovdey, "Like Ruffian."

209 . . . new and deadly challenge. Steven Crist, "Landaluce Dies from Virus," *New York Times,* November 29, 1982.

209 . . . spread far apart. Hovdey, "Like Ruffian."

209 ". . . life-threatening situation." Jon White, "Landaluce Fighting for Her Life," *Daily Racing Form,* November 28, 1982.

210 ". . . she hadn't had anything." Tim Liotta, "Landaluce Loses Her First Race," *San Pedro News-Pilot,* November 29, 1982.

210 . . . experienced some relief. White, "Landaluce Fighting."

210 . . . Male Adapter displayed symptoms. White, "A Close Call."

210 ". . . We never seemed to make any headway." Hovdey, "Like Ruffian."

211 ". . . It's real bad." Christine, "Lukas Was Afraid."

211 ". . . I thought she could." Hirsch, "Reaching Out."

211 . . . Landaluce would not run. Mike Marten, "Eye on Kentucky," *Daily Racing Form,* December 14, 1982.

211 . . . By 8:30 p.m. Hovdey, "Like Ruffian."

212 ". . . I was real scared." Andrew Beyer, "A Horse of a Lifetime Runs Painfully through Lukas' Dreams," *Washington Post,* January 7, 1983.

212 ". . . We're in big trouble." Ibid.

212 . . . Arcadia Methodist Hospital. Hovdey, "Like Ruffian."

212 . . . started to weave. Beyer, "A Horse."

212 . . . her head in Wayne Lukas's lap. Ibid.

212 . . . lay down next to her. Barnett text message.

212 . . . ordered an autopsy. Dave Feldman, "Landaluce's Death Stuns the Horse Racing World," *Daily Oklahoman,* December 1, 1982.

212 ". . . It was the only time." Bobby Barnett, interview by the author, October 6, 2019.

212 . . . called a truck. Bobby Barnett, telephone interview by the author, April 23, 2019.

212 ". . . That's one thing." Hovdey, "Like Ruffian."

212 . . . An hour and a half later. Billy Reed, "Landaluce, Dream That Died, but Not Easily Forgotten," *Louisville Courier-Journal,* November 30, 1982.

20. Grieving

Epigraph: Billy Reed, "Landaluce, Dream That Died, but Not Easily Forgotten," *Louisville Courier-Journal,* November 30, 1982.

214 . . . early Sunday morning. Bill Christine, "Lukas Was Afraid Something Might Happen," *Los Angeles Times,* November 29, 1982.

214 ". . . I just feel so sorry." Steven Crist, "Landaluce Dies from Virus," *New York Times,* November 29, 1982.

214 . . . in Hollywood Park's infield. Bill Christine, "Landaluce Dies of Mysterious Virus," *Los Angeles Times,* November 29, 1982.

214 . . . printed and inserted. Edward "Kip" Hannan, email to the author, May 23, 2020.

214 . . . calls flooded the Wayne Lukas barn. Christine, "Landaluce Dies."

214 . . . speak with the Associated Press. Dolores Wood, "Filly Landaluce Dies of Virus," AP, *Wilmington Morning News,* November 29, 1982.

215 ". . . It was like losing." Laura Cotter, telephone interview by the author, August 11, 2018.

215 ". . . We'd like to talk." Dave Feldman, "Landaluce's Death Stuns the Racing World," *Chicago Sun Times/Daily Oklahoman,* December 1, 1982.

215 ". . . The loss is devastating." Christine, "Landaluce Dies."

215 . . . canceled their flight. Crist, "Landaluce Dies."

215 . . . At their Anacacho Ranch. Marcia Fuller French, telephone interview by the author, August 12, 2021.

215 . . . on local channels. Alan Buchdahl, telephone interview by the author, September 24, 2020.

215 . . . crowd of twenty-eight thousand. Gary West, "The Beautiful Landaluce: What Might Have Been," *Shreveport Journal,* December 8, 1982.

215 ". . . Landaluce's death was greeted." Jon White, "Landaluce Leaves as Quickly as She Ran," *Daily Racing Form,* December 1, 1982.

216 . . . next to Landaluce throughout. Robert Henwood, "Death on a Sunday," *BloodHorse,* December 4, 1982.

216 . . . sentimental favorite. Russ Harris, "Landaluce, Unbeaten Filly, Dies of Virus," *New York Daily News,* November 29, 1982.

216 . . . wasn't properly prepared. Jay Hovdey, "Like Ruffian, in the Worst Way," *Thoroughbred Record,* December 1, 1982.

216 . . . offer condolences. Reed, "Landaluce, Dream That Died."

216 . . . victory in the Lassie was replayed. Gordon Jones, "Virus Is Only Rival to Defeat Landaluce," *Los Angeles Herald Examiner,* November 29, 1982.

216 . . . a memorial shrine. Crist, "Landaluce Dies."

216 . . . the cause of death. Mike Marten, "Autopsy Expected to Reveal Landaluce Died of Pneumonia," *Daily Racing Form,* November 30, 1982.

216 ". . . At times, almost everyone." West, "The Beautiful Landaluce."

216 ". . . People openly wept." Reed, "Landaluce, Dream That Died."

216 ". . . a bloodless exercise." Hovdey, "Like Ruffian."

217 ". . . ignored the race." West, "The Beautiful Landaluce."

217 . . . eulogizing the filly. *World News Tonight,* courtesy of ABC News archives, featuring Dick Schaap, aired November 28, 1982.

217 . . . So did Dan Rather. "Seattle Slew," in *Thoroughbred Champions: Top 100 Racehorses of the Twentieth Century* (Lexington, KY: Blood-Horse Publications, 1999), 45.

217 ". . . It looks like." Jon White, "A Close Call," *Daily Racing Form,* December 2, 1982.

217 . . . appeared to have recovered. Christine, "Lukas Was Afraid."

21. Getting Through

Epigraph: Billy Reed, "Landaluce, Dream That Died, but Not Easily Forgotten," *Louisville Courier-Journal,* November 30, 1982.

218 . . . to receive counseling. Bob Ehalt, "Landaluce: Unforgettable Brilliance, Unimaginable Heartbreak," *America's Best Racing,* August 31, 2016.

218 ". . . a lot of sad people." Bobby Barnett, telephone interview by the author, April 23, 2019.

218 ". . . After you've been around." Steven Crist, "Trainer Relying on Quality," *New York Times,* April 10, 1983.

218 ". . . kind of deadens you." Andrew Beyer, "A Horse of a Lifetime Runs Painfully through Lukas' Dreams," *Washington Post,* January 7, 1983.

219 ". . . captivating not only." Tim Liotta, "Landaluce Loses Her First Race," *San Pedro News-Pilot,* November 29, 1982.

219 ". . . become a legend." Russ Harris, "Landaluce, Unbeaten Filly, Dies of Virus," *New York Daily News,* November 29, 1982.

219 ". . . a national heroine." Bill Christine, "Landaluce Dies of Mysterious Virus," *Los Angeles Times,* November 29, 1982.

219 ". . . fire of her father." Reed, "Landaluce, Dream That Died."

219 ". . . So formidable was Landaluce." Andrew Beyer, "Landaluce's Story: A Half-Told Tale," *Washington Post,* December 2, 1982.

219 ". . . greatest ever of her sex." "Virus Kills Unbeaten Landaluce," *Hackensack (NJ) Record,* November 29, 1982.

219 ". . . crushed." Jon White, "Ironic Match," *Daily Racing Form,* December 5, 1982.

219 . . . continued to stream. Reed, "Landaluce, Dream That Died."

219 . . . more than five hundred letters. Joe Hirsch, "Everyone's Loss," *Daily Racing Form,* December 13, 1982.

219 . . . letter to the editor. "Token Coverage of Racing," letter to the editor, *Baltimore Evening Sun,* December 6, 1982.

219 . . . In a letter. Lanny R. Middings, "Death of Landaluce Mourned," letter to the editor, *Los Angeles Times,* December 4, 1982.

219 ". . . great big sacks of mail." Marcia Fuller French, telephone interview by the author, August 12, 2021.

220 ". . . There may have been pneumonia." Mike Marten, "Multiple Blood Clots, Shock Cited as Cause of Landaluce's Death," *Daily Racing Form,* December 1, 1982.

220 ". . . We don't know for sure it was a virus." UPI, "Clots Led to Death of Filly, *New York Times,* November 30, 1982.

220 ". . . widespread interest." Marten, "Multiple Blood Clots."

220 ". . . had a respiratory infection." Bill Christine, "Verdict on Landaluce: Blood Clots Responsible," *Los Angeles Times,* November 30, 1982.

220 ". . . Every vital organ." Randy Galloway, "Horse Fans Drape '82 in Black," *Dallas Morning News,* November 30, 1982.

221 ". . . mysterious virus." An online query by the author at Newspapers.com for keywords "Landaluce" and "virus" for articles in the year 1982 yielded more than three hundred results as of August 9, 2020.

221 . . . had afflicted Seattle Slew. Joe Hirsch, "Moment to Remember," *Daily Racing Form,* November 30, 1982.

221 . . . more veterinary research. Kent Hollingsworth, "What's Going on Here," *BloodHorse,* December 4, 1982

221 ". . . We found an intestinal infection." Mike Marten, "Strong Bacteria Cause of Landaluce's Death," *Daily Racing Form,* December 10, 1982.

221 . . . hemolytic E. coli. Hemolytic bacteria are those that destroy red blood cells.

221 ". . . not always totally effective." Marten, "Strong Bacteria Cause of Landaluce's Death."

221 . . . only gentamicin showed any potential. Tracy Gantz, "An Infection, Not a Virus," *BloodHorse,* December 18, 1982.

222 ". . . beginning to take effect." Jim Murray, "Landaluce: a Real-Life Love Story," *Los Angeles Times,* December 7, 1982.

222 ". . . gut feeling." Alan Buchdahl, email to the author, September 22, 2020.

222 ". . . She's got her head in the feed tub." "Landaluce in Excellent Condition after Oak Leaf," *Daily Racing Form,* October 26, 1982.

222 . . . blood tests taken. Jay Hovdey, "Landaluce Leaves Lasting Memories," *Daily Racing Form,* January 12, 1983.

222 . . . erroneous cause of death. Colitis is inflammation of the large bowel in horses, not to be confused with colic, which is any undiagnosed

abdominal pain. Colitis is a diagnosis, while colic is a symptom (see acvim.org/Portals/0/PDF/Animal%20Pwmer%20Fact%20Sheets /LAIM/Colitis%20in%20Adult%20Horses.pdf and succeed-equine .com/education/gi-health-care/health-risks/colic-in-horses/).

222 . . . fallen out of use. Succeed Veterinary Center, "Colitis X in Horses" succeed-vet.com/equine-gi-disease-library/colitis-x-horses.

222 . . . Colitis X was not the cause. Dr. Rick Arthur, email to the author, December 3, 2019; Wayne Lukas, interview by the author, October 6, 2019.

222 . . . double-edged sword. Dr. Rick Arthur, email to the author, July 9, 2020.

223 . . . spiral into secondary conditions. Dr. Rick Arthur, email to the author, September 8, 2020. Modern veterinary medicine relies on polymerase chain reaction (PCR) to identify viruses or bacteria from their DNA, a process that was not available in 1982. Still, viruses are difficult to culture even today, especially postmortem, and proper identification requires immediate sampling. The time it took for Landaluce to travel to UC Davis alone might have made it impossible to find the correct organism. (Dr. Rick Arthur, email to the author, September 9, 2020).

223 ". . . We are determined." "Landaluce Memorial Service on December 12," *Daily Racing Form,* December 4, 1982.

22. Futurity

Epigraph: Jay Hovdey, "A Boy with a Bright Future," *Thoroughbred Record,* December 15, 1982.

224 . . . had not slept well. Ibid.

224 ". . . a prize worth winning." Joe Hirsch, "Roving Boy Has a Lot at Stake Sunday," *Daily Racing Form,* December 11, 1982.

224 ". . . You look like a banker." Jay Hovdey, "When Stars Roved the Futurity," *Daily Racing Form,* December 23, 2002.

225 . . . Invited by Laura Cotter. Jon White, telephone interview by the author, June 9, 2020.

225 . . . he would stay behind. Bobby Barnett, telephone interview by the author, April 23, 2019.

225 . . . appeared on the cover. "Hollywood Park Pays Tribute to Landaluce," Hollywood Park official racing program, December 12, 1982.

226 . . . only time in his career. Laffit Pincay, text message to the author, July 31, 2020.

226 . . . today's overwhelming favorite. Jay Hovdey, "Like Ruffian, in the Worst Way," *Thoroughbred Record,* December 1, 1982.

226 . . . alongside its waterfall. Mike Marten, "Landaluce Is Buried in Hollywood Infield," *Daily Racing Form,* December 14, 1982.

226 . . . near tears. Tim Liotta, "Landaluce Rites Given at Hollypark," *San Pedro News-Pilot,* December 12, 1982.

226 . . . Exercise riders. Hovdey, "A Boy."

226 . . . written by track publicist. Alan Buchdahl, email to the author, September 22, 2020.

226 ". . . one of the most remarkable efforts." *Hollywood Park: The Landaluce File,* video footage compiled and edited by Edward "Kip" Hannan, courtesy of Hollywood Park.

228 . . . nearly forty well-wishers. Tim Liotta, "Roving Boy's Victory Creates a Mob Scene," *San Pedro News-Pilot,* December 13, 1982.

228 . . . graciously congratulated. *Hollywood Park: The Landaluce File,* Hannan video, with ESPN footage, December 12, 1982.

228 . . . a hard piece of dirt. Associated Press, "Copelan Returned to Ocala Farm for Rehabilitation," *Miami News,* December 17, 1982.

228 . . . damaged his cornea. Mike Marten, "Eye on Kentucky," *Daily Racing Form,* December 14, 1982.

228 ". . . as if someone had taken a rasp." Mike Marten, "Roving Boy Outgames Desert Wine; Copelan Fifth in Hollywood Futurity," *Daily Racing Form,* December 14, 1982.

228 ". . . would have stopped an elephant." Joe Hirsch, "If Copelan Can Keep Pace with Hooper He'll Do Okay," *Daily Racing Form,* January 12, 1983.

228 . . . dirt streamed down his face. Ibid.

228 . . . never winning a race there. Bill Christine, "Flying Partner, a Top Filly, Is Retired," *Los Angeles Times,* October 21, 1982.

228 ". . . Winning Horse of the Year." Bill Christine, "Copelan's Future Looks Bright after Good Prevue," *Los Angeles Times,* November 28, 1982.

229 . . . fell victim to a slump. Madelyn Cain, *Laffit: Anatomy of a Winner: The Biography of Laffit Pincay, Jr.* (Pasadena, CA: Affirmd, 2008), 158.

229 ". . . I've been working hard." "Pincay Taking Two Days off but Will Ride on Weekend," *Daily Racing Form,* December 16, 1982.

229 ". . . Wayne was distraught." *Laffit: All about Winning* (Six Furlongs, 2005).

229 ". . . once in a lifetime horse." Randy Galloway, "Horse Fans Drape 82 in Black," *Dallas Morning News,* November 30, 1982.

228 . . . would be several months. Steven Crist, "Santa Anita Derby Won by 7–2 Marfa," *New York Times,* April 11, 1983.

229 . . . imprinted with an image of Luce. Jay Hovdey, "She, Too, Left Us Too Soon," *Spur,* January/February 1983.

230 . . . catered Christmas dinner. Bobby Barnett, telephone interview by the author, April 23, 2019.

230 . . . unwrapped a present. Laura Cotter, telephone interview by the author, August 11, 2018.

230 . . . donating proceeds from the sale. Jay Hovdey, "Picavet Had Brush-strokes with Greatness," *Daily Racing Form,* July 6, 2016.

230 . . . best racing filly. Cotter interview.

23. Eclipse

Epigraph: Andrew Beyer, "Landaluce's Story: A Half-Told Tale," *Washington Post,* December 2, 1982.

231 ". . . more howling than usual." Bill Christine, "The Eclipse Awards Are Supposed to Cover It All," *Los Angeles Times,* December 22, 1982.

231 . . . the first horse to win. Steven Crist, "Race Still on for Horse of Year," *New York Times,* October 18, 1982.

231 . . . so exhausted. Mike Marten, "Fight for Top Billing," *Daily Racing Form,* November 1, 1982.

232 ". . . Conquistador Cielo was probably." Andrew Beyer, "In Just World, Eclipse Belongs to Landaluce," *Washington Post,* December 18, 1982.

232 ". . . no Horse of the Year." Steven Crist, "Eclipse Voting Is Wide Open," *New York Times,* January 2, 1983.

232 ". . . the year of Landaluce." Beyer, "In Just World."

232 . . . In 1965. Judy L. Marchman, "Moccasin," in *Horse Racing Divas: From Azeri to Zenyatta, Twelve Fillies and Mares Who Achieved Racing's Highest Honor,* ed. Staff and Correspondents of the *Blood-Horse* (Lexington, KY: BloodHorse Publications, 2011), 104.

233 . . . The first and only two-year-old. Steve Cady, "Secretariat Is Horse of Year, Topping La Prevoyante in Poll," *New York Times,* December 27, 1972.

233 . . . Busher in 1945. Steven Crist, "The Cup Is Born: The 1980s," in *Champions: The Lives, Times, and Past Performances of America's Greatest Thoroughbreds,* ed. Daily Racing Form LLC (New York: Daily Racing Form Press, 2016), 312.

233 ". . . somewhat of a popularity vote." Christine, "The Eclipse Awards."

233 ". . . California is lightly represented." Crist, "Eclipse Voting."

233 ". . . most hotly contested vote." Andrew Beyer, "Conquistador Is Horse of the Year," *Washington Post,* January 5, 1983.

233 ". . . underscoring the growing strength." Ibid.

234 ". . . Landaluce had to be." Ed Bowen, email to the author, May 2, 2020.

234 ". . . How could the secretaries?" Dave Feldman, "Eclipse Award Almost Was a Sham," *Chicago Sun Times* syndicated in *Miami News,* January 6, 1983.

234 . . . first since the filly Idun. Edward L. Bowen, "Leslie Combs II," in *Legacies of the Turf: A Century of Great Thoroughbred Breeders,* vol. 2 (Lexington, KY: BloodHorse, 2004), 140.

235 . . . twenty-three more. "D. Wayne Lukas to Receive Breeders' Cup Sports and Racing Excellence Award," *Paulick Report,* August 24, 2018.

24. Legacy

Epigraph: Bob Mieszerski, "Landaluce Stakes a Special Race for Lukas," *Los Angeles Times,* July 3, 1999.

236 . . . failed to win a race. Steven Crist, "Trainer Relying on Quality," *New York Times,* April 10, 1983.

236 . . . two unraced fillies. Ibid.

236 . . . returned to the races. Steven Crist, "Santa Anita Derby Won by 7–2 Marfa," *New York Times,* April 11, 1983.

237 . . . to meet a young fan. James Litke, "Lukas Moves to the Top with Derby Win," AP, *Rutland (VT) Daily Herald,* May 8, 1988.

237 . . . first in the nation. Christina Bossinakis, *Sermon on the Mount: The Wisdom and Life Experiences of Hall of Fame Trainer D. Wayne Lukas* (Lukas Enterprises, 2019), 138.

237 . . . Against the advice of his agent. Madelyn Cain, *Laffit: Anatomy of a Winner: The Biography of Laffit Pincay, Jr.* (Pasadena, CA: Affirmed, 2008), 168–75.

237 . . . more yearlings by Slew. Carlo DeVito, *D. Wayne, The High Rolling and Fast Times of America's Premier Horse Trainer* (New York: Contemporary, 2002), 116.

237 ". . . perhaps the least gifted." Neil Milbert, "Trainer: Colors Won't Fade," *Chicago Tribune,* May 19, 1988.

238 ". . . As excited as we are." *World News Tonight,* courtesy of ABC News archives, featuring Ray Gandolf, aired April 11, 1988.

238 ". . . an emotional affair." Litke, "Lukas Moves."

238 ". . . In Lukas' mind." Dave Anderson, "Four Men on a Filly at the Kentucky Derby," *New York Times,* May 8, 1988.

238 ". . . become a little more callous." John Eisenberg, "Landaluce Is Gone, But Lukas Never Will Forget," *Baltimore Sun,* May 17, 1988.

239 ". . . ranked Landaluce as number two." Steve Davidowitz, *The Best and Worst of Thoroughbred Racing* (New York: Daily Racing Form, 2007), 148.

239 ". . . one of the greatest." Bob Ehalt, "Landaluce: Unbelievable Brilliance, Unbelievable Heartache," *America's Best Racing,* August 31, 2016.

239 ". . . abbreviated body of work." Jon White, telephone interview by the author, June 9, 2020.

239 ". . . she might not only have been." Jim Murray, "Landaluce: A Real-Life Love Story," *Los Angeles Times,* December 7, 1982.

25. Forever a Champion

Epigraph: Natalie Voss: "A Wild Ride with Seattle Slew," *Paulick Report,* October 4, 2016.

240 . . . renamed the Hollywood Lassie. Bill Christine, "Frankel Is Still on the Fence with Northrexford Drive," *Los Angeles Times,* February 3, 1983.

240 . . . Santa Anita may revive it. Amy Zimmerman, telephone interview by the author, September 8, 2020.

240 ". . . I'm thrilled." Bill Christine, "Hollywood Park Gets Breeders' Cup," *Los Angeles Times,* February 23, 1983.

240 . . . renovation project. Associated Press, "Hollywood Park Owners Plan Major Renovations," *Asbury Park Press,* October 26, 1983.

240 . . . enlarging both the outside. "First Running of Breeders' Cup Ball," *Los Angeles Times,* September 24, 1984.

240 . . . extending the main track. Joe Hirsch, "Hollywood Park 'State of the Art,'" *Daily Racing Form,* June 25, 1984.

240 . . . new tunnels. Mike Marten, "Hollywood Plans $100 Million Project," *Daily Racing Form,* October 27, 1983.

240 . . . a concessions area. Christine, "Hollywood Park."

241 ". . . trees were uprooted." Jay Privman, "Hollywood on the Rise," *Racing Times,* April 26, 1991.

241 . . . Also during Everett's tenure. Bill Christine, *Los Angeles Times,* as seen in *El Paso Times,* "1986 Kentucky Derby Winner Ferdinand Didn't Get the Fond Farewell He Deserved," October 29, 1988.

241 . . . between its north and south tote boards. Bill Christine, "Great
    Communicator Laid to Rest in the Infield at Hollywood Park,"
    Los Angeles Times, November 13, 1990.
241 . . . Hubbard immediately began. Larry Bortstein, "R. D. Hubbard:
    Iceman Cometh to Sunny Cal," *Orange County Register,* January
    24–January 30, 1991.
241 . . . Two massive lakes. Hollywood Park 2012 Media Guide, 12–13,
    yumpu.com/en/document/view/5187515/2012-media-guide
    -hollywood-park.
241 . . . Hubbard also removed. Mike Marten, "Hubbard: 'Forget about the
    Past,'" *Daily Racing Form,* February 20, 1991.
242 . . . many major news outlets. Jack Shinar, "Native Diver Monument
    Moving to Del Mar," *BloodHorse,* December 18, 2014; Steve
    Andersen, "Hollywood Park Makes Plans for Auction, Moving
    Horse Graves," *Daily Racing Form,* December 23, 2013; Beth
    Harris, "After 75 Years, Hollywood Park Hosts Final Races," AP,
    Santa Fe New Mexican, December 23, 2013.
242 . . . said he believes. Wayne Lukas, interview by the author, October 6,
    2019.
242 . . . family was never contacted. Barry Beal, telephone interview by the
    author, July 26, 2021.
242 ". . . get her casket shipped." Fuller French, telephone interview by
    the author, August 3, 2021.
242 . . . unsuccessful in locating. Eual Wyatt Jr. telephone interview by the
    author, November 3, 2019.
242 . . . none were ever received. Joel Cunningham, interview by the author,
    October 12, 2018.
242 . . . Construction has begun. Joel Cunningham, interview by the
    author, October 13, 2020.
244 . . . still stand today. Zimmerman telephone interview.

Epilogue

245 . . . riding point-to-point races. Robert Yates, "Nicholl Solid and True
    as Top Lukas Assistant," *BloodHorse,* March 23, 2018.
245 . . . withdrawn just weeks before. Robert Yates, " Knee Surgery Puts
    Bravazo out of Dubai World Cup," *BloodHorse,* March 1, 2019.

Index

Horses in History

Series Editor: James C. Nicholson

For thousands of years, humans have utilized horses for transportation, recreation, war, agriculture, and sport. Arguably, no animal has had a greater influence on human history. Horses in History explores this special human-equine relationship, encompassing a broad range of topics, from ancient Chinese polo to modern Thoroughbred racing. From biographies of influential equestrians to studies of horses in literature, television, and film, this series profiles racehorses, warhorses, sport horses, and plow horses in novel and compelling ways.